Searching for Literacy

"Professor Graff is among the most influential social historians of our time and has been a trailblazer within the growing field of literacy studies for years. Given his amazing intellectual scope and experience, his newest book should draw attention to critical issues in international educational systems. I would encourage anyone interested in literary practices and education to read this book."
—Sigurður Gylfi Magnússon, *Professor of History, University of Iceland; author of* Wasteland with Words; Minor History and Microhistory

"Harvey Graff is unquestionably the most important historian of literacy in our lifetime. His work is consistently original, provocative, and groundbreaking. In Searching for Literacy, Graff explores the origins of a field, its urgent concerns, questions, and contributors. This is a book for anyone interested in understanding what Graff has called the continuities and contradictions of literacy—what these are, who has engaged them, and what fundamental lessons remain to be learned."
—John Duffy, *Professor of English, University of Notre Dame, USA; author of* Writing from these Roots: Literacy in A Hmong-American Community

"The Literary Myth does what first-class scholarly books should do: it provides a probing and well-documented argument about the issue at hand, but it also educates the reader about the topic more generally…. In the close to thirty years since I discovered The Literacy Myth, … every single one of Harvey's books and articles … has taught me things I didn't know and helped me think differently or more broadly."
—Mike Rose, *Graduate School of Education and Information Sciences, University of California, USA; author of* Lives on the Boundary and The Mind at Work; *Conference on College Composition and Communications 2017, Tribute to Harvey J. Graff*

"In *Searching for Literacy: The Social and Intellectual Origins of Literacy Studie*s, Harvey J. Graff offers a timely and provocative analysis of how literacy is persistently deployed without documentation or definition. Tracing the development of literacy studies across disciplines and fields, Graff urges educators and scholars to resist literacy myths and connect with the historical insights that ground this area of study."
—Patrick Berry, *Syracuse University, USA; author of* Doing Time, Writing Lives: Refiguring Literacy and Higher Education in Prison

"A necessary, magnificent book, written by America's greatest specialist in the history of literacy. Since 1979 Harvey Graff has been a world authority on literacy studies, a discipline in the History of Culture that is enriched by this new book. A useful work for the education and culture sector, rigorous and interdisciplinary: it addresses literacy in various fields of knowledge."

—Diego Moldes, *Madrid, Spain; writer, film historian, student of print and literacy in European history*

Harvey J. Graff

Searching for Literacy

The Social and Intellectual Origins of Literacy Studies

palgrave
macmillan

Harvey J. Graff
Department of English
The Ohio State University
Columbus, OH, USA

ISBN 978-3-030-96980-6   ISBN 978-3-030-96981-3   (eBook)
https://doi.org/10.1007/978-3-030-96981-3

Cover illustration: Terry Vine

This Palgrave Macmillan imprint is published by the registered company Springer Nature Switzerland AG.
The registered company address is: Gewerbestrasse 11, 6330 Cham, Switzerland

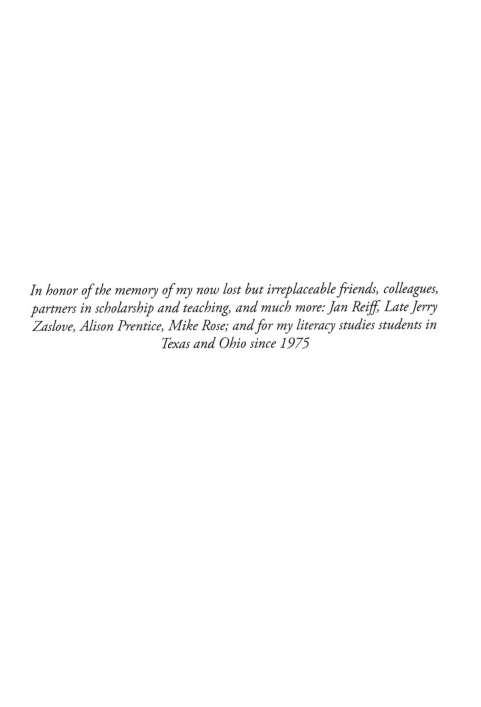

In honor of the memory of my now lost but irreplaceable friends, colleagues, partners in scholarship and teaching, and much more: Jan Reiff, Late Jerry Zaslove, Alison Prentice, Mike Rose; and for my literacy studies students in Texas and Ohio since 1975

Preface

A few years ago, when a very bright and avidly reading eight-year-old friend announced that she had named her new stuffed bear and its cub Bakey and Bearey, I asked her how she spelled the words. Memorably and instructively, she replied, "I don't worry about spelling." She shed more light on questions of literacy than she realized.

This book is the culmination of a series of inquiries and critiques that began in the early 1970s with a graduate seminar paper at the University of Toronto that examined the usefulness of nineteenth-century census data for the historical study of literacy. Michael B. Katz's contribution was formative. Prompted by the seminal works of Carlo Cipolla, Lawrence Stone, and Roger Schofield; UNESCO goals, economic development plans, and modernization theories and debates; and critical efforts to reform schools, my interest was captured and held by the history of literacy. For many years, Roger Schofield and Egil Johansson helped to guide me. I have written about this intellectual trajectory in "The Literacy Myth at Thirty" (2010).

My influential first book, *The Literacy Myth: Literacy and Social Structure in the Nineteenth-Century City* (1979, reprinted with a new introduction in 1991), was followed by a number of books and essays, in particular a general history of literacy in the western world, *The Legacies of Literacy: Continuities and Contradictions in Western Culture and Society*

(1987), and the essay collections *The Labyrinths of Literacy* (1995) and *Literacy Myths, Legacies, and Lessons* (2011). Over time, my primary interests shifted to include the history of childhood and youth (*Conflicting Paths: Growing Up in America*, 1995), urban history (*The Dallas Myth: The Making and Unmaking of an American City*, 2007), and the study of interdisciplinarity (*Undisciplining Knowledge: Interdisciplinarity in the Twentieth Century*, 2015). That recent work deeply influenced the understanding that permeates this book.

Try as I did, I could not leave literacy behind. Speaking and teaching internationally, I continued to write about literacy, the history of literacy, literacy studies, and literacy's inseparable relationships with almost all aspects of the human sciences and human societies.

In 2004, I became the inaugural Ohio Eminent Scholar in Literacy Studies and Professor of English and History and founded LiteracyStudies@ OSU. This university-wide interdisciplinary initiative represents a unique effort to develop both a formal and informal network of academic and public, faculty, student, and staff programs that stimulate the critical, historical, and comparative study and discussion of literacy.

The Literacy Myth laid part of the foundation for an important but incomplete intellectual, ideological, and cultural movement called the New Literacy Studies. Early, prominent texts such as Brian Street's *Literacy in Theory and Practice* (1984) and Colin Lankshear's *Literacy, Schooling and Revolution* (1987) depended explicitly on it. This book, written 40 years later, criticizes and suggests revisions of the New Literacy Studies. The historical scholarship of Mary Jo Maynes, Rab Houston, and Sigurdur Gylfi Magnusson, among others, including my students Kelly Bradbury, Michael Harker, Victoria Clement, and Di Luo adds to our understanding.

This work is a hybrid. It does not pretend to be a complete history of literacy or literacy studies. Rather, it is a critical account of the development of interests, approaches, methods, and understandings of literacy within and across fields, disciplines, and interdisciplines throughout history with an emphasis on the early modern and modern eras. It is a revisionist study. I argue, in brief, that literacy and literacy studies both are historical developments and must be understood in those terms. Those developments have had a profound impact on our traditions of thinking about and understanding literacy and how we study it. Literacy studies, especially in its academic, institutional, and policy forms but also in popular parlance, has lost a sense of its critical foundations. This lack of consciousness hinders, sometimes tragically, recent and contemporary efforts at promoting literacy and developing brave new notions.

Searching for Literacy: The Social and Intellectual Origins of Literacy Studies is addressed explicitly to explication, criticism, and revision of those traditions of understanding and study, both past and present. It proceeds by examining aspects of interests in literacy over time and across the dimensions of linguistics; anthropology; psychology: reading and writing across modes of communication, expression, and comprehension; "new" literacies across digital, visual, performance, numerical, and science domains; and history. In conclusion, it points to the value of new directions along the lines of negotiation and translation.

An innovative and fascinating exploration of many of the most relevant questions, well-suited to an advanced undergraduate or graduate course in literacy and literacy studies could be built around these texts, all of which are discussed in this book: my own *The Literacy Myth*; Jack Goody and Ian Watt's "The Consequences of Literacy" (1968); Ruth Finnegan's *Literacy and Orality* (1988); Sylvia Scribner and Michael Cole's *The Psychology of Literacy* (1981a); Shirley Brice Heath's *Ways with Words* (1983, 1996); Johanna Drucker's *Graphesis* (2014); Michael Clanchy's *From Memory to Written Record* (1979,1993); Deborah Brandt's *Literacy in American Lives* (2001); and Mike Rose's *The Mind at Work* (2004). Many other suggestions appear in this book.

Columbus, OH, USA   Harvey J. Graff

Acknowledgements

I acknowledge the contributions of LiteracyStudies@OSU and the endowment of the Ohio Eminent Scholar position at Ohio State University.

The first outline for this book took shape while I was Birkelund Fellow in 2013–2014 at the National Humanities Center in the Research Triangle, North Carolina. Conversations with others interested in literacy, both directly and in conjunction with the research and writing of *Undisciplining Knowledge*, whetted my interests, forced my focus, and fueled my energies toward an effort to reshape critical studies of and thinking about literacy. This thrust was confirmed during my time in August 2014 as visiting professor at the University of Minas Gerais and the State University of Rio de Janeiro in Brazil (thanks in particular to Ana Galvao).

I thank the late Michael B. Katz, Ian Winchester, Ian Davey, the late Jerry Zaslove, Shirley Brice Heath, Deborah Brandt, Brian Street, John Duffy, the late Mike Rose, Johanna Drucker, the late Jan Reiff, colleagues and students in the University of Texas at San Antonio's Division of Bilingual and Bicultural Studies, and most recently my colleagues and students in Ohio State University's LiteracyStudies@OSU initiative. At Ohio State, I also thank my colleagues the late Chris Zacher, Kay Bea Jones, Marcia Farr, Ed Adelson, Steve Acker, Ann Hamilton, Jared Gardner, Elizabeth Renker, Beverly Moss, Brenda Brueggeman, Steve

Rissing, Phil Binkley, Brian Joseph, Peter Shane, Ruth Colker, Alan Farmer, and Sarah Neville; graduate research assistants Nora McCook, Sean Kamperman, and Michael Harwick; and LiteracyStudies@OSU Assistant Director Susan Hansen.

I am grateful to my superb opthalmologists Tom Mauger, Andrea Sawchin, Paul Weber, and Rebecca Kuenen, who keep me seeing, and therefore reading and writing, and my physicians Cynthia Kreger, Peter Zafirides, and Rebecca Jackson.

Once again, I thank Grey Osterud for her peerless editorial contributions and sage publishing advice. And I thank my Palgrave Macmillan editor Cathy Scott and her team.

Finally, I again thank Vicki Graff who's been my partner for 52 years, about whom I wrote in *The Literacy Myth* in 1979, "my most loyal supporter and most vocal critic, for whom there are no appropriate words of gratitude. She will understand."

Columbus, Ohio   Harvey J. Graff
December, 2021

Contents

Part I

Searching for Literacy Studies

1

Back to Basics

In the popular and political imaginary, literacy is a *sine qua non* of culture and progress, for individuals, societies, nations. It exists in dizzying varieties; there are hundreds of proclaimed literacies. But literacy also seems to resist universal transmission. The reasons commonly given are as many as they are contradictory. They range from individual to institutional and political failings (Graff and Duffy 2007; Hamilton 2012).

Literacy's place in popular culture is one tellingly ambiguous sign. Corporate capitalism celebrates reading and writing in normative, consumer, and durable terms—for its own benefit.

These proclamations are revealingly, though poorly, expressed. Other voices are more mixed.

In their prime time and website videos promoting a line of "Kids" pens, BIC Pens declares awkwardly and apparently without irony, "Fight for your WRITE." Tritely playing with the concept of "right," the company announces unequivocally: "Writing helps children become more confident, creative and awesome! Writing is an important learning tool that gives children the power to share their thoughts and ideas with the world in a meaningful way. That's why BIC wants parents, teachers and caregivers to join us and Fight For Your Write!"

Why Fight For Your Write with BIC?

Join BIC on our mission to save handwriting and Fight For Your Write. Writing is an important vehicle for communication because it distinguishes us and promotes individuality. Did you know that writing is also a critical learning tool for children? Writing helps kids become better readers, boosts their confidence and sparks their creativity. Together we want to show children just how great writing can be and how great they can be![1]

But write what? Communicate what? How does writing do this? Are we even meant to take this seriously? These promotions are so badly written that they seem to parody the very arguments they make.

The bottom line is "PRODUCTS. Transform Boring Into Fun with These Amazing BIC® Products—Colorful and Bold Pens and Pencils with Personality." With no evidence, we are to believe that

The perfect BIC® pen, pencil or marker can make a child feel inspired to write. At BIC, we understand how our products can reflect a child's personality, express what they want to become one day, or just let the world know, "Purple is my signature color." We offer so much variety and style; kids and adults will be amazed by what they find.

"Fight For Your Write," indeed.

In an age with an expert to cite on any subject, BIC's efforts to back up its claims are laughable at best.[2] The vague and unfocused nature makes these claims almost impossible to support. That provides an important clue to exaggerated estimates of the value of literacy when taken out of meaningful contexts. It is also a powerful clue to the uses and abuses of literacy—reading and writing across modes of communication and comprehension—as an object of commodification and consumption.

Is it noteworthy that BIC's claims for writing with its Kids pens are virtually the same as those of the promoters of laptops, tablets, and other electronic devices—their marketplace competitors?

Does this translate into anything more than a high-tech effort to sell low-tech pens under the thin cover of "Join us. Support our mission to save handwriting"?[3]

Without a word about the relationship to its own profitability, Scholastic, the large publisher of school-age and school-related print and digital materials, promotes "A Child's Right to Read" and an effort to "Encourage a child to Read Every Day."[4] Not surprisingly, with false personalization, it informs consumers that "Your Purchase Puts Books into the Hands of Kids."

Selling "five books that shaped your life," it asks "What's Your Bookprint?"

Even more emphatically, its deterministic formula for a better world—"Read Every Day. Lead a Better Life"—embellishes "The Reading Bill of Rights." Adopting and all but parodying the discourse of human rights used in governmental and NGO national and local literacy campaigns, this declaration is part of "Scholastic's global literacy campaign" to sell books. Breathlessly, Scholastic begins a mixed metaphorical roster of "beliefs" with this prelude:

> Today we live in a world full of digital information. Yet reading has never been more important, for we know that for young people the ability to read is the door opener to the 21st century to hold a job, to understand their world, and to know themselves. That is why we are asking you to join our Global Literacy Call to Action. We call this campaign "Read Every Day. Lead a Better Life." We are asking parents, teachers, school- and business-leaders, and the general public to support their children's right to read for a better life in the digital world of the 21st century.

Literacy is "the birthright of every child in the world as well as the pathway to succeed in school and to realize a complete life." Every child has a right to a "'textual lineage'—a reading and writing autobiography which shows that who you are is in part developed through the stories and information you've experienced." "We believe that in the 21st century, the ability to read is necessary not only to succeed but to survive—for the ability to understand information and the power of stories is the key to a life of purpose and meaning." But, apparently, not to write particularly well or to appreciate literacy in the context of actual lives.

Meanwhile, Swedish furniture and housewares giant IKEA addresses parents, pushing the power of its "bookbook" (aka product catalogue) to sell its products, including books, pens, desks, and bookcases. Its paean to the catalogue in the form of a traditional printed and bound book is meant to be poetic and amusing. The video is clever. A sweet Swedish voice announces, "Once in a while something comes along that changes the way we live, a device so simple and intuitive, using it seems almost familiar.... . It's a bookbook."[5]

Under the heading "Books & games," IKEA also sells print: "Home improvement *books* for you, coffee table *books* for a rainy day and bedtime *books* for your favorite little bookworms... ." But the ad can do no better than play obviously with the terms and elements of so-called smartbooks and ebooks.

From Sales to Performance

On other hand, a very different viewpoint emerges in rap artist Kanye West's breakthrough album. Celebrating "The College Dropout," West memorably describes poor African American young people, lacking BICs and IKEA:

> You know the kids gon' act a fool
> When you stop the programs for after-school
> And they DCFS, some of 'em dyslexic
> They favorite 50-Cent song "12 Questions"
> We scream: "rocks, blow, weed, park", see, now we smart
> We ain't retards, the way teachers thought
> Hold up, hold fast, we make more cash
> Now tell my momma I belong in that slow class
> Sad enough we on welfare
> They tryna put me on the school bus with the space for the wheelchair

As a result:

> Drug dealin' just to get by
> Stack ya' money 'til it get sky high
> (Kids, sing! Kids, sing!)
> We wasn't s'posed to make it past 25

Joke's on you, we still alive
Throw your hands up in the sky and say:
"We don't care what people say."[6]

West evokes a more practical and gritty everyday reality than BIC and
IKEA for a different population whose use of reading and writing connects much more closely to survival than to consumption. His world's
"uses of literacy" constitute a different set of spaces (Hoggart 1961).

No less memorably, and likely in response to West, comic and video
artist Weird Al Yankovic defends good grammar and criticizes "Word
Crimes." He directs us to another putative dimension of literacy. To the
critics of prescriptive and inflexible grammar, who hold one reflexive definition of literacy, Weird Al was instantly anathema. But it is quite likely
that he raised his voice and his fancy video technology in parody, satiriz-
ing such censures.[7] Not surprisingly, scholars missed this move. Listen:

If you can't write in the proper way
If you don't know how to conjugate
Maybe you flunked that class
And maybe now you find
That people mock you online
[*Bridge:*]
Okay, now here's the deal
I'll try to educate ya
Gonna familiarize
You with the nomenclature
You'll learn the definitions
Of nouns and prepositions
Literacy's your mission
And that's why I think it's a
[*Chorus:*]
Good time
To learn some grammar
Now, did I stammer
Work on that grammar
You should know when
It's "less" or it's "fewer"

Like people who were
Never raised in a sewer
I hate these word crimes
Like I could care less
That means you do care
At least a little
Don't be a moron
You'd better slow down
And use the right pronoun
Show the world you're no clown
Everybody wise up![8]

Consider the contradictions. Superficially, the clash between West and Weird Al is cavernous. The one celebrates success—of a sort—but to which reading, writing, and arithmetic may contribute in noncanonical, unschooled ways. The other promotes proper grammar and condemns orthographic and stylistic gaffes. Both are long traditions, albeit differently valued and certified as proper or not. Is it odd to ask if Yankovic might lean toward a strict literacy with some levity? By smiling at the new word games, as well as word crimes of text speak and much more, does he in effect point us in new directions?

These examples also suggest that inclusive and useful definitions of literacy must be anchored in reading *and* writing across languages, symbol or sign systems, media, and domains of communication. By *reading*, I refer to the means and modes of understanding or comprehending— that is, making meaning. And by *writing*, I refer to the means and modes of expressing or communicating meaning. Those symbols and media include but are not limited to traditional alphabetic, numeric, and visual systems; some are embodied in humanity, the physical and the constructed environment. They may be spoken, written, printed or pictorially formed, electronically produced and distributed. None exists in isolation from the others. In performance, each practice shapes the others. Literacies are interactive, dialectically related, and require translation and negotiation, as I will explain in this book.[9]

Literacy Now

Today few subjects attract the attention or spark responses as powerful as literacy does. Claims of literacy's and illiteracy's presumed consequences surround us. Few pressing issues—whether individual and collective well-being, social welfare and security, and the state of the nation, domestic or foreign—escape association with literacy. Divisive issues of politics, and of race, class, nationality, gender, or geography constantly run up against it (Graff 2011b).

Despite literacy's acknowledged importance, its powers on the one hand, and the dangers of its diminution, on the other hand, are taken out of context and consequently exaggerated. Literacy is seldom defined. This adds to the illusion of its efficacy and the underlying confusion (Graff 1979, 1981a, 1981b, 1987, 1991, 1995, 2010, 2011a).

We live at an awkward and challenging moment in the history of literacy and the study of literacy. It is also a critical time for literacy as we now understand and practice it. At once, we are told relentlessly by press, pundits, and policy wonks that *literacy is declining* and the threats to civilization are dire. The indicators of decline are mixed and often far from measures of reading and writing: from school completion rates, grade levels, and diverse test scores, local, national, or international, and all but unimaginable anecdotal examples often from social media. Individual wellbeing, economic competitiveness, and national security are all at stake. The problem, it sometimes seems, is worst in the advanced societies. But to other commentators, it lies in the underdeveloping areas. We are not forced to choose among them, of course. Any such competition harms all.

At the same time, we thrive in a new era of a seemingly endless flowering of many or multiple literacies. They range from the "'new' literacies" of "new media" of visuality, screens, moving and animated images, numbers and symbols, to assertions of literacies, of some kind or other, of every imaginable subject, from aural to emotional, food, sex, culture, and countless others. And we are also told, even less clearly and coherently, that literacy, as we have known it, is irrelevant in the age of post-everything. I have compiled a list of almost five hundred "literacies" that I have seen mentioned *in print* (Graff 2011b).

No wonder confusion is rife. In this context, it is not surprising that a newly proclaimed field of literacy studies—home for almost three or four decades of an avowedly revisionist "new literacy studies"—seems to lack direction (Graff 1979; Street 1984; Barton 2006). Is it ironic that a field of inquiry rooted in fundamental dichotomies—literacy versus illiteracy and literacy versus orality; autonomous conceptions of literacy as universal versus ideologically driven approaches to literacy; global versus local manifestations of literacy—veers back and forth between them? Literacy studies never quite breaks free of dominant presumptions or stakes out fundamentally new grounds for understanding. Despite repeated recognitions of the ideological nature of the subject (sometimes termed "the bias of literacy,") prominently by my own book *The Literacy Myth* in 1979 and Brian Street's *Literacy in Theory and Practice* in 1984, the study and understanding of literacy remains riddled with unacknowledged ideological assumptions. The most pervasive and persistent pivots around a "great divide," as Goody and Watt (1968) conceived it in "The Consequences of Literacy" (originally published in 1963). It remains unfortunate that Street's important argument that different views of literacy tend to understand it as "autonomous" as opposed to "ideological" obscured the fact that both the "autonomous" or universal, ahistorical, and uncontextual *and* the "ideological" approaches are themselves riddled with ideological assumptions. The reigning assumptions and their confusions are displayed, for example, from UNESCO to the *Cambridge Handbook of Literacy* (Olson and Torrance 2009), and the United States National Center for Family Literacy, which despite its name is a private charitable foundation. Given the importance of literacy and its complicated dimensions, the power of assumptions is inescapable. But they need to be taken into account consistently for honest and useful scholarship and subsequent policy and practice.

As an academic, and also a public interest, literacy studies obsessively proclaims its novelty. But as this book shows, *it is not new*. Interest in, studying, speculating, and worrying about literacy has a long and formative history. To an unappreciated extent, recent literacy studies are also rooted fundamentally in its own disciplinary and multidisciplinary past. It campaigns relentlessly for recognition, identification, institutional location, and funding. It also has striking applied and commercial elements. It is tied, at least in part, to quests for national economic and cultural superiority. And it promotes its commitment to making a better world. And yet, it ignores and neglects to build on its own heritage and genealogy.

At the same time, literacy studies neglects disciplinary and interdisciplinary relationships of its recent founding and to which it seeks to contribute—and their conflicts and divides. This derives from and simultaneously results in *neglect of its own history*, long and short term. Major divisions, and with them, missed opportunities, often persist powerfully. These include problems of parts and wholes, and definitions, discourse, and relationships. Promotion and exaggeration, and gross comparisons or distinction making, resulting in what I have defined as a *literacy myth* (a well-known misconception), are rampant. In repeating claims for its importance, literacy's students and proponents too often either or both implicitly or explicitly undercut their own efforts. This is one among many contradictions (Graff and Duffy 2007; Graff 1979, 2010, 2012, 2014, 2015).

Searching for Literacy

Searching for Literacy: The Social and Intellectual Origins of Literacy Studies explores these issues from an original critical, historical, and comparative perspective. Informed by and following from my series of studies in the history of literacy and my latest book, *Undisciplining Knowledge: Interdisciplinarity in the Twentieth Century*, it asks how the study and understanding of literacy and literacies have developed (Graff 2015). But it also inquires more broadly into what we might call the social and historical understanding of the production and organization of knowledge with literacy as its focus.

In this book, I argue that the condition of literacy studies is more expected than ironic or paradoxical. That does not lessen its consequences. It is one result of the failure of a fragmented field of study to learn from its own history, on one hand, and to seek out critical relationships between and among approaches to literacy and different modes of reading and writing, on the other hand. It also speaks to the fundamental power of what I termed "the literacy myth," the exaggerated expectations of the power of literacy—that is, the ability to read and write—by itself (Graff 1979; see also Graff 2010, 2011a).

These problems matter. Why they matter should, I hope, be obvious. Literacy, I assert, is too important to be left to its proponents alone, from compositionists and digital specialists to pedagogues, on one hand, and to policy pundits, development economists and sociologists, and purveyors of books and other accoutrements of literacy and schooling, on the other. The evidence, however masked and muddled, is clear: literacy *alone* does not lead to development, health, and progress, either for individuals or for society. If literacy is to be viewed as a human right, a recent call to arms, then it must follow, or at least be inseparable from, the rights to life, shelter, safety, nourishment, and basic well-being. In other words, literacy must always be viewed as *one among other* fundamentals and *always* in interaction with other key factors.

Too often that is not the case, and the costly failures surround us. Many axiomatic formulas or prescriptions simply do not take this basic understanding and its overwhelming logical and empirical support into account. It has proven too easy (and on occasion too profitable) to do so. With some sympathy, I point to the pronouncements and programs of UNESCO, especially Education for All and Literacy for Life (see Arnove and Graff 2008). With less sympathy, I point to BIC or IKEA or those who compete to supply textbooks and laptops to the world. When the focus shifts to conceptualizing relationships, much changes. That is a necessary but very tardy step.

What is to be done? This book is not a guide to policy. Rather it is a critique and a series of (admittedly incomplete) steps on the road to revisioning literacy *and* the study of literacy in relationship to each other. Some would call my concerns epistemological, how we understand, how we know. My concern lies principally with literacy and what has come to be called literacy studies, a very loose cluster of diverse interests in literacy and literacies of all kinds within universities, government agencies, and nongovernment organizations, a disorganized set of topics and researchers across disciplines and departments with aspirations to both disciplinarity and interdisciplinarity, recognition, and organization. In significant part, I am interested in the historical sociology, organization, and production of knowledge (Graff 2001, 2011a, 2015).

My method in *Searching for Literacy* combines criticism and historical understanding. In inquiring into the roots and webs of interests in literacy over time and across fields of study, I probe understandings and rediscover leads, openings, and understandings that have been lost, for example, from linguistic anthropology; psychology; literature and composition; science, numeracy, and graphics; and movement and performance to history, in chapters that focus on these fundamental subjects. Despite a rhetoric and some genuine efforts at interdisciplinarity and integration, more than a century of disciplinarization and departmentalization has led to substantial separation and its deleterious consequences. Among the questions asked in this book is how we may learn from the past to fashion new understandings of the present and new paths to the future.

Literacy Studies Past and Future

Literacy studies' overarching *and* underlying discourse and assumptions link it inseparably to the presumption of change, progress, and advancement, whether of individuals or larger collectivities. Dominant thinking about literacy is governed by an image—an epistemology, if you will—of change. Theories, expectations, metaphors, and analogies almost always have this set of associations at their core. The linkage dates at least from the Greek classical era. The modern heritage or legacy is overwhelmingly positive. That set of presumed "consequences," following Jack Goody and Ian Watt, or "implications," as Goody imprecisely revised his formula, has long dominated approaches and interpretations, obscuring more complicated or differing relationships (Goody and Watt 1968; Goody 1968). Both progressive and conservative proponents agree on this, even when their versions of the "proper" acquisition, practices, and uses of literacy differ sharply.[10]

Closer, critical examination and shifts in emphasis reveal a different set of relationships and promote other understandings. The image is not wrong but *partial*, incomplete, distorting *when taken by itself*. Literacy's uses and impacts are also aligned with continuities and control. The three dominating millennial thrusts across literacy's long history are government, religion, and trade or exchange, and their developing needs. These forces contradict or, often, reshape literacy's linkages with progressive change. In a few words, literacy's impacts are dialectical and contradictory, seldom simple or unmediated.

Similarly, literacy has at least as often been associated with the life of groups as with the individualistic legacy that dominates our powerful inherited images. On the one hand, we must focus on the *collective* as well as individual uses of literacy, as people throughout the ages have done in their everyday and more exceptional practices. On the other hand, both the collective and the individual dimensions influence how the other acquires, uses, and is affected by reading and writing. Neither exists alone. Consider schooling or religious or governmental practices, or popular reading culture, or the collective aspects of artistic and scientific endeavors. How the interrelationships and their balances shift is a matter for questions and study at any point in time or place. Simple images quickly give way.

Dominant images emphasize literacy for liberation (which can be quite restrictive) and individual advancement, and less often for collective progress (or conservative reaction). The hugely simplified temporal association of classical Athenian democracy with the incomplete literacy of male citizens (and the distortions of the search for confirming evidence) is an epochal case in point (Harris 1989). However incomplete an association, it stimulated a powerful, indeed determinative influence and set of expectations over the past two millennia. The approximate temporal relationships and seminal (but perhaps unrepresentative) individual examples of legendary Greek and Roman thinkers and (sometimes) writers prompted a parallel association between the emergence of Greek philosophy, drama, and science following (by centuries) the development of the Greek alphabet (Goody and Watt 1968; Ong 1958). Eric Havelock (1963) and his uncritical followers see the remaking of the human mind by the invention and spread of a Greek alphabet. Similar patterns echo in the images of the impact of print and now electronic media.

Although scholars of India and China point to the breakthroughs in science and other intellectual domains with nonwestern alphabets and probably lower levels of general literacy, the linkages with literacy in the establishment and operation of the Greek and Roman empires suggest greater ambiguities (Gough 1968; Harris 1989). Control and restriction are as much a part of the legacies and uses of literacy as liberation and progress, as Paulo Freire powerfully reminds us in his seminal work. That confusion goes hand in hand with those who conflate the impacts of restricted or limited and mass literacy, for example, on intellectual or scientific-technological advances or even the circulation of information (Clanchy 1993; Eisenstein 1979; Grafton 1980; Grafton et al. 2002; Harris 1989; Houston 2002; Vincent 2000).

Recognizing the ongoing relationships among the media, especially but not only the oral, on one side, and the written, printed, and electronic, on the other side, adds to a transformed understanding. Instead of the ahistorical and anti-human notion of world-redefining (and formulaic) shifts *from* one dominant medium (or communicative-cognitive regime) *to* another—quintessentially the oral to the written and onward—the oral *never* loses its importance and lifeshaping impact. Nor does writing in whatever form of performance, reproduction, distribution, or transmission totally replace it. Too often understandings of literacy's development and impact take the formula of a transition or transformation from X to Y, often if not always in the form of a dichotomy. The following chapters explore these complications. Despite more than a millennium of constructs of a dichotomous remaking of the known world, speech across diverse media and writing across other domains continue to interact, shaping and reshaping each other. It is no accident that ethnographers never cease to rediscover that people still talk ... and then pat themselves on the back for their perspicacity and powers of observation. Multiple, multimodal, and "new" literacies call out for comparative study; that is, in relationship and interaction with each other, as they are actually used.

Remaking literacy studies requires an adjustable, multi-focal historical lens. Often longer term, it moves between the wide angle and the close focus, the larger and the local. It refuses to dichotomize apparent oppositions that turn out to be critical relationships when examined directly. Similarly, it requires the study and assimilation of historical and contemporary investigations to replace the appropriation and repetition of images, illusions, and icons. Seemingly powerful and formulaic shorthands—from "oral to literate," "the domestication of the savage mind," or "the world on paper," with scant regard for source criticism, contextualization, or representativeness can stand no longer. The deeply rooted faith in the power of literacy itself must be understood as itself a historical development. The power and impact, along with the quantity and quality of literacy—among the media—need to be demonstrated, and not simply presumed and equated with expected outcomes. Powerful but incomplete and misleading dichotomies must be replaced with complicated narratives.

Literacy and literacy studies are best understood with more attention to a longer chronological span of intellectual and socio-cultural development. It demands a broader, more dynamic focus on literacy's place and play among a wide array of disciplines and institutional locations. Subfields in disciplines or interdisciplines that deal with literacy include reading, writing, anthropology, child and human development, cognitive studies, formal and sociolinguistics, comparative and development studies, communication and media studies including popular culture studies, science and mathematics, and the visual and performing arts. How seldom they address one another. Cross-, multi-, and interdisciplinarity are among the grounds for comparative studies of literacy.

Literacy studies also suffers from an "internalist" bias. How easily literacy is conceptualized as an "independent variable" in the tradition of Brian Street's autonomous model. Once there is literacy, all else follows—more or less. The need for study dramatically declines.

"External" factors and developments—sometimes listed as affecting levels of literacy, most famously by Lawrence Stone (1969) in a roster of seven elements—demand more systematic (and less random or superficial) attention.[11] Social, cultural, demographic, and political economic forces—such as wartime demands or anticipated economic or civic needs, consequences of global cross-cultural contacts and colonialism, the cycles of the "discovery" of new social problem—all combine in fact and perceptions, often with contradictions, and with shifting currents within and across disciplines. Sometimes they stimulate changing views. Yet, studies of highly localized, limited populations, times, and places, and ecological macrocorrelations of highly aggregated, often ambiguous quantitative data are seldom compared or contrasted. Causes and consequences are seldom identified or clarified. In the context of universities and their organization of knowledge, those shifts in interest and approach should lead to criticism and comparison, different assertions, and sometimes institutional articulations both within and outside the boundaries of departments or divisions that take the name of interdisciplinarity. Literacy's relationships, for example, with demographic behavior, economic performance, or political participation are among the telling cases in point.

Historicizing Literacy Studies

A more complete and useful approach to literacy studies begins *no later than the 1920s and 1930s*, not the 1970s and 1980s. It looks back carefully to the period spanning the modernizing currents of mid-eighteenth century through the early twentieth century. It embraces a longer glance back to the Renaissance and also classical antiquity. It locates in historical context the dynamic building blocks for our expectations, understandings (including theories and policies), institutions, and expectations that culminate in modern literacies and their complications, and literacy studies, the principal disciplines and where and when they cross.

Modern arrangements and judgments, typically institutionalized in distinct fields of study, grew from the foundational currents of Renaissance rediscoveries of scholarship and knowledge and Enlightenment emphases on human malleability, perfectionism, learning capabilities, environmentalism, and institutionalism. They were partly reinterpreted by Romanticism's deeply divided recognition of the power and significance of the "other," the alien or primitive within ourselves and in "strangers," both within the modernizing West and in "newly discovered" regions. Questions about language—and its media and forms—and social order lay at the core of both.

The beginnings and foundations of literacy studies also lay in "civilization's" encountering many "Wild Children" (*enfants sauvages*), noble or savage, and South Sea islanders and other indigenous peoples whom explorers confronted around the world. The reading and writing of the "primitives"—across media and modes of understanding—was sometimes recognized. Inseparable were missionaries (whose work in creating alphabets and written languages initially to "translate" the Bible in aid of their proselytizing is fundamentally a part of literacy studies and linguistics); and conquerors, colonizers, and colonists. They all deployed early (and later) modern notions of Western literacy and its expected influences in their efforts at expansion, "conquest," and domesticating and elevating the primitive and different. Herein lay often missed points of contact between psychology and anthropology, among other fields.

Then and later, at home and abroad the poor, "minorities," immigrants, and others became more threatening than those farther afield. In anthropology and the arts, the primitive and the oral were grounds for celebration at times, complicating positive associations of literacy and negative associations of illiteracy. Strong currents from the Enlightenment and Romanticism intertwined, sometimes contradicting but sometimes supporting expectations about progress and modern development—and their connections with literacy (written culture). Herein lay, in part, the origins of modern social science, the arts, and literature.

From earlier eras, including the Renaissance and classical antiquity, came, haltingly at first, the conviction that writing, and the reading of it, were, at least in some significant circumstances, superior to other means of communication, especially the oral. On one hand, this was a functional development, but, on the other hand, personal and eventually collective cognitive change might follow, some persons of influence thought. So commenced early literacy studies, its theories and institutions.

The first general uses of reading and writing derived from the needs of religion, government, and commerce. Slowly there developed a faith in the powers of formal instruction in places called schools, initially for the relatively few, primarily boys but with informal tutelage for others including girls. Some agendas stressed socialization for citizenship and its correlates. Other agendas emphasized literacy in terms of useful or necessary practices or abilities, from clerks to clerics, rhetors to rulers.

Over time, places for instruction expanded to include many more and to focus especially on the young. This was an epochal conjuncture, with a powerful influence on future generations, and the realms of learning. In these formulations, literacy stood at the center of training that embraced social attitudes and control, and civic morality, along with at least rudimentary intellectual practices, and training in skills for productive contributions to economy, polity, and society. The tools began with simplified alphabets that helped to link signs and sounds to words and sentences, and expanded to include paper, pens, and various means of reproducing and circulating texts that were first handwritten and later printed. The superiority of technology and the inferiority of the "unlettered" stood as certainties, framing constructions of literacy. Literacy's story, right and wrong, came to occupy the center (though often implicitly) of the rise of civilization and progress in the West and over time the rest of the world.

These elements became inseparable as they joined capitalism's efforts to remake the world—and the word, written, printed, and reproduced—in the image of the marketplace and its institutions (with other images and sounds). Equally inseparable was the quest to remake the young, in particular, for the strange new world. These efforts mark, and also serve as representations of, literacy in the traditions that emerged to study and understand literacy from the Renaissance (or earlier) forward. They also stimulated uses of literacy, in conjunction with other media and collective action, for resistance and reform.

Not surprisingly, the development and institutionalization of disciplines in the nineteenth- and twentieth-century Western university incorporated the understandings of literacy to which they were the heirs, especially but not only in the social sciences—anthropology, linguistics, psychology, sociology, economics, politics—and the humanities—classics, history, literature, philosophy. Early relationships resisted efforts at change. The resulting disciplinary fragmentation not only contributed to efforts to build interdisciplinary literacy studies, but also limits them. They underwrite the many contradictions—what I call "the literacy myth," for one—in the place of literacy in Western cultures, and the lives of many persons yesterday and today.

Disciplining and Undisciplining Literacy Studies

Possibilities and limits on opportunities for novel understanding stem from the interplay within and across what I call "disciplinary clusters." (The humanities, arts, social sciences, and basic sciences constitute major disciplinary clusters.) No less important is the sometimes very dynamic interplay—critical and complementary—between disciplines. Of this, the key disciplines of anthropology, linguistics, and psychology provide powerful examples. Among them, orality and oral literature, everyday and privileged writing practices, the ubiquity of "reading" across multiple media, and the search for cognitive and noncognitive "implications" of literacy are telling. So, too, is literacy's active presence as values, ideology, and cultural, economics, and political capital. Destabilizing times can become opportunities to advance or to fall from favor for disciplinary approaches, and moments for interdisciplinary movements—and, importantly, literacy and literacies. These are the focus of this book, and the stimuli for writing it.

For literacy studies, across the past two centuries at least, one of the most powerful forces has been the fear, and often the certainty, that literacy is declining (or not rising), and that with it, families, morality, social order, progress, and socioeconomic development are also declining. This accompanied one of the most momentous transformations in the history of literacy and its study: from a premodern order in which literacy was feared and (partly) restricted, to a more modern order in which illiteracy (or literacy gained and practiced outside of formal institutional controls) constitutes a great threat.

When taken comparatively, and further heightened by international conflict or competition, social disorder and division, international migration of "aliens," rising fertility and mortality, failure of "human capital" to grow, and similar circumstances, literacy levels all become flashpoints for study and action to reverse the dreaded tide. Schools and popular culture attract attention which has in turn the potential to propel disciplinary action and conflict, and, sometimes, interdisciplinary efforts.

The apparently endless "crisis" of literacy in the mid- to late twentieth and early twenty-first centuries is inseparable from Cold War and more recent international anxieties, global economic restructuring and collateral social and cultural change, communicative and media transformation, and both new and persisting inequalities. Seemingly unprecedented "social problems" become calls for and stimulants of interdisciplinary "solutions." Literacy campaigns stir passions in the underdeveloping and developed worlds. Literacy's roles as either or both causes or consequences are very tricky to unravel, a complication in literacy studies' development.

For literacy studies, these complications often impinge on one or another of the "great divides" prominent among approaches that see literacy—almost by its very nature—as universal, unmediated, and transformative in its impact (the autonomous model). Often cited are reading or writing as the "technology of the intellect," the power of the Greek alphabet, the impact of print, cognitive shifts from alphabets, writing, or reading, and the like. Constructing this tradition of study and understanding—comparatively—was relatively uncomplicated. In recent decades, however, others have emphasized increasingly the socio-cultural influences and contextual effects from literacy as acquisition, practice, and use. Among the elements stressed are psychological theories, schools and other environments, families and communities, cultures of practice, and practice and use of reading and writing among media old and new. The reorientation remains incomplete.

Literacy studies' paths are revealing. In the second half of the twentieth century, in conjunction with other disciplines and interdisciplines, literacy studies has taken social, contextual, cognitive, linguistic, and historical, among other "turns." With the turns came the adoption of signifying

French theorist "godfathers" from Lucien Lévy-Bruhl and Claude Lévi-Strauss to Pierre Bourdieu and Bruno Latour. These developments at times interact with and deepen conflicts among disciplines and promote interest in interdisciplinary resolution. The turns, with inadequate testing and criticism, become dead ends.

Recent years witness an emphasis on the everyday and the practical, including the concept of practice itself. This has led to an incomplete and halting but revealing effort to overturn the dominance of grand theories that stressed the universal importance of the written over the oral, the printed over the written, the literate over the unlettered and untutored—consequences and implications of literacy. Practice and context, explored in a variety of circumstances and traditions, partly supplanted presumptions of the unmediated powers and advantages of literacy.

In part, recent literacy studies' emergence stemmed from perceptions of the inadequacy of earlier conceptualizations and presumptions, the search for new methods and sources on which to base a major revision, and reactions to it.

Literacy studies continues to struggle with foundational dichotomies—the making of myths and images—between oral and literate, writing and print, print and electronic, and literacy as transformative. They continue to guide and divide opinion and orient studies. Consequently, the long-standing neglect of rich research on orality and oral literature to which this book returns is almost as much a mark of the limits of many interdisciplinary endeavors as of the power of disciplines. The proponents of the New Literacy Studies have not reclaimed Albert Lord, Milman Parry, or Lev Vygotsky, among others. The persistence and importance of orality is regularly rediscovered across disciplines, as are the newly fashionable "multiple literacies," new emphasis on multilinguality or translation, and curiosity about visuality. None is new. Nor are the collective foundations of reading, writing, and "written culture." The heterogeneity of constructions of the cognitive domain also plagues literacy studies, another instructive matter of connections.

Among the most important—and least appreciated—critical elements are the absolutely crucial connections among myths and images—historical and contemporary—*and* expectations, and the ways that they are embedded in and come to undergird attitudes, policies, institutions, and judgments. To deal with this set of world-shaping conjunctures, we must cast our nets widely. We need to study literacy and literacies in new ways in their widest living circumstances and relationships, lived and written, experienced and recorded.

It is seemingly easy to study writing and "print." But it has been so hard to study reading and writing as practiced across media and modes of understanding and expression, especially in their formative and fundamental relationships to conceptions, ideologies, policies, institutions, and expectations.

*   *   *

Striving for recognition, literacy studies occupies ambiguous ground, both disciplinarily and interdisciplinarily. In part, this is a question of location. But it is also a question of status. The "rise" of literacy studies, part of its emergence and development, contributes to its presence in many academic departments and disciplines. This holds for education, the social sciences, and the humanities, but also (to a lesser extent) the sciences, medicine, public health, the law, and business. This pattern is problematic in some critical respects. It is dis- and unorganized. In the pantheon of disciplines, centers of interest in literacy studies usually do not rank highly. That the study of literacy, for reasons good and bad, is often seen as basic or elementary does not boost its standing. By reputation, it is often viewed as inseparable from schools or colleges of education.

Proclaimed interdisciplinary literacy studies at times become promotional labels: new, relevant, sexy—in academic terms—and appealing for applied and practical reasons to citizens, governments, and corporations, from "how to" to publishing texts and other aids. Perceptions of crises or at least serious problems with popular literacy abilities add to this mix. Such promotion, which is less problematic in professional schools than other institutions, aims to benefit programs and their home departments, colleges, or universities. It also can provoke negative reactions (Graff 2015).

In addition to education, the social sciences of anthropology, linguistics, and psychology are often the homes of literacy studies and the New Literacy Studies. At one time or another, each of these disciplines has claimed the status of a science, applied if not always "pure" or "basic." Psychology, followed by linguistics, exhibits the greatest ambitions, with strong interests in reading, writing, development, and cognition. All three are divided between scientific and cultural, quantitative and qualitative, cognitive and material, hard and soft orientations. All three stress contemporary and sometimes comparative relevance, usually reserving the strongest claims for the perspectives, methods, and theories of their own discipline, even when also proclaiming their interdisciplinarity. Practitioners in these fields often occupy central places in interdisciplinary literacy centers, programs, or concentrations in Education. Claiming attention, they remain divided and disconnected from historical perspectives. Each is the subject of a chapter in this book.

Searching for Literacy: The Origins of Literacy Studies begins an applied intellectual, cultural, and institutional history, taking literacy studies back to its pre-disciplinary and disciplinary foundations: identifying and probing its roots. Relationships are sought, and with them, clarifications and revisions, new beginnings and steps toward a different future for literacy studies and fundamental literacies. It is an experiment in the social history of knowledge.

Toward that end, in the following chapters, I explore literacy and literacy studies in the disciplinary and interdisciplinary domains of linguistics, psychology, anthropology, literaturereading-writing, arts and sciences, and history. Education is highlighted throughout. I probe both achievements and limits within a historical context of the history of literacy and the history of literacy in the disciplines. In searching for the origins of literacy studies critically, historically, and comparatively, my goal lies in the intellectual and practical reconstruction of the field of literacy studies.

Notes

1. See http://bicfightforyourwrite.com/
2. See the thin "report" from Hanover Research entitled "The Importance of Teaching Handwriting in the 21st Century," with footnotes mainly to newspaper articles, on the BIC website. No specific documentation is provided.
3. On the history of handwriting and its ideologies, see Thornton, *Handwriting in America* (1996).
4. See http://www.scholastic.com/readeveryday
5. See www.youtube.com/watch?v=MOXQo7nURs0
6. See http://genius.com/albums/Kanye-west/The-college-dropout
7. See http://www.youtube.com/watch?v=8Gv0H-vPoDc
8. See http://www.azlyrics.com/lyrics/weirdalyankovic/wordcrimes.html
9. Graff and Duffy (2007) elaborate: "We define literacy here not in terms of values, mentalities, generalized knowledge, or decontextualized quantitative measures. Rather, literacy is defined as basic or primary levels of reading and writing and their analogies across different media, activities make possible by a technology or a set of techniques for decoding and reproducing printed materials, such as alphabets, syllabaries, pictographs, and other systems, which themselves are created and used in specific historical and material contexts. Only by grounding definitions of literacy in specific, qualified, and historical particulars can we avoid conferring upon it the status of myth" (Graff 2011a, 37).

10. Full references to Goody's subsequent writing and the debates over the "Goody thesis" appear in Chap. 3.
11. Compare Stone, "Literacy and education in England" (1969) with Schofield, "Measurement of literacy in pre-industrial England" (1968). Schofield criticized the very general nature of Stone's factors, which ranged from religion to stratification, but was more concerned about primary sources and literacy's role in economic development.

References

Arnove, Robert F., and Harvey J. Graff, eds. (2008) *National literacy campaigns and movements: Historical and comparative perspectives.* New Brunswick, N.J.: Transaction.

Barton, David. (2006) *Literacy: An introduction to the ecology of written language.* Oxford: Blackwell.

Clanchy, Michael T. (1993) *From memory to written record: England, 1066–1307.* 2d ed. Oxford: Blackwell.

Eisenstein, Elizabeth. (1979) *The printing press as an agent of change: Communications and cultural transformations in early modern Europe.* 2 vols. Cambridge: Cambridge University Press.

Goody, Jack. (1968) Introduction: The implications of literacy. In Jack Goody, ed., *Literacy in traditional societies*, 1–26. Cambridge: Cambridge University Press.

Goody, Jack, and Ian Watt. (1968) The consequences of literacy. In Jack Goody, ed., *Literacy in traditional societies*, 27–68. Cambridge: Cambridge University Press.

Gough, Kathleen. (1968) Implications of literacy in traditional China and India. In Jack Goody, ed., *Literacy in traditional societies*, 69–84. Cambridge: Cambridge University Press.

Graff, Harvey J. (1979) *The literacy myth: Literacy and social structure in the nineteenthcentury city.* New York and London: Academic Press.

Graff, Harvey J. (1981a) *Literacy in history: An interdisciplinary research bibliography.* New York: Garland.

Graff, Harvey J., ed. (1981b) *Literacy and social development in the West.* Cambridge: Cambridge University Press.

Graff, Harvey J. (1987) *The legacies of literacy: Continuities and contradictions in Western society and culture.* Bloomington: Indiana University Press.

Graff, Harvey J. (1991) *The literacy myth*, with new introduction. New Brunswick, N.J.: Transaction.

Graff, Harvey J. (1995) *The labyrinths of literacy: Reflections on literacy past and present*, rev. and exp. ed. Pittsburgh: University of Pittsburgh Press.

Graff, Harvey J. (2001) The shock of the "new histories": Social science histories and historical literacies. Presidential address, Social Science History Association, 2000. *Social Science History* 25: 483–533.

Graff, Harvey J. (2010) *The Literacy Myth* at thirty. *Journal of Social History* 43: 635–661.

Graff, Harvey J. (2011a) *Literacy myths, legacies, and lessons: New studies on literacy*. New Brunswick, N.J.: Transaction.

Graff, Harvey J. (2011b) Many literacies: Reading signs of the times. In Harvey J. Graff, *Literacy myths, legacies, and lessons: New studies on literacy*, 15–33. New Brunswick, N.J.: Transaction.

Graff, Harvey J. (2012) Literacy studies and interdisciplinary studies: Reflections on history and theory. In Ralph Foshay, ed., *Valences of interdisciplinarity: Theory, practice, pedagogy*, 273–307. Cultural Dialectics Series. Edmonton, Alberta: AU/Athabasca University Press.

Graff, Harvey J. (2014) Epilogue: Literacy studies and interdisciplinary studies with notes on the place of Deborah Brandt. In Julie Nelson Christoph, John Duffy, Eli Goldblatt, Nelson Graff, Rebecca Nowacek, and Bryan Trabold, eds, *Literacy, economy, and power: Writing and research after Literacy in American Lives*, 202–226. Carbondale: Southern Illinois University Press.

Graff, Harvey J. (2015) *Undisciplining knowledge: Interdisciplinarity in the twentieth century*. Baltimore: Johns Hopkins University Press.

Graff, Harvey J., and John Duffy. (2007) The literacy myth. *Encyclopedia of language and education*, vol. 2, *Literacy*, ed. Brian Street, 41–52; Nancy Hornberger, general editor. Berlin and New York: Springer.

Grafton, Anthony T. (1980) The importance of being printed. *Journal of Interdisciplinary History* 11: 265–286.

Grafton, Anthony T., Elizabeth L. Eisenstein, and Adrian Johns. (2002) How revolutionary was the print revolution? *American Historical Review* 107: 84–128.

Hamilton, Mary. (2012). *Literacy and the politics of representation*. London: Routledge.

Harris, William V. (1989) *Ancient literacy*. Cambridge, Mass.: Harvard University Press.

Havelock, Eric A. (1963) *Preface to Plato*. Cambridge, Mass.: Belknap Press.

Hoggart, Richard. (1961) *The uses of literacy: Changing patterns in English mass culture*. Boston: Beacon.

Houston, R. A. (2002) *Literacy in early modern Europe: Culture and Education 1500–1800*. 2d ed. London: Longman.

Olson, David R., and Nancy Torrance, eds. (2009) *The Cambridge handbook of literacy*. Cambridge: Cambridge University Press.

Ong, Walter. (1958) *Ramus, method, and the decay of dialogue*. Cambridge, Mass.: Harvard University Press.

Schofield, Roger S. (1968) The measurement of literacy in pre-industrial England. In Jack Goody, ed., *Literacy in traditional societies*, 311–325. Cambridge: Cambridge University Press.

Stone, Lawrence. (1969) Literacy and education in England, 1640–1900. *Past & Present* 42: 69–139.

Street, Brian. (1984) *Literacy in theory and practice*. Cambridge University Press.

Thornton, Tamara Plakins. (1996) *Handwriting in America: A cultural history*. New Haven: Yale University Press.

Vincent, David. (2000) *The rise of mass literacy: Reading and writing in modern Europe* Cambridge: Polity Press.

2

Linguistics: Between Orality and Writing

In the beginning, there was the Word. The word was spoken. This has long been said *and* written in different traditions and forms. But our knowledge of this—after the fact—necessarily comes through writing. It also comes through centuries of translation and conflicting interpretations.[1] Therein lies a set of relationships—a conundrum—that plagues specialists yet has prompted inadequate attention by those who study and seek to understand literacy. In the place of those relationships, we have a long legacy of formulaic divides surrounding "*from* oral *to* written or literate" that also presume a historical, even an evolutionary trajectory. The linguistic bases of literacy studies swing from presumption to presumption, antecedent to subsequent. This chapter inquires into those cycles.

To a considerable extent, the basic study of language—the discipline of linguistics, including formal linguistics and sociolinguistics—has divided over the primacy and the determinative influence of *either* the oral *or* the written. Linguistics' roots in religion and foundations in philology are not appreciated by students of literacy. To a surprising degree, they have been dismissed or obscured. This is part of their neglect—or (to the same end) their presumption—of history, and of their acceptance of the primacy of a foundational shift from oral to written. This recognition

© The Author(s), under exclusive license to Springer Nature Switzerland AG 2022
H. J. Graff, *Searching for Literacy*, https://doi.org/10.1007/978-3-030-96981-3_2

helps to explain the failure to notice and probe the *interactions* between the oral and the literate. Interestingly, the ways in which linguistics and psychology have interacted (and failed to intersect) in their approaches to literacy form part of this set of complications.

Sociolinguist James Paul Gee captures this problem in part when he observes in a review article: "In anthropological studies the term *literate* in the dichotomy *literate/nonliterate* came to replace the term *civilized* in the older dichotomy *civilized/primitive* and then how a distinction between nonliterate and literate cultures came to be applied to different social groups within modern, technological societies like ours, characterizing some as having "restricted literacy" and others as having "'full literacy.'" But that is not all. He continues, "The importance of these developments is the link often assumed between literacy and higher order mental skills, such as analytic, logical, or abstract thinking" (1986, 719).

The problem is widespread. The superordinate role of the written is presumed by psychologists Jens Brockmeier and David Olson when they (derivatively and contradictorily) coin the reductive term "the literacy episteme" and declare it of recent origin (Brockmeier and Olson 2009; see also Brockmeier 2000, 2002).[2] But what they call a literacy episteme is centuries old and generally recognized. They write about a certain approach to understanding literacy: "Only within such an overarching order, we suggest, do these practices and problems take on an epistemic form and become subjects of thought and theoretical curiosity as well as public attention…. [Only then] can the social, intellectual, and cultural implications of writing become epistemic objects: 'things' that appear as intelligible objects of theory and investigation and whose investigation is considered to be fulfilling societal demands and cultural interests" (Brockmeier and Olson 2009, 5).[3] When they locate that development in the second half of the twentieth century, they are seriously distorting the understanding of literacy and erasing centuries of attention to literacy.

To the contrary, the Swedish linguist Per Linell (2005) writes pointedly about *The Written Language Bias in Linguistics* (see also Säljö 1988). Others emphasize an oral bias.[4] A review of the early history of linguistics in academic institutions supports the view of a bias toward writing. Given technology (and logocentrism), how could it have been otherwise?

The Biases of Linguistics

Applied linguist Douglas Biber poses the questions in a way that indicates the porousness and variability of the literacy episteme and suggests the bias of literacy *and* the biases of much inquiry. Not mentioning the longevity of the question and its place in religious proselytization, including missionary work, early language studies, and pedagogy, among other fields, he summarizes: "A major issue for discourse studies during the last three decades concerns the ways in which literacy influences language use: are there systematic linguistic differences between spoken and written language that can be associated with literacy as a technology (i.e., writing considered as a physical mode of communication distinct from speech)?" He notes that opinions have ranged from claims that written language is "fundamentally different" from spoken to "recent arguments "that there are "essentially no differences associated with literacy in itself" (2009, 75). Revealingly, he does not explain "literacy in itself." Is this a great divide or a series of divides? Perhaps, by conflating them, he exaggerates their cumulative impact. These issues must be faced if we are to understand literacy.

Biber elaborates, "Earlier research on this question sometimes took an extreme position, arguing that there are fundamental linguistic differences between speech and writing" (2009). The examples he cites often confuse variation with difference.[5] Chronologically, these studies were done in the 1970s and earlier, when the fashionable notion of the literacy episteme placed renewed emphasis on the written. Biber continues: "This view was moderated in the 1980s, when researchers such as Tannen (1982), Beaman (1984), and Chafe and Danielewicz (1986) argued that it is misleading to generalize about overall differences between spoken and written language because communicative task is also an important predictor of linguistic variation; therefore, equivalent communicative tasks should be compared to isolate the existence of mode differences" (Biber 2009, 76).

Yet that shift provided an opening to reinforce, seemingly more subtly, a sense of the divide between the spoken and the written. Along these lines, in *The World on Paper* (1994) David Olson posits a new, writing-based world founded in metaphors and based on exceptional texts, an ahistorical world that purported to be historical, while never asking whose world this was or how they wrote (for a detailed analysis of this work, see Chap. 4). Ignoring social and cultural, political and economic historical context, as proponents of the literacy episteme typically do, this approach is striking in the literalness of its reading of writing. Olson's associate Jens Brockmeier prophesies "literacy as a symbolic space" and a "literate episteme" and equating literacy with a rather restricted view of writing while simultaneously exaggerating its powers (Brockmeier 2000, 2002). The sense of certainty and the unacknowledged developmentalism of their claims are among the most striking features of this new bias toward writing.

As a result, Biber tells a circular story that is more revealing than he seems to notice. Comparing the oral and literate led to views that suggested "few (if any) *absolute* [italics added] linguistic differences between speech and writing" or claims that there are "essentially no linguistic correlates of literacy as a technology." He proposes, rather evasively, that "none of these extreme views is correct. Rather, the spoken and written modes differ in their potential for linguistic variation: speech is highly constrained in its typical linguistic characteristics, whereas writing permits a wide range of linguistic expression, including linguistic styles not attested in speech." Given this recognition, Biber is left to admit, "Thus, written texts can be highly similar to spoken texts or they can be dramatically different. Thus difference is attributed to the differing production circumstances of the two modes: real-time production in speech versus the opportunity for careful revision and editing in writing. As a result, the written mode provides the *potential* for styles of linguistic expression not found in the spoken mode" (2009, 75–76).

In effect, Biber shifts the terms of *his* discourse from modes to styles of expression, changing the grounds of the comparison. Comparing apples and oranges incommensurately, he shifts the discussion (without acknowledgement) away from the central question of the debate with which he began. Demonstrating the "literate bias" of linguistics, he makes the obvious observation that revised or edited writing differs, at least in "potential," from "real-time" speech. We are left to wonder how "real time" applies to historical or other evidence of either speech or writing.

Rather than considering how the oral and the written actually interact and shape each other, or returning to ground-breaking studies of oral composition, scholars like Biber, Brockmeier, and Olson uncritically find grounds for maintaining the divides and the biases of literacy. In so doing, they take us farther away from understanding literacy in theory *and* practice. They demonstrate the practical and theoretical limits of the literacy episteme.

From Literacy to Orality

I suggest a different path to a revised understanding. Those who seek to understand literacy, both past and present, err in failing to take orality seriously. As notions of literacy epistemes (among other biases of literacy studies) suggest, such questions are allied inseparably with the various forms of divides, great and smaller. This is among the reasons why we repeatedly rediscover the persisting importance of talk or speech. But contrary to some sociolinguists who rightly reemphasize the importance of orality, the dynamic and dialectical interactions between and among speech and writing (and other modes of literacy) are most important for understanding literacy, its meanings, and its uses.[6]

In 1973, in an article entitled "Literacy versus Non-Literacy: The Great Divide," anthropologist Ruth Finnegan forcefully responded to Jack Goody and Ian Watt's seminal "The Consequences of Literacy" (1968, first published in 1963). Combining studied ambiguity ("non-literacy") and strong statements, Finnegan looks backward to centuries, perhaps millennia of interest in oral composition and oral poetry in making a strong case for the capabilities and achievements of the non-literate. She also directs attention to a substantial literature on the subject of the oral and the written.

Finnegan's major target was the legacy of "a great divide" between literacy and non-literacy promulgated by Goody and Watt and embedded in the literacy episteme. Although Goody and his supporters qualified some of his most sweeping generalizations, the sense of an epochal (and to some an "epistemic") divide never disappeared. New justifications—registers, styles, tasks, episteme—have been invented. Finnegan reiterates: "When people wish to make a basic distinction between different societies or historical periods, one of the commonly invoked criteria is literacy. ... Other characteristics are also employed (particularly that of technology) but that of the absence or presence of literacy is increasingly stressed." Taking this further, she identifies several powerful assumptions: first, "that the presence or absence of literacy is of absolutely crucial significance of the quality of thought in a given culture."[7] "*Prima facie* it seems obvious that individuals and societies which are without writing also lack literature with all that that implies. In other words, they have no access to that part of culture which we would normally regard as among the most valuable part of our intellectual heritage and perhaps the main medium through which we can express and deepen mankind's intellectual and artistic insight" (Finnegan 1973, 112–114).

To the contrary, Finnegan turns to the non-written literatures of much of the world. She observes, "few who have considered these and similar cases would deny that such cultures possess at least the parallel to what we term literature" (1973, 115). Sketching broadly, she points to oral literature as intellectual expression.

> If then we think of literature as a condition for the flowering of intellectual and perceptive thought it is hard to see any great divide between those societies which happen to use *writing* for literary expression and those which do not.... Far from non-literate societies being radically different in that they lack any medium of thought comparable to our literature, they in fact seem in no essentials different from us in this respect. (122)

She admits that "their literature may—sometimes—be less specialist, less fixed to the verbal invariability of the written word, more tied to specific occasions. But these are all matters of degree, and do not necessarily affect the functions of literature as an expression of thought" (122–123). In some societies, there is specialist education for composition and performance.

But in all cases, literature is part of both everyday and ceremonial, informal and formal culture. "It is no longer possible, therefore to accept the old picture of 'the primitive' (or the nonliterate) as unselfconscious and unaware, incapable of contemplating the world with intellectual detachment" (124).

Although she was attentive to the differences between written and oral literature, Finnegan was seldom heard among literacy scholars. The biases toward written literacy are many and strong. Surrounding common images are a cluster of developmental and hierarchical themes: the passage from oral to written, primitive to advanced, popular to scholarly, informal to formal, young to older, novel to established, immigrant or newcomer to assimilated, potential if not absolute. Orality surfaces in discussions of preliteracy, past and present, and with respect to the "acquisition" of literacy, especially but not only by the young (Schieffelin and Gilmore 1986; Heath 1983; Gee 1996).

Some sociolinguists did hear Finnegan's words. But, if anything, an increasing stress on technology led to an even greater sense of the divide. Even scholars of early civilizations and their languages, such as Eric Havelock, and early modernists, such as Walter Ong, tried to incorporate technology into their schemes. For Ong, this was "the technologizing of the word" (1982). They preceded more recent references to literacy and/or writing as "the technology of the intellect," but may well have followed Marshall McLuhan. Regardless, technology itself was almost never problematized.

Careful *not* to reify deprecating notions of "oral culture," Finnegan considers orality and literacy as information technologies. Responding to the recent celebration of new communication "revolutions" rooted in technology, she observes: "These and similar issues are all too often debated as if they were totally new and unprecedented. Every age, perhaps, likes to think it has its own imminent 'revolution,' and its own sense of engagement in cataclysmic changes, whether for good or ill" (1988, 1).

Finnegan emphasizes:

Now is not the first time in history that there have been arguably far-reaching changes in the technology of communications. Indeed many of the current questions recall the strikingly similar debates about earlier forms of communication. It is often not realized that work by social anthropologists and social historians on the implications or maintenance of "earlier" technologies like oral communications, writing or print can both illuminate current changes and their (debatable) interpretation, and also provide a wider comparative and historical perspective for their assessment.

She reiterates that "current debate does not have to reinvent the wheel, but could proceed more intelligently by building on this earlier theoretical and empirical scholarly work" (1988, 1–2).

Underscoring how quickly we contrast writing as a "form of information technology" with orality and presume the difference and deficiency of what is merely spoken, Finnegan observes that most analyses of writing are "parasitic on an implied opposition to oral communication." She explains: "Oral communication looks at first sight unproblematic and 'natural.' But, like literacy or, indeed computer technology, its use too rests on social and cultural conventions and on a man-made system of communication—in this case the remarkable system of human speech.

It is, certainly, a technology that we take for granted" (1988, 4; see also Street 1984; Gee 1986). She perhaps risks overstating the case for the power of oral communication in the effort to limit the dominant *logo scripto*'s credibility.

Finnegan advances and complicates our understanding of oral communications and their powers while qualifying the seemingly limitless transformative influences of more modern and presumably advanced technologies. Her overarching targets were universal theories of great divides and unmediated impacts.[8] Her critique was based on a wide-ranging knowledge of oral communications in Africa, the South Pacific, and western societies. Especially relevant to the concerns of this book is her argument that "'orality' and 'literacy' are not two separate and independent things: nor (to put it more concretely) are oral and written modes two mutually exclusive and opposed processes for representing and communicating information." Rather, "they take diverse forms in differing cultures and periods, are used differently in different social context and, insofar as they can be distinguished at all as separate modes rather than continuum, they mutually interact and affect each other, and the relations between them are problematic rather than self-evident" (Finnegan 1988, 175).

To this argument, I add that orality and literacy continuously interact and reshape each other in almost every context of human life and history. Speaking, reading, and writing are inseparably intertwined, as writers and teachers, politicians and theologians, and performers and scholars in many other fields outside of literacy studies know full well. Radio, television, and electronic media have promoted presence and sometimes the power of the oral, though not in any simple or uncomplicated way, as the notion of a secondary orality suggests.

Instead of assumed "absolutes" and "potentials," we consider relationships. As Finnegan puts it, "The implication of this is that looking for clear-cut 'consequences' or 'impacts' from these traditional technologies is not likely to be very productive." When there are significant consequences, they "are to be found not primarily in the technologies themselves, but in the way these technologies are liable to be controlled and used. The crucial questions are to do with power, access, national and international inequalities, and people's values and ideas about themselves and about the nature of human destiny … not primarily technical questions but those same age-old tendencies that have formed the constant subject of social, historical and literary studies" (1988, 175–176). This is inseparable from the power, means, extent, and choice of access to the control and use of the means and modes of communications. How seldom the spokespersons of new literacy or writing episteme refer to these factors.

While emphasizing the importance of both the oral and the written, Finnegan also reminds us "that to think of script and speech as the only technologies for representing information, even in the past, is misleading." This is a critical issue to which we will return with respect to reading and writing across the arts and sciences. Human communications are not limited to spoken or written. They are also musical and auditory, whether notated or expressed in other graphic forms.

There is human movement, prominently but not solely the dance. There are the visual and numerical expressions of science and the arts. As Finnegan puts it, "These comprise one whole realm of human experience for which information technologies may be potentially as important as for 'words' and 'propositional information.' The same can be said for visual art and expression. In some cultures, memory and historical awareness are transmitted and represented not through words but through the reflective preservation of particular plastic art forms." Finnegan concludes by reiterating that writing's past, present, and future importance lies not in the medium itself "but because of the way we have chosen to use and regard it, sanctioned by a whole series of educational, economic and political institutions" (1988, 179).

From Speech to Script and Back Again

Finnegan's perspective is neither backward-looking, a manifestation of the relativism of the 1960s and after, nor a postmodern embrace of new technologies. She elaborated an established tradition that is itself a part of the classical legacy. That tradition calls out for reconnection with literacy studies. In part, as Finnegan's writing suggests, the path lies in the intersection and interactions between orality and literacy, especially through the perspective of oral composition in relationship to writing.

Following but also revising Finnegan, David Lurie provides a valuable case in point in his history of Japanese writing (2011). Observing that any sense of "a homogeneous orality is obviously problematic," for him, "the major flaw of the 'great divide' theory (and of mainstream thinking on literacy itself until the 1980s)" is a homogeneous literacy, lumping "together all literacies, arranging various abilities to produce and interpret texts into a hierarchy of partial or primitive literacy developing toward full or genuine literacy." To the contrary, Lurie argues that "the evidence for early inscriptive practice in many societies reveals a variety of relationships with writing." Paralleling Finnegan, Lurie asserts that there is as much diversity among these as there is between any one of them and a putative "primary orality." Appreciation of multiple literacies is "a crucial part of the best-known critique that approaches the orality/literacy paradigm from the literacy side," he concludes (2011, 35). This perspective goes hand-in-hand with an appreciation of what we might call multiple oralities. In his study of early Japanese writing, Lurie follows these relationships into different texts with mixed logographic and phonographic orthography, that is, the intersection of speech and writing.

Singers of Tales, Speakers of Words

Enormously important steps in this direction form part of the legacy of literacy studies, but by and large they are either lost to contemporary students or misapplied by other scholars. In particular, I refer to the ground-breaking, almost heroic studies of Harvard classicist Milman

Parry and his student Albert B. Lord, who discovered the great Serbo-Croatian *Singers of Tales* (Lord 1960) in their quest to learn how Homer composed the *Iliad* and the *Odyssey*. "What distinguished Parry from most earlier Classicists who had posed the 'Homeric Question' was not only his hypothesis that the *Iliad* and the *Odyssey* were originally the products of an oral tradition that was older than any written literature; it was also his formulation of a method for *testing* that hypothesis, a discovery procedure capable of moving the debate from the content of orally produced songs to the actual process through which such songs are produced in performance" (Lord 2000, viii). In Parry's own words from 1935:

> If we put lore against literature it follows that we should put oral poetry against written poetry, but the critics so far have rarely done this, chiefly because it happened that the same man rarely knew both kinds of poetry, and if he did he was rather looking for that in which they were alike. That is, the men who were likely to meet with the songs of an unlettered people were not ordinarily of the sort who could judge soundly how good or bad they were, while the men with a literary background who published oral poems wanted above all to show that they were good as literature. It was only the students of the "early" poems who were brought in touch at the same time with both lore and literature. (quoted in Lord 2000, viii; see also Parry 1971; Lord 1995)

With the assistance of Lord, Parry journeyed to the mountains of Bosnia in 1933 and 1935 with special recording equipment to record variant versions of classic tales.

As Lord recounts, Parry's research on the *Iliad* and the *Odyssey* identified the technique of formulaic epithets. "This work has convinced him that the poems of Homer were traditional epics, and he soon came to realize that they must be oral compositions. He therefore set himself the task of proving, incontrovertibly if it were possible, the oral character of the poems, and in the end he turned to the study of the Yugoslav epics."[9] In 1935, "the aim of the study was to fix the exactness the *form* of oral story poetry, to see wherein it difference from the *form* of written story poetry. Its method was to observe singers working in a thriving tradition of unlettered song and see how the form of their songs hangs upon their having to learn and practice their arts without reading and writing" (Lord 2000, 3).

Lord continued the work that Parry began in the early 1930s. In his *Singers of Tales*, he concluded, "oral epic song is narrative poetry composed in a manner evolved over many generations by singers of tales who did not know how to write; it consists of the building of metrical lines and half lines by means of formulas and formulaic expressions and of the building of songs by the use of themes." This is what Lord mean by "oral" and "oral epic." By formula, following Parry, he refers to "a group of words which is regularly employed under the same metrical conditions to express a given essential idea." "These definitions are but the bare bones of the living organism which is an oral epic.... Various patterns ... emerge to give them form.... The formulas are not the ossified clichés which they have the reputation of being but they are capable of change and are indeed frequently highly productive of other and new formulas.... Themes can be expanded and contracted, and the manner in which they are joined together to form the final product which is the song" (2000, 4).

Turning to the song itself, listen to Lord as he argues:

> In a very real sense every performance is a separate song; for every performance is unique, and every performance bears the signature of its poet singer. He may have learned his song and the technique of its construction from others, but good or bad, the song produced in performance is his own song.... The singer of tales is at once the tradition and an individual creator. His manner of composition differs from that used by a writer in that the oral poet makes no conscious effort to break the traditional phrases and incidents; he is forced by the rapidity of composition in performance to use these traditional elements. To him they are not merely necessary, however; they are also right.... His art consists not so much in learning through repetition the time-worn formulas as in the ability to compose the phrases for the idea of the moment on the pattern established by the basic formulas. He is not a conscious iconoclast, but a traditional creative artist. His traditional style also has individuality, and it is possible to distinguish the songs of one singer from those of another, even when we have only the bare text without music and vocal nuance. (2000, 4–5)

Lord continues, "The term 'oral' emphasizes, I believe, the basic distinction between oral narrative poetry and that which we term literary epic.... Oral, however, does not mean merely oral presentation.... What is important is not the oral performance but rather the composition *during* oral performance." Oral composition and oral performance, to these scholars, is not synonymous with or limited to rote repetition from memory, or memorization, on the one hand, or improvisation, on the other hand. "It is true that also that oral epic is transmitted by word of mouth from one singer to another.... With oral poetry, we are dealing with a particular or distinctive process in which oral learning, oral composition, and oral transmission almost merge; they seem to be different facets of the same process" (2000, 5).

Parry's concern with oral epic poems stemmed from his interest in the centuries-old question of how Homer's tales were composed and transmitted in an era with little evidence of writing and none of records of compositions of the content, complexity, and length of such poems. To answer these questions required revising conceptions of both orality and composition and their relationships, and in turn, of writing. The discovery that the syllabic system known as Linear B was a form of Mycenaean Greek that preceded the development of a Greek alphabet consisting of a limited number of consonants and vowels demonstrated that writing existed at the time of the Homeric poems. It also indicated that writing was apparently not used for literary works or for composition in the terms we have come to recognize it. "Ironically enough, however," wrote Lord, "the proof has come at a time when many scholars realize that the existence of writing or even of a literary tradition does not necessarily mean that Homer's poems belong in the category of 'written' literature; and many realize … that obviously our Homeric texts could not have been preserved had there not been writing in Homer's day" (2000, 9). In fact, we need to think in terms of multiple authors who did not write in the literal sense of the term, and of texts that were variable and changeable but did become more fixed. So-called inconsistencies take on different meanings.

This revised conception of both oral composition and performance and the emergence and spread of writing underlies an understanding of the creation, transmission, and performance of Homer's epic poems; their reception; and, in time, their preservation and fixity in written record, which took hundreds of years. In this dynamic process, neither orality not literacy is stable or fixed. Our conceptions of authors and writers and of the powers of early literary creation all change. Interactions and relationships between speech and writing replace notions of stark transitions and divides.

The example of oral composition, performance, and recording in antiquity is seminal. Parry and Lord's interpretations have been spread widely by Havelock and Ong, among others. There is much debate over the processes of dictation to a scribe, the use of formulas in oral and written composition and performance, and the metricality of Homeric verse.[10] Nonetheless, a little imagination and attention to the facts of composition and performance, in their multiple meanings, prompts an appreciation of revised views of orality and literacy. That has been lacking.

Alphabets and their Legacies

Experts, be they classicists or scholars of oral poetry, differ about the meanings and applications of these studies of the connections between speaking and writing. The full import of these interactive relationships for literacy and literacy studies, I argue, has not been appreciated or assimilated. As Eric Havelock's sometimes brilliant and sweeping interpretations indicate, it is difficult to sustain the insights that become possible from an appreciation of the presence and power of the oral under the growing shadow of writing and the presumptions of its dominance.

For example, Havelock has been claimed prominently by the proponents of the literacy episteme. Yet, in his celebrated *Preface to Plato* (1963), he followed the leads of Parry and Lord in a sympathetic, often sensitive account of "the oral sources of the Hellenic intelligence" (to borrow one of his chapter titles). We will never know how Homer was written down and can only speculate about why, if it is indeed the case, as Havelock put it, that "the Greek alphabet, both at the time of its invention and for many generations after, was not applied in the first instance to transcribing vernacular statements but rather to those previously composed according to the oral rules of memorization" (1977, 371).

Havelock's seminal opening led to inconsistent, even contradictory interpretations of the history of orality and the development and uses of literacy, especially writing. For example, he seems to confuse metricality with formulae, which suggests rather paradoxically that writing systems are more flexible than speaking from memory. The emphasis on Greek literacy dominated over the power of orality, replacing a recognition of mutually shaping interactions. Havelock's reconstruction, which is accepted by some but not all scholars, is based on no direct evidence but an imaginative scenario of a passage from sound to sight, ear to eye (Havelock 1973, 1982, 1983; compare to Harris 1989; Thomas 2009). That begs the question of the relationships between orality and literacy, not the domination of divides that often followed him.

Havelock's emphasis was more apparent in subsequent works with more teleological titles such as *Origins of Western Literacy* (1976), *The Literate Revolution in Greece and Its Cultural Consequences* (1982), and *The Muse Learns to Write* (1986). The shift is clear. With leaps of time and space, logic and evidence, the "invention" of the Greek alphabet enabled not only writing but also literature, democracy, history, philosophy, science, and much more. The divide returns. A single-minded—if dramatically incomplete—triumph of literacy achieved hegemony.

Moreover, proponent of this view went on to argue that the alphabet was "imprinted" on the mind of the Greeks, changing their brains and their cognitive design and destiny as metaphors transcend reality. As "the muse learned to write," orality became secondary, residual, when not lost (and refound). With reference to poetry but not historical evidence, Havelock links first orality and then literacy to "evolutionary pressures [that] moulded the capacities of the human brain." He also noted that "it is possible that if literacy presents us with certain problems, these may not be soluble without reference to the habits of non-literacy" (1980, 91).

Despite this recognition, literacy triumphs, or so Havelock alleged. "The premise that the technology of communication controls the content of what is communicated has been popularized in connection with modern radio, cinema, and television," Havelock observed in 1980. He continued, "I am applying it in a more radical fashion to a shift in the character of the human consciousness which occurred in ancient Greece and which we inherit. Briefly I am arguing that the history of the human mind, as of the human language, falls into roughly two epochs, the pre-alphabetic and the post-alphabetic. The possibilities of the latter took time to realize themselves in Greece and emerged in the writings of Plato and Aristotle. Even then they were not fully realized.... [They] are still going on in our own day" (1980, 97). With references to genes, the brain, and the biological bases of cognition, a number of writers have repeated, reified, and further simplified these claims.[11]

Note the formulaic *from/to* quality of the conceptions of the relationships between orality and literacy. In their classic statements, Parry and Lord, as well as Havelock, place enormous importance on formulaic elements both in oral composition and in memorization and performance. Poetic meter typically lies at the center. With respect to Homer, as Lord summarized, Parry's "discovery of the intricate schematization of the formulas in the Homeric poems has never been challenged; though there have been critics who have not been willing to accept his interpretation of the meaning and implication of the phenomenon of formulaic structure." (Lord 2000, 142; see also Lord 1995, esp. Chap. 8) Of course, the Greek hexameter is "probably the best known meter in all literature" (Lord 2000, 142). The study of lines became a test to determine whether a poetic composition was oral or written, and in the process, basically formulaically, a strength became a limitation. Literate, as opposed to oral compositions, it is argued, are much less formulaic: "A *literary* text will show a predominance of nonformulaic expressions" (130).

Havelock takes a further and different turn. He asserts that the "effects" of the alphabetic and its use in first transcription and then writing "were to go deeper ... affecting the structure of language and thought.... Vocabulary and syntax had been controlled by the pressure to memorize. This limited everything that was said to what could be said rhythmically, and in narrativized form." He continues, equally hypothetically and even more metaphorically: "Once the same speech is placed in documented form, the pressure to memorize is relieved.... Therefore the pressures for poetry as a preservative, and for a restriction to narrative syntax, are relieved also. The twin possibilities exist of a preserved prose, and a prose which no longer tells a story. It can allow itself to express other types of discourse" (Havelock 1986, 6–7).

The conception of speech, ironically, becomes thin as that of writing becomes thick (see also Brockmeier 2000, 2002; Brockmeier and Olson 2009; Olson 1994). Without acknowledging how he has himself moved into his own formulae, Havelock asserts, with respect to written Homeric poems, that "this kind of vocabulary, conceptual and abstract, only became possible as an end product of the literate revolution" (1986, 7).[12]

Formulating Divides

"From oral to written," "speech to script," "poetry to prose," "memory to written record," the divides (great and small) and the teleological trajectories know no limits. The rub, indeed the contradiction, lies in the fact that those who stress the limits of formulae with respect to oral communications and composition contradict themselves when they turn to writing and the impact of literacy. They create new limiting formulae.

Revealingly, following the lead about the role of formulae in oral composition from Homer to Serbo-Croatian singers of tales limits its scope and influence. That difficulty is seldom recognized. First, we appreciate the enormously important discovery of the extent and power of oral composition from the time of Homer to contemporary poets, singers, and speakers around the world in its implications for understanding literacy. Second, that appreciation is accompanied by a debate over the uses and consequences of formulae in oral composition. Together, they set the terms and underscore the opportunities for better understanding. Among other things, they may move our understanding beyond the question of the "absolute" versus "potential" differences between the oral and the written.

Despite scholarly gestures from Parry and Lord, who appreciated the power of the oral, to Goody, Havelock, Ong, and others, the question of ongoing, shaping relationships between orality and literacy disappear into formulaic differences and divides. Havelock delivers a cultural realm of dichotomies that undercuts the richness and complexity of his own emphasis on the preliterate poetic composition: "the muse learns to write," "a text speaks," "preliterate orality is primary" compared to later orality, "Homer becomes alphabetized," orality "erodes."

Though it appears that his work is more often cited than read, Walter Ong (1958, 1967, 1977, 1982) takes up much of the mantle of Havelock but gives it an explicitly religious spin, avowing the "Word" and splitting orality into "primary" and "secondary," direct and interpersonal, and artificially distanced and broadcast. More pointedly, with scant regard to evidence or sociocultural and historical context, he introduces a host of quasi-theoretical oppositions between orality and literacy. His "psycho-dynamics" of orality comprise "further characteristics of orally based thought and expression." In contrast to literacy, for Ong, orality is "additive" rather than "subordinative"; "aggregative" rather than "analytic"; "redundant" or "copious"; "conservative" or "traditionalist"; "close to the human lifeworld" "agonistically toned"; "empathetic and participatory" rather than "objectively distanced"; "homeostatic"; "situational rather than abstract; and interior." Often repeated, the dichotomies become reified and accepted unquestionably despite their tendentious and problematic status. Orality descends into psychological reductionism (for which there is no evidence).

Importantly, in sharp contrast, Finnegan returns constructively to the issue of the "variability" of oral composition, in its dependence on performance, in contrast with the "fixity" of the written. In part based on the study of South Pacific oral literature and in part on a critique of what she sees as the dominant western model in light of Parry and Lord, she revises the terms of comparison: "The most highly regarded and specialist form of poetic composition commonly involved precisely the *opposite* characteristics from what we might expect starting with the prevailing orthodoxy. Much Pacific poetry is composed *prior* to performance, depends for its performance on a fixed and memorized version, and does involve the concept of a verbally 'correct' text" (Finnegan 1988, 90).

Finnegan assures her readers that she is not arguing that this is true of all oral literature in Oceania. Rather, she "throws some doubt on the universalist assumption implicit in the oralformulaic school and its disciples who give the impression that only *one* form—that epitomized by the Yugoslav model as explicated by Parry and Lord—characterizes the composition of oral literature; 'a special technique of composition outside our own field of experience', one which is characteristics of 'all oral poetries' and perhaps, according to some extensions of the theory, of oral prose and oral traditional generally" (1988, 90).

Two points follow, both enormously important for how we begin to revision literacy. First, both orality *and* literacy are variable. Second, they interact, each shaping and reshaping the other. In Havelock's terms, such relationships are central to both preliteracy *and* literacy. They are central to the missing chapters of Parry and Lord. Lord describes such interaction without incorporating it fully into his conceptualization and definitions (2000, 130). Finnegan captures the variability: It is now well established that writing can be used for different purposes and with different philosophies in different societies: there is not just *one* context for writing or one established stage (evolutionary or otherwise) to which it corresponds. The same variety, it seems, applies to oral communication: it too can take a number of different forms and appear with different characteristics in different cultures. (Finnegan 1988, 108) She elaborates, "There is perhaps after all no one abiding set of characteristics that *always* appears in 'oral culture' (any more than in 'literate culture'), but there are instead a number of different options and differing possibilities." They are "exemplified by the varying arrangements that have proved possible for the composition and performance of oral literature…. Though there are a number of differences between oral and written communication, these differences are not necessarily absolute and universal ones" (108).

Finnegan's report on South Pacific oral narrative contradicts expectations, received wisdom, and theories. As she notes, "It is commonly assumed that the technology of writing provides the opportunity for a neutral record of oral forms, or, alternatively, that it is somehow intrinsically opposed to or even 'kills' *oral* literary expression." This is not always the case. In this example, writing was "a formative and creative act rather than a neutral one. It not only turned an oral into a written form, with consequent stress on the significance of verbal text, linear formulation and length as distinct from performance…. At the same time, the increasing availability of these written versions fed into the *oral* literary tradition. In the South Pacific, it seems, there were not (as sometimes supposed) two separate and opposed modes but, both now and in the past, form part of one dynamic in which both written and oral forms interact" (1988, 122).

Is it so different elsewhere? Interactions inform us more powerfully and usefully than stages, divides, and formulae. Literacy studies, if it is to move forward, must reopen this question. A new human communicative and creative world awaits us.[13]

Between the Oral and the Written

That orality and literacy shape and reshape each other dynamically is central to the understanding of the stereotypical "making of literate society." Less well-known but equally telling and instrumental in the progress toward the disciplines of anthropology and linguistics are the understandings and actions of usually Christian, Western, and imperial missionaries as they encountered the proverbial "other"—nonliterate, primitive, uncivilized, and heathen—in historical moments of "contact." Cross-cultural and linguistic translation is often at the core of the interactions.

To begin, Finnegan's South Pacific, especially Fijian, accounts demonstrate interactions between oral and written compositions which in some cases she traces to nineteenth-century missionary activities. For example, "modern Samoan oratory is shot through with biblical references; the popular Fijian *same* are specially composed poems on Christian themes; Christian hymns in local languages are common throughout the area" (1988, 112). Finnegan refers to Africa and Egypt in the "establishment of an oral tradition authenticating the teachings of mission schools." Some legends, such as the *Kaunitoni*, which serves socially cohesive functions of nationalization, have been taken to be a prehistoric oral composition. "But it is no more closely related to Fijian culture than [the flag or coat of arms] it does not, apparently, antedate them" (115).

More generally and historically, "the influence of writing and the interest of foreigners have encouraged the systematic collecting and formulation of stories, often partly moulded by their own interests and preconceptions. In practice, writing has played a major part in the preservation and formulation of so-called 'oral tradition' in the Pacific … for example, the Maori "myths" about creation, the primary gods, the peopling of the world, and the occupation of particular tracts of land by the owners" (Finnegan 1988, 115). This process includes "feedback": the presence within oral forms of material from written sources, especially the Bible. The oral and the written are inseparable.

Donald F. McKenzie's now-classic narrative of the coming of print to the Maori people deepens our understanding. In *Bibliography and the Sociology of Texts*, McKenzie cuts into the process by interrogating a "prime example of European assumptions about the comprehension, status, and binding power of written statements and written consent against the flexible accommodations of oral consensus on the other" (1999, 79).

As a result, the assembled Maori chiefs who, in February 1840, agreed to the Treaty of Waitangi had, in their eyes and minds, a different understanding of the actions and meanings of "signing" and assenting than British agents and observers, then and later. Underlying the complications were the relationships between orality and literacy. First there is orthography and philology. McKenzie observes: "Just imagine the problems of trying to capture strange sounds alphabetically … translat[ing] visually the aural beauty of the originals [Maori words]…. Those spellings are not only aurally inefficient, but to a differently acculturated English ear, they may appear crude and culturally primitive, thus reinforcing other such attitudes…. The absence of a philology (let alone a grammar and syntax for a non-European language) made a rational orthography hard to devise. Yet until there was an orthography, the teaching of reading and writing was obviously impossible, and printing of course depended upon a standard set of letter forms" (1999, 82).

Despite some controversy over whether it was possible to do so, by 1830 the English developed an Anglicized alphabet of five vowels and nine consonants. McKenzie comments, "Those decisions about letter forms were typographically efficient but culturally explosive, for by giving English words a Maori semblance they disguise their quite different conceptual import" (1985, 84). On one hand, missionaries and civil and royal authorities presumed the need to alphabetize and create a basis for writing—for religious proselytization and conversion and for schooling. But on the other hand, given their assumptions about writing and language, both spoken and written, they did not recognize either differences or interrelationships.

During the pre-print years (1815–30) missionaries began to teach reading and writing. "The decision to teach those skills in the vernacular had long since been settled elsewhere in Bengal…. It also seemed an efficient policy." English was hard to learn and "a universal conversation of parent and child, of old and young, was only conceivable if they were bound together by a common speech within which the new learning would pass quickly, unimpeded by language barriers" (McKenzie 19, 84).

The missionaries simultaneously feared and depended on literacy. As to languages: "the missionaries were all too well aware that English would give the Maori access to the worst aspects of European experience. By containing them culturally within their own language, they hoped to keep them innocent of imperial evils." As to the practice and content of reading: "By restricting them further to the reading of biblical texts and vocabulary, they limited the Maori to knowledge of an ancient middle-eastern culture." This entailed more than reading by itself. "At the same time the missionaries enhanced their familiar pastoral role by making the Maori dependent on them morally and politically.... In 1833 William Williams wrote that 'A reading population, whose only book is the Word of God, cannot fail to make a great moral change in the face of the country, as soon as that Word begins to take effect'" (McKenzie 1985, 84). This was an adaptable strategy, too. "Such a vision implied that priority be given to the translation of the Scriptures into Maori. This ideological bias was reinforced by doctrinal strike in 1839–40, just when the policy should have been relaxed but when the Church Missionary Society faced competition from Bishop Pompallier's Catholic mission and press" (85).

It is likely that the missionaries expected the Maori bible to teach a larger audience by oral reading. Text and prayer book printing spread the Bible. Missionaries reported Maori enthusiasm to learn to read and ease in doing so. They expected the Maori to be ready and rapid learners, as did their counterparts elsewhere (Tagupa 1981; Clammer 1976; for comparisons, see Graff 1979, 1991).

Biblical texts did have an impact on Maori consciousness later in the century. But it was not the impact of the written (or spoken) Word that was anticipated. These texts "provid[ed] a new source of imagery in song and story and sharpen[ed] the expression of economic and political pressures on Government" (McKenzie 1999, 85). McKenzie calls the missionaries and teachers naïve, but that may not be most accurate term for their lack of comprehension or mistaken expectations about literacy.

As is apparently the case in Hawai'i and Fiji, expectations and proud announcements of a rapid transition to literacy in a newly created written language were unfounded. "It is as if the very notion of literacy itself compelled a heightened language of self-approval and infinite promise."

The divide was met and transcended rhetorically but not practically. "Victims of their own myths, the missionaries found what they wanted to find, and report what they knew their London committee wished to hear" (McKenzie 1999, 88).

Seeking to understand, McKenzie returns to the oral-literate relationship. He identifies by analogy a critical issue in that complicated connection. "If we reflect that the teaching of elementary reading is primarily oral/aural, because it involves the pronouncing and repetition of letters, syllables, and words (a practice reinforced where there are few books, fewer texts, and group teaching), we can appreciate how oral repetition from memory might masquerade as reading and the Maori—used to an oral tradition—had a most retentive memory" (1999, 91). Underscoring a problem that has persisted over millennia, McKenzie risks reifying the oralliterate divide in attempting to explain why the Maori did not surmount it. He may well be correct in part, but, like the missionaries, he neglects the relationships and mutual influences that sometimes tie speech and writing. Memory and reading or writing are not necessarily opposites. At the same time, contrary to the beliefs of the missionaries, neither are they necessarily complementary. With or without prodigious memories, Maoris may have heard more effectively or efficiently than they read. Writing developed even less.

As in other societies at different points in time where writing was not dominant (and perhaps many more where it was), "the main use of literacy to the Maori was not reading books for their ideas, much less for the access they gave to divine truths, but letter writing. For them, the really miraculous point about writing was its portability; by annihilating distance, a letter allowed the person who wrote it to be in two places at once.... It was the spatial extension of writing, not its temporal permanence, that became politically potent in gathering the tribes and planning a war a decade and more later" (McKenzie 1999, 93). A letter, after all, can be dictated and read aloud to many. The various elements also combined in the making of a literate elite among the Maori over several decades. The value of printing gained recognition among the Maori, too, despite— or because—of the great hope of the missionaries (95–96). For the missionaries, the idea of the printing press long proved more powerful than their ability to use it in practice. They held to both a reading myth and a printing myth.[14]

For the Maori, evidence of the reception of print, including the Bible, indicates that they gave it "a totemic power of warding off not only evil.... Books were also useful for making roll-yourown cartridges" (McKenzie 1999, 107). But schools and print were not so useful. On the part of the missionaries, McKenzie observes, "What we have here is not only disillusionment about the actual extent to which literacy of the most elementary kind had been achieved, but a clear example of the way in which even the most sophisticated technology (print) will fail to serve an irrelevant ideology (an alien religion)." As a result, "The missionaries and their great instrument of truth had failed lamentably to equip the Maori in the one area that really mattered to them—land. Nor was it merely a failure in creating literacy in Maori. In 1844 almost no Maori spoke (let alone read) English" (108–109). The failure was two-fold: lack of distribution of land ownership and promotion of literacy in English. They are not unrelated. In sum, "Historians have too readily and optimistically affirmed extensive and high levels of Maori literacy in the early years of settlement, and the role of printing in establishing it. Protestant missionary faith in the power of the written word, and modern assumptions about the impact of the power in propagating it, are not self-evidently valid, and they all too easily distort our understanding of the different and competitively powerful realities of societies whose cultures are still primarily oral" (109–110). To the contrary, some among the missionaries and their printer showed an awareness of the complications and of the oral-literate interactions, regardless of the halting spread of literacy and the exaggerated power of print.

At the time and for decades thereafter, the interactions between the oral and the written were lost. The Treaty of Waitangi that Maori chiefs signed on February 6 was not a translation of any of five extant English versions, Further, 39 names were added to an English copy of the treaty over the next seven months "which the signatories, being pre-literate, could not have read even if they had known the language" (McKenzie 1999, 111). In fact, the number of signatories is uncertain and many of the names were written by the government clerk for the chiefs. Personal reading of the treaty is no more likely; McKenzie calls it a "chimera."

The Maori responded to a document read out loud to them: "an oral statement, not as a document drawn up in consultation with the Maori, pondered privately over several days or weeks and offered finally as public communique of agreements reached by the parties concerned. Without begging any questions about Pakeha [British colonialists] intent to deceive, even the Maori language itself was used against the Maori" (McKenzie 1999, 113).

Inattention to the relationship between the oral and the written, as well as the failure of the missionaries' literacy campaign of the 1830s, remind us that these questions are of great consequence. The treaty was read aloud but oral discussion was proscribed. The British pronounced a final document—"all who draft documents secure an initiative, determine the concepts, and choose the linguistic terms by which to reveal or conceal them," whereas "a collective oral response is rarely unanimous about details of wording: it tends to assume continuing discussion and modifications, and lacking a documentary form, it is weaker in its power to bind when a group disperses" (McKenzie 1999, 117; compare to Clanchy 1993). The Maori chiefs and the British documents and understanding differed because their words and their understanding differed. This was not a matter of a divide between speech or orality and writing, Literacy did not replace non-literacy; they continued to shape and influence each other. Literacy, orality, and their uses reflect colonial power, and understanding their relationships was and remains fundamental to the foundations of linguistics and other disciplines.

McKenzie reminds all students of literacy that "that spirt [of understanding] is only recoverable if texts are regarded not simply as verbal constructs but as social products. Crucial to that development is Pakeha recognition of their own myth of literacy and recognition of the status or oral culture and spoken consensus." For example, "For many Maori, the spirit of the treaty is best served by the Maori text, in which *kawanatanga* means what it says (governorship, not sovereignty), in which the *taonga* guaranteed by the Crown include all that is materially and spiritually precious, in which Maori and Pakeha share the Queen's protection as equal partners." In that understanding, the treaty in Maori is a sacred covenant. The English versions "distort its effect and remain caught in the mesh of documentary history and juridical process." McKenzie concludes that the Maori always knew "there is a real world beyond the niceties of the literal text and in that world there is in fact a providential version now editing itself into the status of a social and political document of power and purpose. The physical versions and their fortuitous forms are not the only testimonies to intent" (1999, 127–128).[15]

The dynamics of the passage from *Memory to Written Record: England 1066–1307* stands among the formative examples that speak to the heart of these issues. Historian Michael Clanchy (1993) painstakingly captures the dialectics of orality and literacy in his evocation of the shifting relationships not only of memory and written record but also of hearing and seeing, reading and writing themselves, and the emergence of a more "literate mentality." Clanchy explores symbolic objects, spoken versus written words, listening to the word, writing as a work of art, and the relationships between words and images.

In the Americas

The history of the Americas provides equally rich grounds for revisioning the fundamental relationships that interconnect, rather than divide, the oral and the literate, the spoken and the written. Consequential and suggestive encounters are found in many Old World–New World, imperial and indigenous, extended and mutually reshaping episodes of so-called discovery, attempted conquest, and conflict. South America, to pursue one example, is particularly well studied, and the scholarly debates about the Andean collisions between the Spanish and the native peoples of Peru and Columbia are particularly instructive. Their literatures, documents, and debates provide case studies for all who seek to surmount the stultifying and sometimes profoundly misleading legacies of divides, great and otherwise.

In all cases, we find a clash of cultures, languages, and assumptions about the power of the Word and words. Presumptions about the superiority of European languages, alphabets, and systems of writing and about the limits of various native peoples and their languages abound. We also find tales of power and resistance inseparably intertwined with languages, writing, reading, and the uses of literacy. The alphabet and the alphabetization of indigenous languages are inextricably connected with the overlapping and complementary but not always synonymous forces of Christianization and imperial conquest.

The recent historiography reveals a major shift in understanding away from great divide conceptions and uncritical acceptance of European views of the inferiority of local and indigenous languages, oral traditions and communication, and writing systems (when present). There is now a greater recognition and appreciation of their complex interactions and the agency of the indigenous peoples. Recent studies seldom focus separately on the orality of the natives and the literacy of the newcomers, but rather explore resistance and the dynamic interaction between the oral and written (see Hanks 2010; Rappaport 1990; Rappaport and Cummins 2012).

Traditions of linguistics, anthropology, and history are all implicated.

Studies of indigenous literacies in the Andes identify alphabetic literacy dating back five hundred years and other writing systems predating that. Scholars have uncovered a "hidden history" of indigenous literacy. In *The Lettered Mountain: A Peruvian Village's Way with Writing* (2011), Frank Salomon and Mercedes Niño-Murcia examine mountain villagers' writings from Inka times to the present. They elaborate the dimensions and understanding of literacy and challenge stereotypes of orality. They draw attention to a seventeenth-century Quechua-language book that explained ancient priesthood and gods. Contrary to expectations, the archives expose a distinctive legacy of letters that precedes the presence of state schools.

Writing long underlay specifically Andean sacred culture and self-governance. Yet Salomon and Niño-Murcia also demonstrate the power wielded by the nation-state in its writing standards. Those standards developed in relationship with European authorities including academies and cultural institutions, but not with the rural literate or oral tradition (see also Salomon 2001; Seed 1991).

In *Beyond the Lettered City: Indigenous Literacies in the Andes*, Joanne Rappaport and Tom Cummins probe the written record. More in accord with Finnegan's work than the standard narrative, they discover use of formulaic expression deriving from a Spanish legal convention of the colonial period, rather than remnant of an earlier oral tradition. They find litigators "attempt[ing] to advance claims by transcending an imperfect paper trail through expanding the scope of written evidence by means of an appeal to oral tradition.... 'Time immemorial' thus became a colonial indigenous vehicle for asserting what was meant to appear as a more ancient authenticity, legitimizing rights by appeal to customary law and to the oral memory" (2012, 169).

In addition, along the same lines identified by Clanchy in medieval England and Finnegan in the South Pacific, Rappaport and Cummins discover that "oral and symbolic traditions inserted in the documentary record became elements of the scripted past, following European legal conventions through which orality and literacy became intertwined" (2012, 169). Critically, and no less reminiscent of practice and experience today, they report from records of the late 1690s, "once the written record was internalized by Pasto witnesses, it was not all that easy for them to separate those narratives that they had acquired through oral traditions from the evidence that was read to them or commented on by other readers. In effect, we are speaking of a 'paraliterate' system, where literacy involves much more than command of the technologies of reading and writing." They conclude "it is difficulty to extricate orality from alphabetic literacy in dispute documents because by the seventeenth century, the Pastos were inextricably bonded with a colonial culture whose very nature was defined in part by legal discourse. The indigenous respondents, moreover, understood the value of writing and the legal conventions that underlay its use" (169–170).[16]

Rethinking the Relationships between Orality and Literacy

Recent and contemporary approaches in sociolinguistics are heir to long and formative legacies. Beset with internal divisions, some reflecting traditions of the divides between orality and literacy, the field has struggled for a recognized place within linguistics and anthropology (and sometimes education). From its beginnings, it has been mired in conflicts about the nature of language and communication themselves. Much revolves around question of language as oral or speech versus language as written or literate, the deeply rooted question of differences or relationships. For example, despite the recent emphasis on the importance of different languages and translations in the connections between orality and literacy, it is remarkable that recent interest in globalization and global English(es) does not pay attention to the interaction of orality/speech with writing and communication.[17]

A curious but perhaps not surprising chapter in this passage took place in the journey from Dell Hymes's "perspective for linguistic anthropology" (1964a) to John Szwed's "ethnography of literacy" (1981). The oral—speech—was all but lost.[18] Ironically (or perhaps not), a different field developed that should have been but was not connected to literacy: the ethnography of speaking (see Hymes 1962). This approach is encapsulated in the title of a landmark publication, "Poetics and performance as critical perspectives on language and social life," by Richard Bauman and Charles Briggs (1990). The recent fashionable notion of "performing" literacy—as anything and everything is seen as a performance—was not yet in the air. The penultimate chapter of the collection *Explorations in the Ethnography of Speaking* (Bauman and Sherzer 1989) dealt with writing, but the interrelationships of orality and literacy were not a focus of that book.

The role of the oral is taken seriously only in young children's learning (or not learning) to read. That is the obvious exception to the rule.[19] Orality has been considered, often but not always negatively, in studies of minority, racial, gender, and class cultures. This enormously important, sometimes revelatory, research tends to emphasize cultural and communicative differences. For example, it has helped the understanding of cultural clashes and their impact on "school failures." But its focus in general has not been on oral-literacy interrelationships, and when it has, the emphasis falls on the different uses of both orality and literacy from school and "proper" middle-class standards.[20]

In the last three decades, important openings and avenues have been lost in a rush to talk about "literacy events," often out of context, and to do "ethnographies of literacy or writing" that are not ethnography but observation. This stands in contradiction to the scholars, like Shirley Brice Heath, who influenced the beginnings of the tradition, borrowing or adapting from "speech acts" or "speech events." The tradition of difference and of a necessary transition to writing and literacy has obscured them.

I urge a sustained return to those leads. Consider for example, Wallace Chafe and Deborah Tannen's 1987 review essay, "The Relation between

Written and Spoken Language." Beginning with the curious claim that "linguists have been late to realize that differences between spoken and written language are worth their attention," they write off hundreds of years of attention that preceded the disciplinization of linguistics in the twentieth century (1987, 383). In reviewing twentieth-century and more recent research, they certainly document the emphasis on difference, especially in studies of literacy.

Tannen provides a revealing example of the opportunity and the problem in a summary article that begins her edited collection *Spoken and Written Language: Exploring Orality and Literacy* (1982). Divides permeate this realm; interactions and relationships are limited. She recognizes that "all the scholars whose work I have cited point out that literate tradition does not replace oral. Rather, when literacy is introduced, the two are superimposed upon and intertwined with each other. Similarly, no individual is either 'oral' or 'literate.'" She reiterates that "people use devices associated with both traditions in various settings. Goody and Watt suggest that oral tradition is associated with the family and the ingroup, while literate tradition is learned and passed on in the decontextualized setting of the school. Certainly, this is typically true…. But strategies associated with one or other tradition can be realized in any setting and in any mode" (Tannen 1982, 3).

Shifting between notions of public and private as well as literate and oral, Tannen suggests but stops short of a more integrated and dynamic conception. Recognition of the roles of power, authority, hierarchy (including age), social relationships, or institutions is absent. Critical relationships are obscured; where are the complex shaping and reshaping of the oral *and* the literate, the written *and* the spoken? To speak or write of "oral/literate continuum" or the "oral/literate paradigm" (Tannen 1982, 3–4) is only a small step beyond difference or opposition.

Shirley Brice Heath's classic work, *Ways with Words: Language, Life, and Work in Communities and Classrooms* (1983, with a new epilogue in 1996 and updates in 1990 and 2012), remains the most sophisticated demonstration of the dialectically reshaping relationships of the oral and the literate. Disagreements with Health's book typically centered on matters of ideology, concerning the weight placed on race, class, and inequality and on the attention to policy and government. Critics often failed to appreciate what the author explicitly set out to do, and sometimes read it with reference to Heath's silences rather than to her rich ethnographies of speech, writing, and reading. Yet the book continues to command attention both for its examples and its role as an exemplar. Too often, even those New Literacy Studies scholars who rhetorically eschew dichotomies continue to search for them.[21] Together, these matters have distracted their attention away from the centrality of the oral in its inseparable connections with the literate.

Much of *Ways with Words* documents the different relative emphasis on the valuation and the practice of orality and literacy across racial, social class, and community lines in her study sites in the North Carolina Piedmont: the working-class African American and white communities of Trackton and Roadville, and the neighboring white and African American "mainstream" communities. Residents of these communities were all highly supportive of education for their children and regularly made use of reading and writing at least for instrumental reasons. This was true regardless of other class and cultural differences, which varied with respect to the use of reading and writing and the presence of books in the home, reading bedtime stories, or valuing and demonstrating frequent practices ("literate habits") of reading and writing.

Especially compelling is Heath's ethnographic focus on comparison and relationships in arenas including families, civic life, and religious institutions across these communities. In each setting, she explores the interrelationship of orality and literacy, with an unusual absence of explicit judgmentalism. Heath rhetorically captured her interpretive thrusts in the title of a summary article published as *Ways with Words* went to press: "Protean Shapes in Literacy Events: EverShifting Oral and Literate Traditions" (Heath 1982). Questioning conceptions of a great divide, she also commented on how little we knew—and, I add, how little we continue to know—about "the actual uses of literacy" at work settings; regular interactions in religious, economic, and legal institutions; and family socialization of children into uses of literacy. Heath explains: "In the clamor over the need to increase the teaching of basic skills, there is much emphasis on the positive effects extensive and critical reading can have on improving oral language. Yet there are scarcely any data comparing the forms and functions of oral language with those of written language produced and used by members of social groups within a complex society" (1982, 92– 93).

The story she tells for the Carolina Piedmont communities located historically around textile mills is a complicated weave of the oral and the literate, of speech, reading, and writing. They are exemplary but not representative of other communication. Nonetheless, despite our usual expectations for the operations of a bureaucratic society with government functions and work environments governed and structured by printed forms, writing, and now electronic versions, Heath finds assumptions often contradicted by everyday practices that show the written and the oral to be inseparable in practice, if not in theory, from the use of written materials at school, work, medical centers, and government offices. She often finds the written negotiated orally by groups, that is, collectively and socially. The realm of applications and instructions may be governed by writing, but it functions and is lubricated by speech. This is especially true for how people found paid work and much of the training to accomplish it.

To historians of literacy and work, this is not news. But to those who uncritically assume that a modern, industrial and postindustrial world replaces orality, especially "oral tradition," with absolute demands for advanced literacy, this conclusion is unexpected, even anathema. Heath expresses her hypothesis: careful and systematic "examination of the contexts and uses of literacy in communities today may show that THERE ARE MORE LITERACY EVENTS WHICH CALL FOR APPROPRIATE KNOWLEDGE OF FORMS AND USES OF SPEECH EVENTS THAN THERE ARE ACTUALLY OCCASIONS FOR EXTENDED READING OR WRITING" (Heath 1982, 94, capitals in original), She makes the trenchant observation that even persons more accustomed to an oral than a literate environment may well need more training and practice in oral interactions or the mediation of orality and literacy, in the acquisition of work or medical care, for example, than practice in reading and writing by themselves. Heath brilliantly describes the "ever-shifting interactions" of speech, song, reading, and writing in religious practice, as in other forms of cultural activity. These interactions—including reading and responding to written material—are often collective and social, not individual. There are great variations, of course. But the dynamic shaping and reshaping of literacy *and* orality is unmistakable.

None of this implies that literacy—reading, writing, and beyond across different modes of understanding and expression—is not essential. As Heath wrote in the 1980s, today "the traditional distinctions between the habits of those characterized as having either oral or literate traditions may not actually exist in many communities of the United States, which are neither non-literate nor fully literate. Their members can read and write at least at basic levels, but they have little occasion to use these skills as taught in school. Instead, much of their daily life is filled with literacy events in which they must know how to use and how to respond in the oral mode to written materials" (1982, 94).

This argument leads Heath to comment further that "descriptions of the concrete context of written communication which give attention to social and cultural features of the community as well as to the oral language surrounding written communications may discredit any reliance on characterizing particular communities as having reached either restricted or full development of literacy or as having language forms and functions associated more with the literate tradition than with the oral, or vice versa." In Trackton, for example, "written information almost never stood alone" (1982, 94, 99). In her 1990 and 2012 sequels to *Ways with Words*, Heath emphases out-of-school-learning more generally, in a world that is even more mediated by the oral and visual in no small part through the influence of electronics.

Heath concludes that "descriptions of these literacy events and their patterns of uses in Trackton do not enable us to place the community somewhere on a continuum from full literacy to restricted literacy or non-literacy" (1982, 111). This understanding is vitally important. Where I part company with Heath is when she points to "two continua, the oral and the written." Such a conceptualization is not, in my view, sufficient to capture and force us to integrate into our understanding of reading and writing across media and modes of comprehension and expression what she correctly highlights as the "protean shapes in literacy events: ever-shifting oral and literate traditions" (111).

Notes

1. I first used this rhetorical formulation in *Legacies of Literacy* (1987). The similarity between this formulation and the opening of the first chapter in Jack Goody's *Logic of Writing* (1986) is entirely coincidental. Yet the differences between our interpretations of this logocentric view are consequential. While I immediately underscore the principal issues and sources of confusion in understanding literacy, Goody turns a complex historical transformation into a formula.

2. Brockmeier's version of his "episteme" is deeply ahistorical; none of these formulations pays attention to context. Claims of its novelty are self-serving. Brockmeier and Olson's use of evidence is flawed. They confuse and conflate social, psychological, and intellectual issues; the general and specific; and literacy and writing. For one critique of Olson and his presumptions, see Halverson, "Olson on literacy" (1991); Halverson, "Goody and the implosion of the literacy thesis" (1992).

3. Brockmeier and Olson's "Literacy episteme" (2009, 9), declares the existence of a "field" after 1960, but that is not the same as an episteme.

4. For an interesting perspective, included in one of the testaments to the literacy episteme that, looking to the "future of writing" rather than the past and present, actually argues somewhat contradictorily against part of the accepted narrative, see Harris, "Literacy and the future of writing" (2002). See also Cook-Gumperz and Gumperz, "From oral to written culture" (1981), Cook-Gumperz, *Social construction*, 1986.

5. In "Are there linguistic consequences of literacy?" Biber argues: "For example, researchers such as O'Donnell (1974), Olson (1977), and Chafe (1982), argued that written language generally differs from speech in being more structurally complex, elaborated, and/or explicit" (Biber 2009, 75).

6. See the classic work of Basil Bernstein, Dell Hymes, Erving Goffman, William Labov, and their students. For introductions, see Bauman and Briggs, "Poetics and performance" (1990); Goffman, *Forms of Talk* (1981); Hymes, "Introduction: Toward ethnographies of communication" (1964b); Koerner, "Toward a history of modern sociolinguistics" (1991); Labov, *Sociolinguistic patterns* (1972); Shuy, "Brief history of American sociolinguistics," 1990; Szwed, "Ethnography of literacy" (1981).

7. Finnegan quotes then Director-General of UNESCO, Réné Maheu, speaking of the "apparent association between non-literacy and illiteracy" and asserting "one apparent consequence of nonliteracy: lack of literature" (1973, 113).

8. Among her major targets are Goody, Ong, Havelock, and McLuhan.

9. Yugoslavia was the name of the country when Lord published *The Singer of Tales* in 1960.

10. See for example, Lord's chapters on "Writing and Oral Tradition" and "Homer" in *Singers of Tales* (1960). Compare on one hand with Havelock's work and on the other hand with Finnegan, *Literacy and Orality* (1988). See also Lord, *Singer of Tales*, 2000; Parry, *Making of Homeric Verse* (1971).

11. Havelock and Marshall McLuhan were colleagues at the University of Toronto. Among the many influential works on the alphabetization of the brain that acknowledge a debt to Havelock is Maryanne Wolf's *Proust and the Squid* (2007). Havelock's work, which is pervaded by such slippages, is often cited on the "great transmission" or the revolutionary remaking of the human brain.

12. Compare with Lord, *Singers of Tales* (2000, 130) and the extended example of Yugoslav oral poets. Havelock, *Literate revolution in Greece* (1986, 167), refers to "erosion of orality."

13. Finnegan writes: "When we speak of both 'orality' and 'literacy' one or more of three main aspects may be involved: composition, performance, and transmission over time. These three do not always coincide. Thus it is possible for a work to be oral in performance but not in composition or transmission, or to have a written origin but non-written performance or transmission. These various combinations constitute a background to considering different patterns of transmissions…. The differing patterns do not coincide neatly with the distinction between oral and written traditions" (1988, 171–172). See Heath, *Ways with words* (1983); Schieffelin and Gilmore, *Acquisition of literacy* (1986); Tannen, *Spoken and written language* (1982). For examples of inattention to context and oral-literate relationships, see Canagarajah, *Translingual practice* (2013); Blommaert, *Grassroots literacy* (2008).

14. On letter writing, see popular South American films; Besnier, *Literacy, emotion and authority*, 1995; Cancian, *Families, lovers, and their letters* (2010); Henkin, *Postal age,* 2006; Kalman, *Writing on the plaza* (1990); Lyons, *Readers and society*, 2001; Lyons, *Reading culture and writing*

practices (2008); Lyons, *Writing culture of ordinary people* (2013); Romani, *Postal culture* (2013); Scribner and Cole, *Psychology of literacy* (1981); Vincent, *Literacy and popular culture* (1989); Vincent, *Rise of mass literacy* (2000).

15. Contrast the Maori's experience with that in Fiji described by Clammer, *Literacy and social change* (1976). According to Tagupa, "Education, change, and assimilation" (1981), missionaries and officials in Hawai'i presumed that an alphabetic translation and print led directly to mass literacy and expected that cultural and social changes would necessarily follow.

16. For Central and South America, Salomon, "How an Andean 'writing without words' works" (2001), Hanks, *Converting words* (2010), and Rappaport, *Politics of memory* (1990) form excellent case study material. See also Seed, "'Failing to marvel'" (1991). For great divide views, see Mignolo, *Darker side of the Renaissance* (1995); Boone and Mignolo, *Writing without words* (1994). For North America, recent scholarship on native peoples and their encounters with colonists informs the same fundamental questions and follows the same trajectory. Less sophisticated and less influenced by both linguistics and anthropology but now developing rapidly, Native American literacy studies has also been less influenced by scholarship in literacy studies. Regardless, it is ripe for revision with more sustained attention to the interaction between forms of orality and forms of literacy. It also speaks to the importance of non-alphabetic literacies, as Iroquois rituals, Dakota winter counts, and Pacific Northwest coast "totem poles" attest to other forms of record-keeping and a myriad of interactions that demonstrate cross-fertilization between oral and written forms. The colonizers also made deliberate use of cultural misrepresentation as a technique of coercion. Cessions of land, which the indigenous signatories thought of as temporary grants of use rights but which the English enforced as the entire alienation of all property rights, are well-known examples; for a survey, see Calloway, *Pen and ink witchcraft* (2013). For case studies, see Bross and Wyss, *Early Native literacies* (2008); Cohen, *Networked wilderness* (2010); Cushman, *Cherokee syllabary* (2011); S. Lyons, *X-marks* (2010); Morgan, *Bearer of this letter* (2009); Wyss, *Writing Indians* (2000).

17. For example, Canagarajah, *Translingual practice* (2013), repeats such catchwords and phrases as translingual, translocal, global, and cosmopolitan. Jan Blommaert's 2008 pseudo-ethnography, *Grassroots literacy*, also slights these fundamental linguistic dimensions.

18. See also Cook-Gumperz and Gumperz, "From oral to written culture" (1981).
19. Among the large literature, see Schieffelin and Gilmore, *Acquisition of literacy* (1986); Tannen, *Spoken and written language* (1982); Heath, *Ways with words* (1983); Dyson, *Multiple worlds of child writers* (1989); Dyson, "'Welcome to the jam'" (2003); Olson and Torrance, *Cambridge handbook of literacy* (2009).
20. For both examples of oppositions and differences, see Tannen, *Spoken and written language* (1982). The seminal work of Dell Hymes, Richard Bauman, and especially William Labov merits reopening by students of literacy.
21. See Street, *Literacy in theory and practice* (1984). For more on the debate over the New Literacy Studies, see Chap. 3.

References

Bauman, Richard, and Charles L. Briggs. (1990) Poetics and performance as critical perspectives on language and social life. *Annual Review of Anthropology* 19: 59–88.

Bauman, Richard, and Joel Sherzer, eds. (1989) *Explorations in the ethnography of speaking.* 2d ed. Cambridge: Cambridge University Press.

Besnier, Niko. (1995) *Literacy, emotion and authority: Reading and writing on a Polynesian atoll.* Cambridge: Cambridge University Press.

Biber, Douglas. (2009). Are there linguistic consequences of literacy? Comparing the potentials of language use in speech and writing. In David R. Olson and Nancy Torrance, eds, *The Cambridge handbook of literacy*, 75–91. Cambridge: Cambridge University Press.

Blommaert, Jan. (2008) *Grassroots literacy: Writing, identity, and voice in Central Africa.* Milton Park, Abingdon, and New York: Routledge.

Boone, Elizabeth Hill, and Walter D. Mignolo, eds. (1994) *Writing without words: Alternative literacies in Mesoamerica and the Andes.* Durham: Duke University Press.

Brockmeier, Jens. (2000) Literacy as symbolic space. In Janet Wilde Astington, ed., *Minds in the making: Essays in honor of David R. Olson*, 43–61. Oxford: Blackwell.

Brockmeier, Jens. (2002) The literacy episteme: The rise and fall of a cultural discourse. In *Literacy, narrative and culture*, ed. Jens Brockmeier, Min Wang, and David R. Olson, 17–34. Richmond, England: Curzon.

Brockmeier, Jens, and David R. Olson. (2009) The literacy episteme: From Innis to Derrida. In David R. Olson and Nancy Torrance, eds., *The Cambridge handbook of literacy*, 3–21. Cambridge: Cambridge University Press.

Bross, Kristina, and Hilary E. Wyss, eds. (2008) *Early Native literacies in New England: A documentary and critical anthology*. Amherst: University of Massachusetts Press.

Calloway, Colin G. (2013) *Pen and ink witchcraft: Treaties and treaty making in American Indian history*. New York: Oxford University Press.

Canagarajah, Suresh. (2013) *Translingual practice: Global Englishes and cosmopolitan relations*. London: Routledge.

Cancian, Sonia. (2010) *Families, lovers, and their letters: Italian postwar migration to Canada*. Winnipeg: University of Manitoba Press.

Chafe, Wallace, and Deborah Tannen. (1987) The relation between written and spoken language. *Annual Review of Anthropology* 16: 383–407.

Clammer, J. R. (1976) *Literacy and social change: A case study of Fiji*. Leiden: E.J. Brill.

Clanchy, Michael T. (1993) *From memory to written record: England, 1066–1307*. 2d ed. Oxford: Blackwell.

Cohen, Matt. (2010) *The networked wilderness: Communicating in early New England*. Minneapolis: University of Minnesota Press.

Cook-Gumperz, Jenny, and John J. Gumperz. (1981) From oral to written culture: The transition to literacy. In Marcia Farr Whitman, ed., *Variation in writing: Functional and linguisticscultural differences*, 89–109. Hillsdale, N.J.: Lawrence Erlbaum.

Cook-Gumperz, Jenny, ed. (1986) *The social construction of literacy*. Cambridge: Cambridge University Press.

Cushman, Ellen. (2011) *The Cherokee syllabary: Writing the people's perseverance*. Norman: University of Oklahoma Press.

Dyson, Anne Haas. (1989) *Multiple worlds of child writers: Friends learning to write*. New York: Teachers College Press.

Dyson, Anne Haas. (2003) "Welcome to the jam: Popular culture, school literacy, and the making of childhoods. *Harvard Educational Review* 79: 328–361.

Finnegan, Ruth. (1973) Literacy versus non-literacy: The great divide. In Robin Horton and Ruth Finnegan, eds, *Modes of Thought*, 112–144. London: Faber and Faber.

Finnegan, Ruth. (1988) *Literacy and Orality: Studies in the technology of communication*. Oxford: Blackwell.

Gee, James Paul. (1986) Orality and literacy: From *The Savage Mind* to *Ways with Words*. *TESOL Quarterly* 20: 719–746.

Gee, James Paul. (1996) *Social linguistics and literacies: Ideology in discourses.* 2d ed. London: Routledge.

Goffman, Erving. (1981) *Forms of talk.* Philadelphia: University of Pennsylvania Press.

Goody, Jack. (1986) *The logic of writing and the organization of society.* Cambridge: Cambridge University Press.

Goody, Jack, and Ian Watt. (1968) The consequences of literacy. In Jack Goody, ed., *Literacy in traditional societies*, 27–68. Cambridge: Cambridge University Press.

Graff, Harvey J. (1979) *The literacy myth: Literacy and social structure in the nineteenthcentury city.* New York: Academic Press.

Graff, Harvey J. (1991) *The literacy myth*, reprinted with new introduction. New Brunswick, N.J.: Transaction.

Halverson, John. (1991) Olson on literacy. *Language in Society* 20: 619–640.

Halverson, John. (1992) Goody and the implosion of the literacy thesis. *Man* (new series) 27: 301–317.

Hanks, William F. (2010) *Converting words: Maya in the age of the cross.* Berkeley: University of California Press.

Harris, Roy. (2002) Literacy and the future of writing: An integrational perspective. In Jens Brockmeier, Min Wang, and David R. Olson, eds, *Literacy, narrative and culture*, 35–66. Richmond, England: Curzon.

Harris, William V. (1989) *Ancient literacy.* Cambridge, Mass: Harvard University Press.

Havelock, Eric A. (1963) *Preface to Plato.* Cambridge, Mass: Harvard University Press.

Havelock, Eric Alfred. (1973) *Prologue to Greek literacy.* Cincinnati: University of Cincinnati Taft Lectures.

Havelock, Eric Alfred. (1976) *Origins of Western literacy.* Toronto: Ontario Institute for Studies in Education.

Havelock, Eric A. (1977) The preliteracy of the Greeks. *New Literary History* 8: 369–392.

Havelock, Eric A. (1980) The coming of literate communication to Western culture. *Journal of Communication* 30: 90–99.

Havelock, Eric A. (1982) *The literate revolution in Greece and its cultural consequences.* Princeton: Princeton University Press.

Havelock, Eric A. (1986) *The muse learns to write.* New Haven: Yale University Press.

Heath, Shirley Brice. (1982) Protean shapes in literacy events: Ever-shifting oral and literate traditions. In Deborah Tannen, ed., *Spoken and written language: Exploring orality and literacy*, 91–117. Norwood, N.J.: Ablex.

Heath, Shirley Brice. (1983) *Ways with words: Language, life, and work in communities and classrooms*. Cambridge: Cambridge University Press; with new epilogue, 1996.

Heath, Shirley Brice. (1990) The children of Trackton's children: Spoken and written language in social change. In James W. Stigler, Richard A. Shweder, and Gilbert S. Herdt, eds, *Cultural psychology: Essays on comparative human development*, 496–510. Cambridge: Cambridge University Press.

Heath, Shirley Brice. (2012) *Words at work and play: Three decades in family and community life*. Cambridge: Cambridge University Press.

Henkin, David. (2006) *The postal age: The emergence of modern communications in nineteenthcentury America*. Chicago: University of Chicago Press.

Hymes, Dell. (1962) The ethnography of speaking. In Thomas Gladwin and William C. Sturtevant, eds, *Anthropology and human behavior*, 15–53. Washington, D.C: Anthropological Society of Washington.

Hymes, Dell H. (1964a) A perspective for linguistic anthropology. In Sol Tax, ed., *Horizons of Anthropology*, 92–107. Chicago: Aldine.

Hymes, Dell H. (1964b) Introduction: Toward ethnographies of communication. *American Anthropologist* 66: 1–34.

Kalman, Judy. (1990) *Writing on the plaza: Mediated literacy practice among scribes and clients in Mexico City*. Cresskill, N.J: Hampton Press.

Koerner, Konrad. (1991) Toward a history of modern sociolinguistics. *American Speech* 66: 57–70.

Labov, William. (1972) *Sociolinguistic patterns*. Philadelphia: University of Pennsylvania Press.

Linell, Per. (2005) *The written language bias in linguistics: Its nature, origins, and transformations*. Milton Park, Abingdon, and New York: Routledge.

Lord, Albert B. (1960) *The singer of tales*. Cambridge, Mass.: Harvard University Press.

Lord, Albert B. (1995) *The singer resumes the tale*, ed. Mary Louise Lord. Ithaca: Cornell University Press, 1995.

Lord, Albert B. (2000) *The singer of tales*, 2d ed., ed. Stephen Mitchell and Gregory Nagy. Cambridge, Mass.: Harvard University Press.

Lurie, David B. (2011) *Realms of literacy: Early Japan and the history of writing*. Cambridge, Mass: Harvard University Asia Center.

Lyons, Martyn. (2001) *Readers and society in nineteenth-century France: Workers, women, peasants*. Basingstoke: Palgrave.

Lyons, Martyn. (2008) *Reading culture and writing practices in nineteenth-century France*. Toronto: University of Toronto Press.

Lyons, Martyn. (2013) *The writing culture of ordinary people in Europe, c. 1860–1920*. Cambridge: Cambridge University Press.

Lyons, Scott Richard. (2010) *X-marks: Native signatures of assent*. Minneapolis: University of Minnesota Press.

McKenzie, Donald F. (1999) *Bibliography and the sociology of texts*. Cambridge: Cambridge University Press.

Mignolo, Walter. (1995) *The darker side of the Renaissance: Literacy, territoriality, and colonialization*. Ann Arbor: University of Michigan Press.

Morgan, Mindy J. (2009) *The bearer of this letter: Language ideologies, literacy practices, and the Fort Belknap community*. Lincoln: University of Nebraska Press.

Olson, David R. (1994) *The world on paper: The conceptual and cognitive implications of writing and reading*. Cambridge: Cambridge University Press.

Olson, David R., and Nancy Torrance, eds. 2009. *The Cambridge handbook of literacy*. Cambridge: Cambridge University Press.

Ong, Walter J. (1958) *Ramus, method, and the decay of dialogue*. Cambridge, Mass.: Harvard University Press.

Ong, Walter J. (1967) *The presence of the word*. New Haven: Yale University Press.

Ong, Walter J. (1977) *Interfaces of the word*. Ithaca: Cornell University Press.

Ong, Walter J. (1982) *Orality and literacy*. London: Methuen.

Parry, Milman. (1971) *The making of Homeric verse: The Collected Papers of Milman Parry*, ed. Adam Parry. Oxford: Oxford University Press.

Rappaport, Joanne. (1990) *The politics of memory: Native historical interpretation in the Colombian Andes*. Durham: Duke University Press, 1990. 1

Rappaport, Joanne, and Tom Cummins. (2012) *Beyond the lettered city: Indigenous literacies in the Andes*. Durham: Duke University Press.

Romani, Gabriella. (2013) *Postal culture: Writing and reading letters in post-unification Italy*. Toronto: University of Toronto Press.

Säljö, Roger, ed. (1988) *The written word: Studies in literate thought and action*. Berlin: Springer-Verlag.

Salomon, Frank. (2001) How an Andean 'writing without words' works. *Current Anthropology* 42: 1–27.

Salomon, Frank, and Mercedes Niño-Murcia. (2011) *The lettered mountain: A Peruvian village's way with writing*. Durham, N.C: Duke University Press.

Schieffelin, Bambi B., and Perry Gilmore, eds. (1986) *The acquisition of literacy: Ethnographic perspectives*. Norwood, N.J: Ablex.

Scribner, Sylvia, and Michael Cole. (1981) *The psychology of literacy.* Cambridge, Mass: Harvard University Press.

Seed, Patricia. (1991) "Failing to marvel": Atahualpa's encounter with the word. *Latin American Research Review* 26: 7–32.

Shuy, Roger W. (1990) A brief history of American sociolinguistics, 1949–1989. *Historiographica Linguistica* 17: 183–209.

Street, Brian. (1984) *Literacy in theory and practice.* Cambridge: Cambridge University Press.

Szwed, John F. (1981) The ethnography of literacy. In Marcia Farr Whiteman, ed., *Variation in writing: Functional and linguistic-cultural differences*, 13–23. Hillsdale, N.J.: Lawrence Erlbaum.

Tagupa, William E. H. (1981) Education, change, and assimilation in nineteenth century Hawai'i. *Pacific Studies* 5: 57–69.

Tannen, Deborah, ed. (1982) *Spoken and written language: Exploring orality and literacy.* Norwood, N.J.: Ablex.

Thomas, Rosalind. (2009) The origins of western literacy: Literacy in ancient Greece and Rome. In David R. Olson and Nancy Torrance, eds., *The Cambridge handbook of literacy*, 346–361. Cambridge: Cambridge University Press.

Vincent, David. (1989) *Literacy and popular culture: England 1750–1914.* Cambridge: Cambridge University Press.

Vincent, David. (2000) *The rise of mass literacy: Reading and writing in modern Europe.* Cambridge: Polity Press.

Wolf, Maryanne. (2007) *Proust and the squid: The story and science of the reading brain.* New York: Harper.

Wyss, Hilary E. (2000) *Writing Indians: Literacy, Christianity and Native community in early America.* Amherst: University of Massachusetts Press.

3

Anthropology: Reading and Writing from Pictographs to Ethnography

The New Literacy Studies captured attention in the 1970s and 1980s. It is characterized by an "anthropological turn," sometimes termed an ethnographic or a cultural turn. Literacy studies followed trends in many disciplines and fields, from history to sociology and cultural studies, although that was seldom acknowledged. Nonetheless, a casual acquaintance with current studies might lead to the impression that anthropological and/or ethnographic approaches all but dominate research in literacy. That is both inaccurate and ahistorical.

In fact, instead of a "turn," this shift was more of a return. Although not sufficiently appreciated, "Literacy has occupied a central position in the history of anthropological thought," Niko Besnier observes. "During the formative decades of the field and its allied disciplines, literacy was implicated, more or less explicitly, as determinant of differences between 'civilized' and 'primitive' thought and action" (1995, 1–2). Indeed, I contend that as a given, even a categorical preoccupation, literacy was implicated in the development of the discipline more generally and much earlier. Anthropology's conceptualization, definition, scope, and methods were shaped by presumptions about literacy; conversely, and, equally importantly, anthropology has had a significant influence—metaphorical,

© The Author(s), under exclusive license to Springer Nature Switzerland AG 2022
H. J. Graff, *Searching for Literacy*, https://doi.org/10.1007/978-3-030-96981-3_3

methodological, and epistemological—on the study and understanding of literacy. Anthropology's roots in both archeological studies of early writing and in "contact" between Europeans and indigenous peoples are now generally acknowledged. But few historians of the field have taken into account literacy's implicit and unscrutinized place in early anthropology. Explicit awareness and critical understanding of this relationship is certainly called for.[1]

These connections are closely associated with the centrality of linguistics to social and cultural anthropology. In all cases, it is revealing that the relationship is framed in terms of "literacy … as determinant of differences," rather than literacy as a result or a more dialectical or mutually relational construction. That, I argue, is a critical matter. In anthropology, as in other fields of knowledge and modes of investigation, literacy is poorly conceptualized and understood. The costs continue to grow.

Besnier (1995) and Street (1984) represent the important efforts made by New Literacy Studies to revise our approaches to and understanding of literacy in theory and in practice, as Street put it. Together with other commentators, they made significant steps forward that I applaud. At the same time, they fail to make critical distinctions and remain both ahistorical and incomplete. In this, I argue, they represent underlying continuities in the anthropological tradition that need to be recognized, criticized, and revised.

The anthropology of literacy has been characterized by a rhetorically qualified but de facto dichotomy or sense of substantial and continuing difference between *non*-literate or *less* literate societies and *more* literate ones. While that presumed divide has lessened, it has not disappeared. As James Gee and many others have observed, the distinction moved, or actually expanded, from across societies to within societies: "In anthropological studies the term *literate* in the dichotomy *literate/nonliterate* came to replace the term *civilized* in the older dichotomy *civilized/primitive* and … a distinction between different cultures (nonliterate versus literate ones) came to be applied to different social groups within modern, technological societies like ours, characterizing some as having 'restricted literacy' and others as having 'full literacy.' The importance of these developments is the link often assumed between literacy and higher order mental skills, such as analytic, logical, or abstract thinking" (Gee 1986, 719).

That this constitutes a further and significant step is insufficiently appreciated in both older and newer traditions. How this connection between literacy and cognition was asserted, propagated, and widely accepted with little evidence or research is worthy of study in itself. It is surprising that, despite periodic questioning amidst frequent restatement, this question is seldom the subject of inquiry. Nor has it received necessary development and criticism. (This issue is also explored in Chap. 4 on psychology.)

Terms that sometimes take on the power of concepts, such as "full" and "restricted" literacy, are never defined or developed meaningfully. They are abstractions. The possible relationships between and among levels of literacy and cognitive abilities, as well as the cultural consequences of different levels of literacy, are more often unexamined expectations than documented patterns. Yet they are not related to common criticisms of literacy abilities under conditions of mass or popular literacy, or, in turn, literacy's presumed place in social or economic development.

This framing around assumed differences continues to be a problem with the New Literacy Studies as well. Neither Besnier (1995) nor Street (1984) embraces and explores the *relationships* between literacy in theory and literacy in practice. Indeed, they repeat contrasts in anthropological traditions between "civilized," "higher order," and otherwise "advanced" areas and cultures, and their supposed opposites, which are directly linked to literacy and its absence.

Although they cite historical scholarship that points to critical distinctions even within more developed areas, they do not recognize what Gee points out: that a continuing gap between "restricted" and "full" literacy has been presumed to exist *within* European American societies as well. To what extent does this assumption serve as a proxy for class and/or race-ethnicity?

Indeed, notions about "full" and "restricted" literacy rest on the very ideas of "civilization" and "progress" that many scholars have taken great pains to criticize but on which their very enterprise depends. As in so many aspects of literacy's study, another legacy of anthropology's history is at play here: modernization theories that place abstract and unfounded notions about literacy at their center.[2] In various formulations, literacy is cause of modern development and progress—in its various dimensions—or, less often, the consequence. The historical and more recent data cry out for more complicated formulations. As a discipline, anthropology is well placed to contribute.

Traditions of Difference

Despite protestations to the contrary, differences continue to rule. Powerful, though slippery, expectations take the place of critical inquiries (see Olson and Cole 2006; Olson and Torrance 2009). Their bases have shifted from the crude formulation of primitive/civilized to seemingly more sophisticated cognitive and linguistic ones. These powerful conceptions, and the equally strong distinctions and evaluations that accompany them, persist despite our expanded definitions of literacy, literacies, and abilities. This is contradictory. Ethnographies, anthropology's own methodological and epistemological disciplining of context, too often adopt these expectations, leading to a subfield, "the ethnography of literacy or writing," that is separated from broader ethnographies. Another subfield, "the ethnography of speaking" (or speech), is revealingly separate from that of literacy or writing (see Chap. 2.)

The asserted change in understanding represented by current terminology is at least as much a semantic substitution or a rhetorical rewording as it is a replacement for or a substantial revision of concepts of difference. This alleged reconceptualization remains rooted in oppositions rather than useful, complicated human relationships. No doubt the shift from orality to literacy encompasses some fundamental elements. Nonetheless, its formulation is still based on the construction of differences that are allied inseparably with literacy; no less important, it utilizes constructions of literacy that ignore or slight the contexts and varieties of literacy's acquisition, practice, and use. Jack Goody's touted shift from the "consequences" to the "implications" of literacy was meant to capture recent rethinking. But this terminological change does not reflect careful scrutiny of what is "implied" by literacy, to and for whom, with what influence, in what relationships. These matters are very important.

For Goody and for what his critics term the "Goody myth," the power of cultural synonyms—functioning as symptoms, symbols, signs, images—is enormous, even hegemonic, especially in the domain of the anthropological. The "savage mind" is illiterate, non-literate, or preliterate, primitive, uncivilized, in its varying formulations. The "domesticated mind"—a curious choice of words, perhaps a riff on "the cooked" versus "the raw"—is presumed to be the positive opposite pole (Goody 1977, 147; see also 146–162).[3]

The continuing tradition of dichotomous differences is prominently displayed in the title of Jack

Goody's 1977 book, *The Domestication of the Savage Mind*. In this and other constructions, Goody proposes a shift—or a variety of rhetorical and conceptual moves—away from Lucien Lévy-Bruhl's *Primitive Mentality* (1923) and Claude Lévi-Strauss's *The Savage Mind* (1966). In his book, as well as his earlier essay on the "implications of literacy" (1968b), Goody incompletely and unclearly reframed the deterministic arguments of his 1963 essay coauthored with Ian Watt, "The Consequences of Literacy" (1968). Along with subsequent writings, Goody's statements constitute a series of ambiguous assertions that have led to continuing debate over what he meant or implied regarding literacy. When read closely, his revision is quite limited and self-contradictory.[4]

In *The Domestication of the Savage Mind*, "domesticated" is contrasted with "wild." "Wild" and "domesticated" form a table of binaries from Lévi-Strauss's *The Savage Mind* that Goody includes twice (1977, 7 and 147). But how and why domestication occurs is not addressed. Is the distinction between "wild" literacy and "domesticated" literacy clear? How closely does this pairing follow the metaphorical—and muddy—tradition of Marshall McLuhan's "hot" and "cool"? It seems equally contradictory and misleading.

This broad presumption of difference embraces multiple dimensions that are neither admitted nor evaluated. Among them are the individual over the collective, the private over the social, and the silent over the aloud. The images that anthropologists use to illustrate this set of ideas are striking. Rooted in the first part of each pairing, they contrast sharply with traditions of ethnographic research. At the end of the first chapter in *Domestication* is a sketch of a young Chinese boy apparently reading a book. Without comment on the nature of the source—an 1899 publication of the London Missionary Society, Mrs. Arnold Foster's *In the Valley of the Yangtse*—Goody's caption reads, "Domestication as an individual experience." Goody's immediately preceding lines link writing with the formal operations that constitute the essential basis for abstract thought: "I myself ... see the acquisition of these means of communication as effectively transforming the nature of cognitive processes" (1977, 18).[5] That conclusion does not follow from Goody's arguments and his evidence.

Other epochal forms of domestication were collective and material. The circumstances of learning, practice, and use in specific social, cultural, economic, and political contexts are unmentioned. If less than a "great divide," the dichotomy remains. No less important, Goody does not mention the long-standing presumption that non-alphabetic writing systems, such as Chinese characters, limited the effects of literacy on thought. His illustrative example ignores alphabetic systems as well as gender.[6]

Anthropological Legacies of Literacy

This anthropological legacy softens but continues the basic divide. Nodding in the direction of "interactions," as Goody and his followers do, does not change the main message. To use anthropologist Brian Street's (1984) popular phrasing, admitting that literacy is not an autonomous factor does not lessen the implication of a strong divide and the many ways that set of assumptions connects with other cultural presumptions.

From the substitution of literacy for civilized, much else followed. Yet the nature of the relationship between the two terms remains unspecified. Are they equated, seen as inseparably associated, or asserted to be causally connected? Goody's focus on literacy, which is reduced to writing and linked to higher-order thinking processes, is *not* found in Lévy-Bruhl or LéviStrauss. Literacy, particularly writing, actually became more prominent in anthropology over time. Among the questions that are not addressed is whether the *presence* of literacy was more important than the *absence* of illiteracy or nonliteracy.

Far too often unrecognized and unremarked is the pervasive bias toward writing over reading. Simply put: writing leaves evidence of itself; reading does not. That makes it easy to slight context, whether historical, geographic, or social. Collections, archives, compendia—themselves taken as markers of the march of civilization—isolate the products of literacy, separating them from the means and modes of their production. This problem has engaged historians relatively recently, raising many relevant questions about understanding the impact or implications of writing. The possible fallacies are many and powerful (for critiques, see Clanchy 1993; Davis 1975; Steedman 1982, 1999, 2005; see also Chap. 7). That Goody tended to follow LéviStrauss's linguistic focus made it easier for him and his followers to neglect concrete social, cultural, political, and economic contexts.

In fact, to my reading Lévi-Strauss was more aware of socioeconomic factors in his approach to "totemism" than is Goody in his arguments based on classification, lists, and formulae. I also see Lévi-Strauss's conceptualizations as less deterministic. His approach to "dialectical reasoning" and "points of departure," rather than arrival, repays attention (1966, 250, Chap. 9). Goody typically compares cognitive processes in nonliterate societies (often based on observations by himself or others) with mental operations in "modern" or literate societies, with examples, especially historical ones, often taken from secondary sources. This method is almost guaranteed to accentuate differences.[7]

Goody seldom asks who is using writing for what ends in what circumstances. Despite his and his supporters' protests, differences that are presented as opposites or dichotomies rule. Comparisons swing radically over time and space and social groups. This, I aver, is one, but not the only legacy of literacy studies in anthropology.

Literacy's social and cultural relationships take innumerable forms. Anthropologists have seldom specified the causal relationships they presume, which often results in obfuscation. For Goody, "simpler" and "more complex" replace non-literate/literate or primitive/civilized, but rephrasing seldom reduces the strength of the contrast. The lines between dichotomy and difference are not distinct. The specific nature and contributions of literacy are not clarified. Brian Street comments, "the use by social anthropologists in particular of the 'autonomous' model of literacy, notably in the Goody version, affects not only their representation of literacy practices in specific societies but also their descriptions of the processes of social change and the nature of religious and political ideology in those societies" (1984, 6; see also Besnier 1995).

In *The Logic of Writing and the Organization of Society*, his third volume on literacy, Goody wrote: "Once again, one must be careful about drawing the line too sharply. While writing helped to develop new types of formal logical operation, it did so initially by making explicit what was implicit in oral cultures, which were neither pre-logical nor yet alogical except in a very narrow sense of those words." His meaning here is murky: how does writing make explicit what was implicit in oral cultures? His characterization of orality is cast in terms of what it is not—"neither pre-logical nor yet alogical"—rather than in terms that pertain to orality as such. Goody's disclaimers and his own "warnings" raise questions he does not answer or even seem to take on board. He continues, "These warnings are necessary because to overprivilege the European experience by stage theories that cut us off too sharply from other societies leads us to jump to the self-congratulatory assumption that only in one area of the world could modernization have taken place" (1986, 182). He seems unaware that "stage theories" and models of "modernization" were designed on the basis of that assumption and extend it universally.

Similarly, Goody writes repeatedly about the "the influence of a major mode of communication, writing, on social organization" but ignores the human uses of writing in specific contexts (1986, 184). There is a logical fallacy in this view of writing as a technology: writing does not make things explicit, people do. Goody practices special pleading to sustain the sense of difference.[8]

Goody and Beyond

Of these general and long-standing problems in understanding literacy, especially writing, Goody's work is the best but hardly the only example. The recent debate over determinism versus interrelationships in his writings—and in regard to literacy more generally—largely misses the point. I remain mystified by how few scholarly evaluations of Goody's work—particularly historical critiques focused on ancient Greece, medieval western Europe, or either the Near East or Asia—have been published.[9] The range of Goody's work preempts scrutiny, perhaps. Is there also a sense of a commanding literate authority? Or, perhaps, a literacy episteme that serves as a myth?

I remain intrigued not only by the repetition of the claims that Goody significantly revised his "thesis" but also by the contortions that psychologists and educationists engage in to defend his confusing and contradictory arguments. We now have decades of empirical studies that directly counter or substantially qualify Goody's claims. Yet specialization reigns supreme. Significantly, those who most frequently cite Goody are not historians or regional specialists; they are psychologists and educationists with their own interests. And, of course, the ultimate bias of anthropology lies in its historical identification with normatively underdeveloped and historically isolated populations. Genuine ethnographies may be very useful in contemporary efforts to understand and interpret literacy, but they are seldom read in the rush to proclaim that case studies based on brief observation or surveys are ethnographies of literacy or writing (Besnier 1995; Goody 1968a; Schieffelin and Gilmore 1986; Street 1984; Street 1993).

To my reading, contra *Technology, Literacy, and the Evolution of Society: Implications of the Work of Jack Goody* (Olson and Cole 2006) and other defenders, Goody himself has given relatively little ground in his successive volumes. His "strong theory" is generally undiminished. Phrasing admits qualification and specificity, but the logic and argument emphasize difference and generalization.

Commentators from Goody to Gee seize on the easy examples and memorable metaphors of Lévi-Strauss's "savage mind" and Lévy-Bruhl's "primitive" or "prelogical mentality." Goody begins and ends *The Domestication of the Savage Mind* with this example of dichotomy. Interestingly, neither Lévi-Strauss nor Lévy-Bruhl paid much attention to writing. Their concern was with "thought" in a tradition or mode of understanding that contrasts primitive and civilized, traditional and modern, oral and written. Might I suggest that their conceptions of "thought" are more primitive than not? It was Goody who added writing and literacy and introduced a psychological (though not a philosophical) twist on thinking.[10]

Neither Lévi-Strauss nor Lévy-Bruhl attempted to construct an historical account that granted pride of place to the alphabet or the Greeks. Their concerns differed from Goody's. Therefore his turns in their direction and then his criticism of them may be suspect and distracting, even disingenuous. Goody narrowed Lévi-Strauss's distinction between the *bricoleur* and the scientist, images that easily took on lives of their own. At the same time, he exaggerated Lévi-Strauss's differentiation between savage and civilized thought and practice. Furthermore, he had little to say about dichotomies between signs and concepts, myth and art as opposed to science and history.[11] Goody's method and understanding of literacy, indeed his scholarly method in general, more closely resemble those of a *bricoleur* than a scientist. This is not necessarily bad except when presenting itself as something else.

For example, Goody's chapter "Following a formula" is a formulaic, stereotypical description of difference between the oral and the literate, not, as his 1987 book puts it, an examination of *The Interface Between the Written and the Oral*. In stating his key points, Goody repeatedly uses such phrases as "must be different," "meant," "writing as creating." His arguments skip logical steps and jump from one point to another. The number of the undocumented assertions and assumptions about oral communication and early writing is almost breath-taking. Clearly, the understanding of language must be different in these two situations; the written language is not simply a visual representation of the oral. Some individuals spend more time with the written language than they do with the spoken (Goody 1977, 124). Yet, as this passage shows, Goody imagines and then exaggerates the differences, rather than investigating the relationships between the two.

> While the exigencies of oral composition meant the use of a certain number of set phrases, it seemed wrong to think that the content was necessarily fixed and transmitted by verbatim memory. Rather, it was early writing systems that emphasized copying and repetition, that separated the roles of composer and performer. In the scientific use of the term, formulae were more clearly the product of graphic reductionism. Finally, in the more general sense we saw writing as creating a greater consciousness of form and formalization. But such formalization, always conserving, was not always conservative, for it was an essential prerequisite of the rapid growth of knowledge in the last five thousand years, lying at the basis of central developments in the arts but more especially in the sciences. Writing is critical not simply because it preserves speech over time and space, by abstracting

its components, by assisting backward scanning, so that communication by eye creates a different cognitive potentiality for human beings than communication by word of mouth (1977, 127–128; for more examples, see 144–145).

In this and many other instances of short and long term transformations, a number of alternative historical and anthropological descriptions and explanations are possible, even preferable. Typically, they incorporate dynamic interactions between the oral and written, include the social and the collective dimensions, and recognize the place of practice, human choices, actions, and their effects. (For discussion of these alternative view, see Chap. 7.)

To the contrary, Goody was usually uninterested in social and historical context, interactions and more proximate chronology or timing, and the interplay of reading, writing, and speech. His favored examples from science and medicine are cases in point (see, for example, 1977, 144–145). While denying dichotomies, he continued to flirt with them, especially with a psychological or cognitive twist.

In the final chapter of *The Domestication of the Savage Mind*, Goody pointed to "the potentialities or literacy" and "the possible outcome of changes in the means of communication." He stated the case through a sweeping set of dichotomies with both logical and chronological leaps and rhetorical flourishes: "From whatever vantage point we view this change, the shifts to writing and then to print must be considered of critical importance in both formalizing and increasing the flow of information that has been a precondition of many of the features that differentiate the prehistoric societies of the Neolithic and Paleolithic from the 'modern' civilisations that followed" (1977, 148). Jumping over five millennia and eschewing human actions and inactions, Goody unconvincingly denies dichotomies. His approach to literacy and writing remains essentialist, as his frequent use of "intrinsic" indicates (149, 151). In the end, he is reduced to caricature in an effort to justify his argument.

Goody's world, past and present, is a world of "two cultures," literate and oral, scientific and traditional, continuous and discontinuous: a world without mutual reciprocal human interactions.

Is that in fact a world without human agency, indeed without history itself? Does "communication" work so simply and directly? History is all but abolished by this level of formulaic generalization. We end in a cage shaped by determinism and reductionism, which are inseparably interrelated.

For an anthropologist presenting historical cases and citing published studies, Goody's neglect of social and cultural context, time, and place is striking. Even when he was writing, Goody was not current with the relevant anthropological and literary scholarship, so he relied on formulae. His work on literacy and writing roams widely across continents and millennia, from antiquity to the Middle East, Africa, Asia and the Pacific, and medieval Europe without attention to distinctions. The disjuncture between evidence and analysis, on the one hand, and conclusions and high-level generalizations, on the other, is disturbing. Only in that way can the evolution, transcendence, and dominant power of writing be asserted.[12] "Potentialities" and "tendencies" replace a single "great divide" (1986, 185; 1987, Chap. 12). This constitutes a small step toward understanding literacy, but it is insufficient to fill our need for comparative, critical, historical, and contextualized studies.[13]

Unfortunately, Goody's work, from "The Consequences of Literacy" (1968) through (ironically) *The Theft of History* (2006), continues to stand as history *and* anthropology when it is neither. It remains an often cited but less often studied compilation, an anthology of sorts, which reflects—and, in some ways, distorts—an earlier stage in the history of writing and knowledge. In my view, it has limited the impetus to advance the direct study of literacy past and present. It has supplied a set of easy answers rather than setting out an active agenda for researchers.

Theories and Practices

In his 1984 book *Literacy in Theory and Practice*, anthropological linguist Brian Street challenged Goody's foundational formulations. Street called attention to two conceptions of literacy: an "autonomous" or independent and universalistic view that he associated with Goody and certain philosophers, psychologists, and linguists; and an "ideological" approach that he linked to a more contextual, historical, and practice-oriented view (for definitions, see 1, 3, 6, 24, 95). Street mounted a striking critique of the tradition of the "great divide," the dichotomy between literacy and orality, literate and illiterate, and civilized and primitive that characterizes the autonomous model. Citing on one hand, recent critical studies by linguistic anthropologist Shirley Brice Heath (1983), cross-cultural experimental psychologists Sylvia Scribner and Michael Cole (1981), and myself (1991) and, on the other, his own research on different practices of secular and religious literacy in Iran during the 1970s, Street's argument was partly successful. He is often credited with launching the New Literacy Studies and qualifying the claims of "strong theories" of literacy. Street's predominant interests lay in linguistics, not sociology, economics, or history.

Unfortunately, the thrust of Street's critique was blunted by his labeling the approach to literacy that Goody and a number of psychologists and linguists adopted as an autonomous conceptualization as opposed to a definition of literacy as ideological. It retained, indeed, underscored a fundamental dichotomy. Street did not clearly state that both autonomous and ideological models are ideological, that is, they express a normative vision or set of ideas or ideals. Depending on summaries of research, his definition of the ideological model was also underdeveloped. Replacing one problematic and rather unclear dichotomy with another was insufficient to achieve the goal of revising or rethinking. It proved to be confusing and obstructed the necessary debates (see, for example, Olson and Torrance 2009). The subsequent literature— and much of the New Literacy Studies—has perpetuated this problem.

In my view, neither term served its purpose well, either descriptively or conceptually. Too often lost in the new dichotomy is the simple but powerful point that *both* the autonomous *and* the ideological conceptions are themselves ideological in theory and in practice. Naming them did not remedy that complication. Street did not follow his own opportunity to probe that very point.

That in turn led to confusion between the problem of conceptualizing literacy in theory versus studying literacy in practice. This stood among the complications that Street wished to clarify. They are related at every point. The very question of the relationships of theory and practice and how the two shape and reshape each other was neglected. That matter has received the least attention in the discussions that followed, which accords with the central themes of this book. And that absence has had a powerful impact on efforts to study and understand literacy. It is possible that the problem of literacy's relationships to different ideologies has actually worsened in the last several decades.[14] Moreover, an unquestioned belief in literacy in itself, the deeply held and understandable valuation of literacy (in the form of the literacy episteme, if not the literacy myth) has reinforced the great reluctance of those who might know better to give ground on the seemingly overwhelming, all-but independent transformative significance of literacy. They include scholars, teachers, moralists, psychologists and political economists who hold developmental views of individuals and societies, policy makers, and many others.

A significant opportunity for critical reflection passed by without sufficient appreciation or exploration. The publications of national governments and UNESCO as well as many schools and activists seldom reflect the criticism of the autonomous model of literacy. "Literacy in context"—as a revised and "domesticated" understanding of *both* theory *and* practice—uncritically took its place. Together, the presumptions of the literacy episteme or myth, combined with economic pressures, concerns about both developing and developed nations, fears of cultural decline and assumed threats to national security, have contributed to blunting what might have offered a new, constructively critical edge.

Despite the importance and validity of much of Street's and subsequent scholars' criticisms of the standard narrative of literacy, most often the response was to offer qualifications and claim that strong positions stopped short of adopting or advocating autonomous views—or that autonomous views themselves might not be ideological.[15] I suspect that, even in the last decades of the twentieth century and the early decades of the twenty-first, many scholars wished to disassociate themselves from positions that were labeled ideological. This attribution, even when intended non-derogatorily, was deemed unnecessarily risky if not downright suspect.

No new model, by any name, replaced the older autonomous formulation. Divides or various parsings of dichotomies that eschew the absolute or universal came to rule, though not always comfortably. Overarching dichotomies, such as autonomous versus ideological or theory versus practice, continued firmly, albeit more often implicitly, in place. This problem underlies the limits of, and the limited ethnographies of literacy.[16]

Local Literacies and Limits

In the first decades of the New Literacy Studies, with a heady spirit of remaking the study of literacy and with it literacy as we know it, locally based research was initiated in many areas in the world.[17] Among the best known are two very differently designed and conducted landmark ethnographies: Shirley Brice Heath's 1983 study of several Piedmont communities in the United States South; and Sylvia Scribner and Michael Cole's 1981 study of the Vai people in Liberia (discussed in Chap. 4). Among the many studies conducted in one or another ethnographic vein, Street edited two collections of research in developed and underdeveloped areas (1993, 2001).

Yet within another decade or two, the pendulum swung in the other direction. In part, this is the normative operation of academia and specialization, and studies of literacy followed other scholarly trends, often at some distance. In this instance, however, the assumptions and programs of governments, NGOs, and corporate commercial interests were also involved. Underlying them all was the standard narrative of literacy's overarching importance and discomfort that too much concern with social context and a close local focus was limiting.

An exceptional if perhaps unintended example is Deborah Brandt and Katie Clinton's "Limits of the local: Expanding perspectives on literacy as a social practice" (2002). This article exemplifies the tensions within literacy studies, as it simultaneously shows the field's adherence to academic fashions and the limits of the New Literacy Studies as a critique of ideology and practice. Caught between "limits" and "expansion," to use their own words, the authors dance around dichotomies. Exaggerating—perhaps more as metaphor than literal terms—the distance between the "local" and "global" (their fashionable terms of opposition), they criticize the New Literacy Studies for accentuating the local. This essay followed but perhaps misinterpreted the outpouring of locally focused case studies from the 1980s to the 2000s, many but not all under the New Literacy Studies banner.

Brandt and Clinton begin with a personal touch:

> Two admirers of the socio-practice paradigm take a critical look at it. We argue that in an attempt to suppress what was most suspect and repugnant in Great Divide concepts—namely, a claim for an autonomous status for literacy as a technology detached from context—the new paradigm has created conceptual impasses that make it hard to account fully for the workings of literacy in local contexts. We will argue, in fact, that the new paradigm maintains its own, tacit great divide—one that assumes separations between the local and the global, agency and social structure, and literacy and technology. (2002, 338) In my view, this is neither accurate as description nor sustainable as argument. The shortcomings of those studies did not lie in their localism but rather in their isolation of literacy from specific socioeconomic and historical contexts and from the human activities in which they are embedded and within which they are meaningful.

The authors recognize that the New Literacy Studies are built in part on a failure to transcend fundamentally dichotomies. But at the same time, their criticisms in many ways miss the point. They continue, "Our aim ... is to come to terms with certain aspects of literacy that have been under-theorized in social-practice perspectives—particularly its ability to travel, integrate, and endure. We want to understand literacy's transcontextualized and transcontextualizing potentials." Dichotomizing theory and practice, this language wanders from a discourse of "paradigms" and "account fully" (a statistical concept) that nods in the direction of science and social science, a path they do not follow, to a muddy if fashionable discourse of "travel," "integrate," and "endure." These are metaphors, not "new analytical concepts that can more readily explain how literacy, always locally manifested, nevertheless can function to delocalize or event disrupt local life" (Brandt and Clinton 2002, 338). I do not know what they mean by "transcontextualized" or "transcontextualizing" and "delocalize" or "disrupt." Do they mean relationships? And, if so, between what and what? They allude to very different traditions of social theory, but the provenance of those traditions (from "social-practice" to "actor-network") is not noted, nor are their differences acknowledged.[18]

Most important, the assertion of "tacit great divides" is an unfounded extrapolation that, in the end, may reify differences rather than reduce them. To focus on "the local" is not to deny an "other," whether globally or otherwise constructed. Revealingly, Brandt and Clinton never define social practice, context, local, or global. They write as if their meanings are self-evident, when each term has multiple dimensions and is found in a variety of traditions of research and interpretation. The authors' conceptual confusions are evident (see, for example, 2002, 340). They also confuse practice approaches to literacy with social practice and social actor network theories.

Owing in part to Street's reliance on dichotomies, Brandt and Clinton misleadingly write of "reversals" in a presumed shift from an autonomous to an ideological model. In an inexplicable statement, they declare: "Out of these two major reversals—the move from text to context and the unification of orality and literacy—came concepts central to much literacy research today" (2002, 342). Orality and literacy are never "unified." Their effort to separate literacy event and literacy practice is no more comprehensible. Literacy events exemplify and constitute literacy practices, a conceptualization whose usefulness was probably already exhausted. Overattention to literacy events has had the unfortunate effect of taking literacy out of its social and cultural contexts and away from its practices. Instead, literacy researchers' emphasis shifted to locating and "reading" texts—a term that is now applied to many forms of expression, not just to written documents—in context(s) that may include everything from the reading audience to the societies and cultures in which texts were produced and are received. They declare that in this way they are critiquing and revising the presumption of a "great divide" between orality and literacy. Yes, text and context can be confused or dichotomized; they need to be related dynamically. But I fear that Brandt and Clinton are caught in their own semantics, however ironically.

The anthropological twists and turns reveal the missing connections within literacy studies. It is fitting that this gap is seen clearly in the ethnographic domain. So often one set of dichotomies or divides or differences replaces others. "Expanding perspectives on social practice" may prove limiting, along with the incomplete New Literacy Studies that it seeks to criticize. The problem is conceptual and, even more fundamentally, epistemological. The crux of conceptualization pivots on the *relational*—dynamic, dialectical, mutually reshaping, plural—oral *and* literate, texts *and* contexts, local *and* "other" dimensions and origins, rather than the "global," which in itself becomes static and reified. Literacy is turned into an object and essentialized. Literacy in and of itself not does not travel, integrate, or endure; that conception is divorced from life and action. Rather, the human uses of reading and writing, as well as their effects, must command our attention (see also Street 2003a, 2003b).

Renaissance and Recovery?

Anthropology has played a crucial but curious role in the study of literacy. Its own prehistory embraces the Renaissances of the classical material and intellectual legacies, often coupled with presumptions of the depths from which "civilized" peoples had risen, from pre-alphabetic and preliterate, wild and primitive. Renaissances of learning include those of the Middle Ages, often associated with the twelfth century; the early modern era in the fifteenth and sixteenth centuries; and, in some constructions, powerful currents in the eighteenth and nineteenth centuries. Overlapping chronologically with the "expansion of Europe" and "contacts" between peoples who had previously been separated, the various encounters with the "others" came at the time of the more recent Renaissances. Both periods, more familiarly the latter, are deeply intermeshed with the origins of anthropology.

The legacies are multiple and contradictory. There is the long history of divides, greater and lesser, and of varying degrees of difference. Here lies the superiority of the literate and the civilized. But that tradition is more complicated and bears further examination. The fact and the image of the classical (or more recent) great orator-scholar-politician and Plato's suspicions of the effects of writing are a part of this tradition.[19] So, too is the celebration of memory and the intricate systems to advance memory (for example, Ong 1958; Yates 1966). A third element includes the legacies and the image of writing by dictation to a professional scribe and groups of the learned, the religious (whether orthodox and reformed), pious and literary women, and families working over texts and discussing fundamental questions collectively and orally, often, but not always, with written or printed texts present.

Another significant current amid difference is the celebration of the noble, creative, original, but nonliterate *savage*, periodically rediscovered and privileged in art, literature, and philosophy, among other domains. This Romantic notion is another form of reversal, both symbolic and real. It has shaped visions and understandings of literacy and illiteracy in complex and contradictory ways. For example, it underlies an association of reading and writing with a loss of spontaneity, creativity, innocence, and naturalness. A part of nineteenth-century explorations of exotic places, as well as of Romanticism, its nationalistic cousin, it lingered longer in the arts, especially in painting, among the Fauvists and various schools of abstraction and primitive realism. That example, too, bears examination. (This is part of the legacy of Lévy-Bruhl.) The noble savage has a place in the history of psychology and was memorably captured in film in the story of Victor, *L'Enfant Sauvage*, by Francois Truffaut (1970), one of many untutored or untrained Wild Children who play a part in this drama.

A third current may be even more complicated but no less consequential. This is the recognition of differences that fall well short of great divides and inevitable divergences. Sometimes an appreciation of the variety of other civilizations, languages, and traditions grew out of contact and encounters. This legacy comes in part from missionary efforts to bring the European word of god to those seen as in need of it, although it does not preclude recognizing the imperial purposes to which secular authorities sought to bend their activities. Beyond the many interpretive challenges presented by this history, I point to the striking array of endeavors conducted by missionaries and others well in advance of, or in some cases in opposition to, colonial officials: to learn local languages and sometimes, writing systems; to translate the Bible and other key texts into those languages; alternatively or simultaneously, to instruct indigenous persons in European languages so they could read and understand both the scriptures and civil documents; and to teach laypersons how to interpret and apply a written text to lived experience. Speaking to issues of translation in the broadest sense, these efforts touched many parts of the world.

Herein lay in significant part the origins of linguistics (discussed in Chap. 2), a major impetus for translations in both directions, and more or less systematic efforts to school indigenous peoples. These activities suggest important paths toward new understandings and to promoting literacy itself. In many areas in Africa and the Americas, for example, indigenous persons trained in missionary churches created their own syntheses of Christian, Old Testament, and indigenous (supposedly "traditional," but actually transformative) forms of spiritual practice and then recorded and transmitted them to others, often at a distance. What matters most is what people *did* with the tools that were made available to them, not the missionaries' or colonialists' intentions.

As the discussion in Chap. 1 suggests, this powerful legacy is insufficiently appreciated and incompletely understood. As a partial history, the commonly accepted narrative obscures variations in approaches to local, native, and indigenous languages and their multifarious array of writing systems. The early anthropologist-missionaries who sometimes sought to learn local writing systems in order to educate, promulgate, and indoctrinate did not completely dismiss or castigate those they encountered as savage or wild; rather, they saw them as untutored and alien from European civilization. To play with words that capture the space they inhabited, however awkwardly, and the conceptual opportunities that focusing on them may offer us even today, there was space to play, space to build upon. These efforts varied greatly in practice and in results, as well as in the degrees of respect for and comprehension of indigenous cultures. Lines between colonization and proselytization blurred; an element of conquest or coercion was present in most contexts. Yet many undertakings involved reading, writing, and translation that was mutually instructive. This history is a partially lost tradition that progressive literacy sponsors and instructors have rediscovered.[20]

It is a relatively small step to the issue of literacy's place in constructions and understandings of cultural difference and pluralism more generally, past and present. A renewed interest in the anthropology or, if one prefers, ethnographies of literacy could focus more or less simultaneously on practices of reading and writing across media and on modes of understanding and communication across cultures, places, times, and other lines of differentiation and aim to develop theories of literacy based on those patterns of similarities and difference. Literacy—reading and writing as activities, not static attainments—would be conceptualized and studied as both theory and practice, in dynamic relationship to each other. Such research would be parallel or at least systematically constructed, designed with collaboration and comparison in mind. That would be a truly new literacy study, as well as a greater pursuit and practice of pluralism and democratic tolerance.

The current faddish pursuit of an anthropological perspective, too often reduced to a matter of using ethnographic methods, tends to serve mostly as a metaphor for a relatively undefined cultural approach. At other times, it has stood for an unfocused blend of history, psychology, and linguistics. In the hands of Jack Goody, anthropology was substituted for history, to the detriment of both. The actual anthropological study of literacy has been diminished as a result.

The familiar dichotomies, beginning with the stark separation of primitive versus civilized and the expectation of a consequential passage from one condition to another signified by literacy, remain powerful even after criticism and rhetorical dismissal. Determinism may have been replaced by looser constructions, but the sense of an unavoidable difference if not absolute or universal divide remains, as do reductionism and essentialism.

The history of anthropological studies of literacy is open to broader conceptualizations and understandings. These alternative currents within the field, both at the roots of the discipline and in its twentieth century disciplinarization and institutionalization, have significant implications for literacy studies.

Traditions of Ethnographies

An anthropology of literacy remains a vision for future research. In the likely form of an ethnography, it has long been promised, but the promise remains largely unfulfilled (Heath 1983; Street 1984; Besnier 1995; Barton and Hamilton 1998; Barton et al. 2000). John Szwed proposed "The Ethnography of Literacy" in 1981. Responding to the widespread sense of a "literacy crisis" and observing considerable uncertainty over the meaning and course of reading and writing, he wrote: "The stunning fact is that we do not fully know what literacy is. The assumption is that it is simply a matter of the skills of reading and writing does not even begin to approach the fundamental problem: What are reading and writing for? Is the nature of the ability to read and write something on which there is in fact near agreement?" (1981, 14).

Szwed faced these unresolved questions squarely: "I propose that we step back from the question of instruction, back to an even more basic 'basic,' *the social meaning of literacy*: the roles these abilities play in social life; the varieties of reading and writing available for choice; the contexts for their performance; and the manner in which they are interpreted and tested, not by experts, but by ordinary people in ordinary activities." Following the recent trend in language studies, he remarked that "it is not enough to know what a language looks like and to be able to describe and measure it, but one must also know what it means to its users and how it is used by them" (1981, 14). To that end, he pointed to the value of ethnography (20; for his cautions, see 20–23).[21] Szwed wrote on the eve of the publication of Shirley Brice Heath's *Ways with Words* (1983) and Brian Street's *Literacy in Theory and Practice* (1984). Szwed had no idea what would attempt to pass as ethnographies of literacy, reading, writing, and also speech and language. What he called for differs profoundly from interviews of unsystematic samples of individuals about their reading or writing, schooling, or "habits," and short-term periods of classroom or other observation as "mini" or "micro" ethnographies. Indeed, the notion of "mini" or "micro" effectively contradicts the very conception of ethnography.

Beginning in the late 1960s, a number of small-scale studies in an ethnographic tradition pointed, more or less, toward an anthropology of literacy, typically in practice but sometimes in theory or their interactions.[22] Although the number of investigations of developed societies and areas has grown, most ethnographies examined less developed areas and minority, immigrant, and other subcultures, peoples, and places within more developed nations. They exemplified traditional assumptions that ethnography is synonymous with highly localized case studies involving onsite research focusing on relatively isolated groups. This set of anthropological assumptions is now outdated (Van Maanen 2004). Although assumptions of lesser abilities and isolation—whether by choice or by colonial oppression or neglect—are somewhat less overwhelming, they remain present in research into less and more developed places alike. Selections of questions and methods and of subject populations are interrelated.

We have learned much about the literacies of Buddhist villagers in northeast Thailand, Islamic students in the western Sudan, nomads in Somali and India, writing and astrology in

Madagascar, multilingual literacies in rural Eritrea, economic uses of literacy in northwest Bangladesh, power and gender in rural Pakistan, conceptions and uses of literacy in a Papuan New Guinean village, Arabic literacy and secrecy among the Mende of Sierra Leone, literacy and cultural identity in the Horn of Africa, and literacy and ethnic identity in Alaska, for example. The basic themes in locally conceptualized studies are clear. Variation, agency, the power of tradition, the quests for identity, and the conflicts of gender in struggles for power are illuminating. Language and discourse, transitions from non-literate to literate, and secret or nonsanctioned uses of writing are highlighted. Contexts are often narrowly inscribed and underconceptualized with respect to practice and theory. Most recently multiple literacies, especially in electronic or digital media, attract major interest.

There is certainly a greater awareness that views and practices of literacy are ideological and that understanding often conflates autonomous and ideological conceptions, theory and practice. With the major exception of work sponsored by or associated with David Barton's Literacy

Research Centre at Lancaster University in England and Heath's southeastern United States Piedmont case study, the great majority of ethnographies remain focused on small groups and subcultures; those examining literacy are increasingly situated in school.

Niko Besnier's fascinating 1995 study, *Literacy, Emotion, and Authority: Reading and Writing on a Polynesian Atoll*, exemplifies recent work. Reflecting shifts in approach, Besnier examines the movement of the Nukulaelae from non-literacy to literacy through the perspective of social practice. He emphasizes how a small, isolated Polynesian community with virtually no access to print technology became immersed in literacy over a century. In the process, with evidence ranging from personal letters to tee-shirts, he underscores the diverse forms and uses of reading and especially writing according to social and cultural needs and local circumstances. Letter writing and the expression and regulation of emotion is a special theme. As the publisher states, this "case study, which has implications for understanding literacy in other societies, illuminates the relationships between norm and practice, between structure and agency, and between group and individual" (Besnier 1995).

Toward Anthropologies of Literacy?

Both similar and different are the major projects of David Barton, his colleagues, students, and associates. Touching almost all bases are the titles of two books: the collection *Situated Literacies: Reading and Writing in Context* (Barton, Hamilton, and Ivanič 2000) and *Local Literacies: Reading and Writing in One Community* (Barton and Hamilton 1998). Risking the charge of being overcritical of research published more than fifteen years ago, I ask: Is it enough simply to say that literacy is "situated" and that studies of literacy must be "situated in context" without making more specific statements of a conceptual, comparative, and critical nature? Asserting that "all literate activity is indicative of broader social practices" and that "reading and writing in one community" constitutes or is constituted by "local literacies" (Barton and Hamilton 1998, 1) is, I think, insufficient for advancing the field.

Consider the specific contexts in which these projects are situated. These range disconnectedly from photographs to time, prisons, farmers' livestock transactions, children's text projects, and an electronic community. Consistency and comparability across cases are largely absent.

Separation and differentiation predominate over relationships and critical interactions. As a result, the New Literacy Studies is at risks of deserving the criticism proffered by Brandt and Clinton, despite its own incoherence. This approach leads to a proliferation of studies of different topics, analogous to today's "many" or "multiple literacies." The critical and the historical dimensions are lacking. Crucial relationships within and among case studies are slighted.

Binaries ebb and flow amid a sea of subjects.

Without discounting the very real value of the empirical research reported in many studies, especially works like *Local Literacies*, their limits are telling. Reflecting the orientation of the researchers in social linguistics and their explicit commitment to the "social practice" emphasis of the New Literacy Studies, this engaging study offers windows into "literate practices" that follow four featured interviewees across the domains of school experiences, community work, "living a local life," and "leisure and pleasure."[23] Barton and Hamilton discuss how Harry, Shirley, June, and Cliff use literacy in their daily lives, including local media, participation in public activities, families, schools, other institutions, and leisure. We learn a great deal—but primarily about a few persons.

Local Literacies is propelled by its pursuit of six propositions which the authors see as central to the New Literacy Studies and which Barton outlined in his earlier book, *Literacy: An Introduction to the Ecology of Written Language* (1994). In their explication, they contribute to a "theory" of literacy as social practice (Barton and Hamilton 1998). In my view, these propositions constitute an emphasis or perspective rather than a theory.

1. Literacy is best understood as a set of social practices; these can be inferred from events that are mediated by written texts.
2. There are different literacies associated with different domains of life.
3. Literacy practices are patterned by social institutions and power relationships, and some literacies become more dominant, visible and influential than others.
4. Literacy practices are purposeful and embedded in broader social goals and cultural practices.
5. Literacy is historically situated.
6. Literacy practices change, and new ones are frequently acquired through processes of informal learning and sense making.

Barton and Hamilton take steps forward but partly reverse them. Axioms often substitute for criticism and reconceptualization. This is captured in the book's first words: "Literacy is primarily something people do, it is an activity, located in the space between thought and text. Literacy does not just reside in people's heads as a set of skills to be learned, and it does not just reside on paper, captured as texts to be analysed. Like all human activities, literacy is essentially social, and it is located in the interaction between people" (1998, 1).

Literacy "is"; "Literacy does not"; what people "do with literacy." Is there a contradiction here with the collateral stress on people's practice and agency? Or is there confusion? This phrasing leans toward an independent or at least separate entity called literacy that acts, rather than individuals and groups of people reading and writing, comprehending and making meaning, communicating and expressing, across media and modes of communication for various purposes and ends. The human, the interactive, the relational at the core of understanding literacy are downplayed or missing in these constructions.

Consider the first three points.

With respect to the first: do texts mediate, or do people, institutions, traditions, ideologies, social and political relationships do so? The danger here is that of giving texts a quality of nearautonomy. There is a further complication with the empirical emphasis on inference: what is the role of theory or cultural expectations in inference? How powerful are the presumptions and propositions? Further, neither here nor elsewhere is the foundational analogy and metaphor for the literacy practice and events approach in linguistics and ethnographies of speech addressed and elaborated. The relatively unattended relationship between reading, writing, and speaking, between literacy and orality, is critical here.

With respect to the second point, tellingly absent is any consideration of the existence and status of "different" literacies, not only in their relationships with "different domains of life" but also with each other. The risks include the seemingly endless proliferation of literacies that meet no consistent definitions or qualities. When Barton and Hamilton refer to cooking, community, family, meetings, and campaigning literacies, for example, do they refer to the uses of reading and writing in these activities? Constructions of home, work, and community literacies are similar. How do these different literacies relate to one another; do they influence or help to shape each other? This form of a social practice approach tends to separate and differentiate when I think we need to interrelate and integrate. None of these literacies is independent of the others.

With respect to the third point, I call for a sharper and more focused understanding of what Barton and Hamilton suggest when they write,

"Literacy practices are patterned by social institutions and power relationships, and some literacies become more dominant, visible and influential than others." How and why does this operate, and with what
consequences? They acknowledge that vernacular, everyday literacies have
important relationships to dominant literacies, but they do not probe
those connections. Neither vernacular nor dominant literacies are autonomous or independent. These relationships are dynamic, dialectical, historical, and ongoing. Barton and Hamilton contradictorily refer to a
"divide," but also to "a great deal of imposed literacy. When they continue, "We have found it useful in this discussion to contrast dominant
and vernacular practices, but the divide is not clear-cut," they fudge key
questions instead of confronting or resolving them. In this vein, they
refer to the state, commerce (under which they include newspapers), and
religion (1998, 256–257). Clearly, this is an ongoing and ever-present set
of complex relationships, which can be viewed as matters of negotiation.
To suggest otherwise risks trivializing the larger context of lived literacy
experiences and the place of reading and writing in life.

Missing, or at least slighted, is how different complexes of the uses of
literacies), with their power relationships, institutional associations, associations with traditions and ideologies, actually shape the others. This
goes well beyond "impinging" and "imposition," or participating in
bureaucratic practices. Barton and Hamilton make a start when they
write of practices that tend toward "the sense of trespassing across the
social boundaries of appropriate reading and writing." But the critical
relationships disappear when they continue: "What is interesting here is
how people make literacies their own, turning dominant literacies to
their own use, by constant incorporation and transformation of dominant practices" (1998, 256–257). They lose the dialectic and intermedia-
tion. The binaries that the New Literacy Studies sought to reject continue
to reign, though perhaps somewhat more subtly. The now-dated discursive forms or rhetoric from cultural studies—trespassing, incorporation,
transformation, disruption, oppositional—all suggest some form of
agency but muddle matters of purpose and distract from our understanding of literacy.

Such issues raise questions for the fourth point, that "Literacy practices
are purposeful and embedded in broader social goals and cultural

practices" (Barton and Hamilton 1998, page).With respect to graffiti, for example, what is its purpose; how does it become incorporated in broader institutions and practices; and how does that transform its purpose?

The fifth proposition—literacy is historically situated—is woefully neglected in *Local Literacies*.

Similarly, the final point—"Literacy practices change, and new ones are frequently acquired through processes of informal learning and sense making" (Barton and Hamilton 1998, page)—while true, immediately forgets the critical issue of how new and old literacies are interrelated and shape one another. Indeed, the New Literacy Studies is characterized by its emphasis on multiple or multimodal literacies, most often digital or electronic, which are typically referred to as "'new' literacies." Numerical, visual, spatial, performance, or expressive uses of reading and writing, broadly defined, are rarely addressed. About their intersections and relationships we know far too little.

Obviously, digital media are important. They do "impinge" on practices of literacy. But the combined rush to praise *or* condemn the new practices has largely missed the great opportunity to explore their relationships and to understand how print and electronic literacies shape each other. What has precedents, and what is unprecedented? Mass mediation, visual communication, motion pictures, and animation are not new; they are mediated by traditional alphabetic and alphanumeric modes of expression. Variant word and spelling forms have many precedents. How are they related? How do their influence, shape and reshape each other? The New Literacy Studies so far have failed to prove its value here. (For further discussion, see Chaps. 5 and 6.)

I am asking a great deal, certainly. But am I demanding too much of local and ethnographic studies? The founders of ethnography would say no. The more recent, often cited defenses of these approaches, from Clifford Geertz (1973, 1983) and Sherry Ortner (1995, 1999, 2006), on the one hand, to Carlo Ginzburg (1980), on the other, would also say no. I am not asking that every study consider all bases or all relationships; that is impossible. But I am strongly suggesting that significant steps might be taken by sustained recognition of the centrality of critical, comparative, and historical conceptualizations. In part, this is a matter of attention, recognition, emphasis, probing complicated relationships—in other words, of theory *and* practice.

For this effort, we have an important precedent which repays examination. Published more than thirty years ago, fifteen years before *Local Literacies*, and subjected to many criticisms, not always fairly, Shirley Brice Heath's *Ways with Words: Language, life, and work in communities and classrooms* (1983) stands as the model for an anthropology and ethnography of literacy (see also Heath 1990, 2012).

Ways with Words (discussed in Chap. 1) is a comparative study encompassing three neighboring communities—Roadville, Trackton, and Townspeople—whose residents are white and African American; working class and middle class; mill workers, white collar, and farming. It examines diverse patterns of family life and socialization, community relationships, religious participation, and speech and educational patterns. Developed from a sociolinguistic framework, it is distinguished by the duration of the ethnography as well as its comparisons. *Ways with Words* is not an easy model for ethnographies of literacy.

At the same time, Heath's combination of the conceptualization and execution of a critical, comparative ethnography of literacy with explicit attention to language, to culture including religion, race, class, community, and to work is unique. It repays close attention. Especially compelling is the interplay between the oral and literate, the collective and the individual, the intersections of generations, and the multiple, overlapping contexts for reading, writing, speech, and both personal and social action. *Ways with Words* reveals what it means to see literacy as social practice, embedded in everyday life and social institutions in their complementarity and oppositions; in the complicated relationships across cultures, classes, races, and socioeconomic and geographic settings; as constituted by old and new forms of reading and writing across media and modes of communication; in broad communicative, cultural, and political economic circumstances. In sum, to explore literacy and literacies in their many but related contexts.

Heath, Smith, Barton, and others have shown us a path. The ethnographies of literacy, in partial contrast to ethnographies of speech and communication, are largely stillborn, so far. Nonetheless, a new frontier lies ahead.

Notes

1. Although it is not my focus in this book, anthropological and historical studies suggest how much can be learned about literacy's importance from specific studies of the extent of development that occurs even with "restricted literacy." Classic works developing this theme include Besnier, *Literacy, emotion, and authority* (1995); Finnegan, "Literacy versus non-literacy" (1973); Finnegan, *Literacy and Orality* (1988); Goody, "Introduction: Implications of literacy" (1968b); McKenzie, *Bibliography and the sociology of texts.* (1999). Recent studies on early writing are even more eye-opening; there has been a virtual revolution in understanding, quite relevant to the approach in this book. See, for example, Houston, *Shape of script* (2012); Lurie, *Realms of literacy* (2011); Postgate, *Bronze Age bureaucracy* (2013); Schmandt-Besseret, *Before writing* (1992); Schmandt-Besseret, *How writing came about* (1996).

2. An earlier tradition of "literacy thresholds" is now gone. See Graff, *Literacy myth* (1979) Chap. 5, for discussion. The key work on "thresholds" was by C. Arnold Anderson. This concept fell under the broad arms of modernization theory, updated, more or less, in human capital and neoliberal conceptions. The question of the relationship of anthropology—and literacy studies and other developmental approaches more generally—to modernization theory merits more attention. Elements persist in UNESCO campaigns and publications.

3. Goody remarks that the dichotomy of Domesticated/Wild requires "comment," but never offers any.

4. Compare the first and last chapters of *Domestication of the Savage Mind.* It presumes to state conclusions; as a result, it precludes critical inquiry. All this supports (or derives from) the literacy episteme. For an indication of Goody's influence, consider these raw citation counts from searches in JSTOR limited to articles and books (excluding pamphlets, reviews, and miscellany, as of 5/22/2015): Domestication of the Savage Mind: 2906; Logic of Writing and the Organization of Society: 1323; Literacy in Traditional Societies: 1274; Interface between the Written and the Oral: 1269.

5. Goody does not explain what he means by "formal operations," so readers do not know that this is a type or level of cognitive processing that Piaget's model of cognitive development finds emerging in children

around age 10. Goody does not acknowledge either the simple fact that children can become literate when they are much younger or Piaget's finding that this developmental process occurs cross-culturally, regardless of other differences. Nor does he explain his reference to "individual" as opposed to collective or cultural experience, which in this context suggests an unexamined equation of individualism with progress.

6. See Goody's other work and compare, for example, with Gough, "Implications of literacy in traditional China and India" (1968); Lurie, *Realms of literacy* (2011).

7. A review of the appropriateness of the comparisons Goody makes would be interesting.

8. Consider especially Goody, *Logic of writing* (1986), 184–185.

9. See, for example, Collin, "Revisiting Jack Goody" (2013); Collin and Street, "Ideology and interaction" (2014); Halverson, "Goody and the implosion of the literacy thesis" (1992); Olson and Torrance, *Cambridge handbook of literacy* (2009); Olson and Cole, *Technology, literacy, and the evolution of society* (2006); Street, title (year.)

10. That was Goody's 1960s innovation. In effect, he anglicizes the French scholarly tradition. With scant effort to develop the case, Goody all but equates writing with thought. See the works of Goody cited here and the more recent formulations of the "literacy episteme," which are cited and discussed in Chap. 2.

11. Overall, Goody's interest in classification is very different from Lévi-Strauss's. In addition, I believe that Goody misreads Lévi-Strauss on history.

12. Goody's references to Weber and Polyani are insufficient for his points but indicative of his "method." Readers might review his *Logic of Writing and the Organization of Society* (1986), a 185-page "essay," or *Interface Between the Written and the Oral* (1987), a 300-page book. Strikingly, his own presentation and summary of his major arguments (1986, 171) is quite similar to his criticisms of his critics.

13. For a book that makes an important beginning but stops short and reintroduces dichotomies and neglects history, see Collins and Blot, *Literacy and literacies* (2003).

14. See, for example, such defenses of Goody as Olson and Cole, *Technology, literacy, and the evolution of society* (2006); Collin, "Revisiting Jack Goody" (2013). See also Brandt and Clinton, "Limits of the local" (2002).

15. Among a huge, uneven literature, see the works of David Barton, Colin Lankshear, Peter McLaren, and Ira Shor. A selection of relevant work is included in Cushman et al., *Literacy* (2001). The New Literacy Studies literature lacks cohesion and synthesis. It is deeply divided by divergent emphases on place, race, gender, age, ethnicity, new or old literacies or media, activepassive, agency-social justice-social control, informal-institutional, and ideology-autonomy lines.

16. See, for example, Heath and Street, *On ethnography* (2008).

17. Some fields within psychology, linguistics, and education were barely touched by the New Literacy Studies' currents.

18. This is especially the case regarding Bruno Latour's social actor network theory. There is no mention of the large critical literature that Latour's work generates nor an argument for its specific relevance to literacy studies. This reflects the sociology of knowledge in the field and unclear notions of literacy as "technology."

19. See, for example, Havelock, *Preface to Plato* (1963); Harris, *Ancient Literacy* (1989).

20. Relevant here are tensions within the writing of Paulo Freire. See Bartlett, *Word and world* (2010).

21. Szwed did not attend to the power of conceptions about literacy in shaping both uses and how we think about "habits" and practices, or the complicated relationships between literacy and language studies. He followed the pioneering footsteps of Hymes, Labov, and others in ethnographies of speech. See Basso, "Ethnography of writing" (1974); Clammer, "Towards an ethnography of literacy" (1980), Schieffelin and Gilmore, *Acquisition of literacy* (1986); Street, *Cross-cultural approaches to literacy* (1993); Street, "Ethnography of writing and reading" (2009).

22. The major collections of studies are Goody, *Literacy in traditional societies* (1968); Street, *Cross-cultural approaches to literacy* (1993); Street, *Literacy and development* (2001); Schieffelin and Gilmore, *Acquisition of literacy* (1986); Barton, Hamilton, and Ivanič, *Situated literacies* (2000). Major monographs include Heath, *Ways with words* (1983); Besnier, *Literacy, emotion and authority* (1995); and Barton and Hamilton, *Local literacies* (1998).

23. Note that I do not say theory or model; viewing literacy as a social practice does not constitute a theory.

References

Bartlett, Lesley. (2010) *The word and the world: The cultural politics of literacy in Brazil*. Creskill, N.J.: Hampton Press.

Barton, David, and Mary Hamilton. (1998) *Local literacies: Reading and writing in one community*. London: Routledge.

Barton, David, Mary Hamilton, and Roz Ivanič, eds. (2000) *Situated literacies: Theorising reading and writing in context*. London: Routledge.

Basso, Keith H. (1974) The ethnography of writing. In Richard Bauman and Joel Sherzer, eds, *Explorations in the ethnography of speaking*, 425–432. Cambridge: Cambridge University Press.

Besnier, Niko. (1995) *Literacy, emotion and authority: Reading and writing on a Polynesian atoll*. Cambridge: Cambridge University Press.

Brandt, Deborah, and Katie Clinton. (2002) Limits of the local: Expanding perspectives on literacy as a social practice. *Journal of Literacy Research* 34: 337–356.

Clammer, J. (1980) Towards an ethnography of literacy: The effects of mass literacy on language use and social organization. *Language Forum* 4: 24–51.

Clanchy, Michael T. (1993) *From memory to written record: England, 1066–1307*. 2d ed. Oxford: Blackwell.

Collin, Ross. (2013) Revisiting Jack Goody to rethink determinisms in literacy studies. *Reading Research Quarterly* 48: 27–38.

Collin, Ross, and Brian V. Street. (2014) Ideology and interaction: Debating determinisms in literacy studies. *Reading Research Quarterly* 49: 351–359.

Collins, James, and Richard K. Blot. (2003) *Literacy and literacies: Texts, power, and identity*. Cambridge: Cambridge University Press.

Cushman, Ellen, Eugene R. Kintgen, Barry M. Kroll, and Mike Rose, eds. (2001) *Literacy: A critical source book*. Boston: Bedford/St. Martin's.

Davis, Natalie Zemon. (1975) Printing and the people: Early modern France. In Natalie Z. Davis, *Society and culture in early modern France*, 189–226. Stanford: Stanford University Press.

Finnegan, Ruth. (1973) Literacy versus non-literacy: The great divide. In Robin Horton and Ruth Finnegan, *Modes of Thought*, 112–144. London: Faber and Faber.

Finnegan, Ruth. (1988) *Literacy and Orality: Studies in the technology of communication*. Oxford: Blackwell.

Gee, James Paul. (1986) Orality and literacy: From *The Savage Mind* to *Ways with Words*. *TESOL Quarterly* 20: 719–746.

Geertz, Clifford. (1973) *The interpretation of cultures.* New York: Basic Books.

Geertz, Clifford. (1983) *Local knowledge: Further essays in interpretive anthropology.* New York: Basic Books.

Ginzburg, Carlo. (1980) *The cheese and the worms: The cosmos of a sixteenth century miller.* Baltimore: Johns Hopkins University Press.

Goody, Jack, ed. (1968a) *Literacy in traditional societies.* Cambridge: Cambridge University Press.

Goody, Jack. (1968b) Introduction: The implications of literacy. In Jack Goody, ed., *Literacy in traditional societies*, 1–26. Cambridge: Cambridge University Press.

Goody, Jack. (1977) *The domestication of the savage mind.* Cambridge: Cambridge University Press.

Goody, Jack. (1986) *The logic of writing and the organization of society.* Cambridge: Cambridge University Press.

Goody, Jack. (1987) *The interface between the written and the oral.* Cambridge: Cambridge University Press.

Goody, Jack. (2006) *The theft of history.* Cambridge: Cambridge University Press.

Goody, Jack, and Ian Watt. (1968) The consequences of literacy. In Jack Goody, ed., *Literacy in traditional societies*, 27–68. Cambridge: Cambridge University Press.

Gough, Kathleen. (1968) Implications of literacy in traditional China and India. In Jack Goody, ed., *Literacy in traditional societies*, 69–84. Cambridge: Cambridge University Press.

Graff, Harvey J. (1979) *The literacy myth: Literacy and social structure in the nineteenthcentury city.* New York and London: Academic Press.

Halverson, John. (1992) Goody and the implosion of the literacy thesis. *Man* (new series) 27: 301–317.

Harris, William V. (1989) *Ancient literacy.* Cambridge, Mass: Harvard University Press.

Havelock, Eric A. (1963) *Preface to Plato.* Cambridge, Mass: Belknap Press.

Heath, Shirley Brice. (1983) *Ways with words: Language, life, and work in communities and classrooms.* Cambridge: Cambridge University Press, 1983; new epilogue, 1996.

Heath, Shirley Brice. (1990) The children of Trackton's children: Spoken and written language in social change. In James W. Stigler, Richard A. Shweder, and Gilbert S. Herdt, eds, *Cultural psychology: The Chicago symposia on human development*, 496–510. Cambridge: Cambridge University Press.

Heath, Shirley Brice. (2012) *Words at work and play: Three decades in family and community life.* Cambridge: Cambridge University Press.

Heath, Shirley Brice, and Brian V. Street. (2008). *On ethnography: Approaches to language and literacy research.* New York: Teachers College Press.

Houston, Stephen D., ed. (2012) *The shape of script: How and why writing systems change.* Santa Fe, N.M.: School of Advanced Research Press.

Lévi-Strauss, Claude. (1966) *The savage mind,* trans. Librarie Plon. Chicago: University of Chicago Press.

Lévy-Bruhl, Lucien. (1923) *Primitive mentality,* trans. Lilian A. Clar. London: Allen & Unwin. Lurie, David B. (2011) *Realms of literacy: Early Japan and the history of writing.* Cambridge, Mass.: Harvard University Asia Center.

McKenzie, Donald F. (1999) *Bibliography and the sociology of texts.* Cambridge: Cambridge University Press.

Olson, David R., and Michael Cole, eds. (2006) *Technology, literacy, and the evolution of society: Implications of the work of Jack Goody.* Mahwah, N.J.: Lawrence Erlbaum.

Olson, David R., and Nancy Torrance, eds. (2009) *The Cambridge handbook of literacy.* Cambridge: Cambridge University Press.

Ong, Walter. (1958) *Ramus, method, and the decay of dialogue.* Cambridge, Mass: Harvard University Press.

Ortner, Sherry. (1995) Resistance and the problem of ethnographic refusal. *Comparative Studies in Society and History* 37:173–193.

Ortner, Sherry, ed. (1999) *The fate of "culture": Geertz and beyond.* Berkeley: University of California Press.

Ortner, Sherry. (2006) *Anthropology and social theory: Culture, power, and the acting subject.* Durham, N.C.: Duke University Press.

Postgate, Nicholas. (2013) *Bronze Age bureaucracy: Writing and the practice of government in Assyria.* Cambridge: Cambridge University Press.

Schieffelin, Bambi B., and Perry Gilmore, eds. (1986) *The acquisition of literacy: Ethnographic perspectives.* Norwood, N.J.: Ablex.

Schmandt-Besseret, Denise. (1992) *Before writing,* vol. 1, *From counting to cuneiform.* Austin: University of Texas Press.

Schmandt-Besseret, Denise. (1996) *How writing came about.* Austin: University of Texas Press.

Scribner, Sylvia, and Michael Cole. (1981) *The psychology of literacy.* Cambridge, Mass: Harvard University Press.

Steedman, Carolyn. (1982) *The tidy house.* London: Virago

Steedman, Carolyn. (1999) A woman writing a letter. In Rebecca Earle, ed., *Epistolary selves: Letters and letter writers, 1600–1945*, 111–133. Farnham, Surrey: Ashgate.

Steedman, Carolyn. (2005) Poetical maids and cooks who write. *Eighteenth-Century Studies* 39: 1–27.

Street, Brian. (1984) *Literacy in theory and practice.* Cambridge: Cambridge University Press.

Street, Brian V., ed. (1993) *Cross-cultural approaches to literacy.* Cambridge: Cambridge University Press.

Street, Brian V., ed. (2001) *Literacy and development: Ethnographic perspectives.* London: Routledge.

Street, Brian. (2003a) The limits of the local—"autonomous" or "disembedding"? *International Journal of Learning* 10: 2825–2830.

Street, Brian. (2003b) What's "new" in new literacy studies? Critical approaches to literacy in theory and practice. *Current Issues in Comparative Education* 5: 77–91.

Street, Brian V. (2009) Ethnography of writing and reading. In David R. Olson and Nancy Torrance, eds, *The Cambridge handbook of literacy*, 329–345. Cambridge: Cambridge University Press.

Szwed, John F. (1981) The ethnography of literacy. In Marcia Farr Whiteman, ed., *Variation in writing: Functional and linguistic-cultural differences*, 13–23. Hillsdale, N.J.: Lawrence Erlbaum.

Van Maanen, John. (2004) Ethnography. *Social Science Encyclopedia*, 3d ed., 320–322. London: Routledge.

Yates, Frances. (1966) *The arts of memory.* London: Routledge.

4

Psychology: Between Mind and Culture

From Eric Havelock to Walter Ong to Jack Goody, we have strong, determinist theories of the consequences and implications of literacy, reading and/or writing. Both directly and indirectly, they address the psychology of literacy, itself a vague and abstract construction. In most cases, they aim to inform or explain the impact of reading and writing—as a "technology of the intellect"—on the mind or the brain (these formulations are not careful), cognition, understanding, the sense of self, and meaning making. A long, complex tradition has been embodied in the writing of psychologist David Olson, most fully when he attempted to take on the role of a historian in his 1994 book, *The World on Paper*. This perspective and its presumptions were extended in 2009 with the *Cambridge Handbook of Literacy* coedited by Olson and Nancy Torrance.

Psychology is an old area of human interest with deep roots in history, from theology to politics, and warring traditions that emphasize either human nature—what is innate, original, endowed, or internal—or nurture and environment. Both theoretical and empirical traditions overflow with these clashes. Major currents have tended to lurch from one divide another. Confusions are common, for example, among forms of cause and effect and judgments of neutrality, danger and risk, and benevolence.

H. J. Graff, *Searching for Literacy*, https://doi.org/10.1007/978-3-030-96981-3_4

The field is full of conflicts. It swings back and forth between the oppositions, and sometimes the contradictions, of foundationalisms, determinisms, innatism, instinctualism, genetics and inheritance, cognitivism,
materialism, environmentalism, and currents of romanticism, self- and
other-determinism, and human agency.

Questions about the nature and nurture of humans will never be
resolved to the satisfaction of all. Too many strong assumptions interfere
with observations on subjects that typically are hard to study and harder
to assess—for reasons other than the interference of prior assumptions
and conceptions imported from other fields. Many assumptions exist on
both ends of the spectrum of "hard" (or absolutist) and "soft," sometimes
phrased as "hard wired" versus cultural, from the structure and operation
of the brain to "imprinting" on the young. They are far from solely
empirical, despite the proclamations of the scientists of cognition and
psyche. Most of these factors impinge on questions relating to the acquisition, practice, and uses of literacy and literacies.[1]

An example that has become very popular in our own age of the brain
or cognitive neuroscience is the notion, for which classicist Eric Havelock
is often credited, that the invention of the Greek alphabet and/or Western
writing systems more generally led to changes in the human brain. In
various inconsistent formulations, these psychologists argue that the
brain changed under the influence of writing, either in itself or in conjunction with the standardization of the alphabet, with a reduced number of vowels and consonants. The alphabet, it is contended, made
reading and writing, as we know them, possible or at least easier (hardly
the same thing). Reading, in turn, is also claimed to have changed the
human brain, mind, or thought. These terms are used interchangeably
despite the fact that they are not synonymous. The specific character of
those relationships is seldom stated with any precision.

The slippage is palpable. Child reading and language researcher
Maryanne Wolf, author of the popular book *Proust and the Squid: The
Story and Science of the Reading Brain*, writes: "The classicist Eric Havelock
and the psychologist David Olson assert the thought-provoking hypothesis that the efficiency of the Greek alphabet led to an unparalleled transformation in the actual content of thought. By liberating people from the
effort required by an oral tradition, the alphabet's efficiency 'stimulated

the thinking of *novel thoughts*'" (2007, 65). The idea (which is not a hypothesis) is Havelock's (1977, 1980), which Olson adopted.[2]

Before many pages, Wolf repeats that the alphabet and/or reading had changed the brain as if it were proved. Near the end of her book she shifts from writing to reading and from neurons to culture and asserts, "The reading revolution, therefore, was both neuronally and culturally based, and it began with the emergence of the first comprehensive writing systems, not the first alphabet" (2007, 217).[3] Wolf offers no direct evidence for this conclusion; in fact, there is none.

The research she reports projects backward chronologically from the present and horizontally to "all comprehensive writing systems."[4] This matter cannot be studied by scans of individuals' brain activity today; indeed, scans are inconclusive even for much simpler brain functions and provide no basis for inferences about processes of cognitive development in the past. What cannot be ascertained empirically nevertheless threatens to become an established truism with dramatic implications.[5]

Some aver that the evolving, ever pliable brain may change with the putative transformation from oral to literate, speaking of the "literate mind" or "literate brain." The brain, it is said, is in danger of changing again today under the impact of digital media. Journalist Nicholas Carr ponders "What the Internet Is Doing to Our Brains" in his provocative *The Shallows* (2010). (See also Baron 2015). Have humans evolved from an oral to a literate and now to a digital mind? Is that a good or a bad thing? Of none of this is there direct or persuasive evidence. But with respect to matters of reading and writing, that absence seldom obstructs arguments and beliefs. Is that complication also central to the "literacy episteme"? That brings it close to what I term the "literacy myth."

The studies that claim neurological or brain-based connections to or from literacy form one strong psychological tradition. The new "hard wired" approach is experimentally dependent on modern brain-scanning technology, but it fits comfortably with much older metaphors for the transformations presumed to follow from reading and writing. More common, however, is a second tradition or wave that emphasizes connections rather than dramatic ruptures. The two, superficially opposed, can work together, as Wolf's work implicitly presumes.

Reflecting a centuries-old legacy that highly, if inconsistently and selectively, values the ability to read and to write, albeit for varying purposes, the psychology of literacy has recently been presented as the stuff of a literacy episteme—or, in my view, a literacy myth. As summarized by Jens Brockmeier and David Olson (2002, 2009) and Brockmeier (2000, 2002), with references to Havelock, Goody, Innis, McLuhan, Ong, Derrida, and many others, the literacy episteme is equated with a "culture of literacy" and "a cultural discourse." It is also equated with writing. As argued in Chap. 2, this conception is misleading and unhelpful for a psychology of literacy.

Recently, Brockmeier and Olson have proposed a miscellany that seems to be neither cultural nor historical, despite their assertions: "We define what is meant by the literacy episteme, proposing that is only within such a larger cultural-historical trajectory that we can capture the astonishing rise of a set of activities and issues subsumed under the notion of literacy (or writing) to an area of academic and applied inquiry that, by now, is well established.... Only within such an overarching order, we suggest, do these practices and problems take an epistemic form and become subjects of thought and theoretical curiosity as well as public attention." They go on, repeatedly asserting "only" without explaining why: "Only within the literacy episteme can the social, intellectual, and cultural implications of writing become epistemic objects: 'things' that appear as intelligible objects of theory and investigation and whose investigation is considered to be fulfilling societal demands and cultural interests" (Brockmeier and Olson 2009, 5, accompanied by numerous citations). How do they know that preliterate or nonliterate people were incapable of reflecting on their own thought processes?

They continue, no more clearly or concretely, with implications for a psychology of literacy: "The literacy episteme is an historical *a priori*. It defines the terms under which we conceptualize what we have called a fully developed 'culture of literacy'" (Brockmeier and Olson 2009, 7–8) But there is no such thing as "an historical *a priori*." That presents an enormous problem for their notion of an episteme and undermines the assertions that follow: "To see literacy as an episteme rather than as simply a skill, a competence, a social practice, or a universal good—that is, as a frame rather than a content—has brought to the fore two ideas that had been absent from academic and public discourses on language. One is that writing is a peculiar form of language and not simply a secondary representation of speech … The other idea is that the prototypical form of written language—extended, monological prose, traditionally conceived of as a dominant feature of our civilization and hallmark of high culture—is an historical form" (8).

Neither of these ideas is new, even in this restatement original. Both are debatable and debated. But the form of the proposed or supposed episteme propels formal written literacy forcefully to the fore. Ironically or contradictorily, literacy is accorded more undifferentiated power by the diffuseness and disconnection of this approach. As Brockmeier and Olson put it with respect to writing, their incomplete synonym for literacy:

> Many different theoretical and empirical approaches have been developed to investigate this growing spectrum of literacies. At the same time, however, research has also aimed at looking for the common basis of these diverse activities to determine both what is distinctive about writing as opposed to alternative means of expression, communication, and reflection, and the psychological competencies that may be general to many of them. The goal of this research is a more precise understanding of what we may mean by something as vague yet as important as literate competence as the ability to use written language as a form of life. (2009, 18)

What is meant by "the ability to use written language as a form of life"? The literacy episteme translates Goody and Watt's essay and the later works of Goody for the late twentieth and earlier twenty-first centuries. This is what some observers have termed the "Goody thesis" and in at least one case the "Goody myth." (See Chaps. 2 and 3.) It is the un- or understated foundation for David Olson's work, including the coedited *Cambridge Handbook of Literacy* (Olson and Torrance 2009).

If not entirely "autonomous," as in the original Goody formulation, writing—not literacy—remains conceptualized as distinctive and superior. The "implications" of writing, therefore, are boundless, unconstrained by history or culture or actual uses. As Chap. 2 showed, this flaw is fundamental to Goody's thinking from *The Domestication of the Savage*

Mind (1977) to his surveys that emphasize writing (1987).[6] Goody's work from 1963 on fundamentally underlies the literacy episteme.

The so-called episteme's claims are built on a rhetorical foundation with written discursive supports and paper wallcovering and roof. Presented by Olson as *The World on Paper*, it is labeled cultural and historical but it does not stand on historical evidence or understanding or exist in historical or cultural context. Arguing against no one, Brockmeier and Olson return to Samuel Johnson as their touchstone, as they declaim that despite the end of the supposed dominance of a certain tradition of privileged writing, "literate practices flourish like never before" and there is "a renewed interest in and recognition of the diverse forms and uses of this most recognizable of all human technologies: the written word" (2009, 18–19) Long live writing, but whither their episteme?

Whose World on Paper?

David Olson expresses his debt to the work of Goody in many places, most prominently in the first words of his contribution to the 2006 festschrift, *Technology, Literacy, and the Evolution of Society*: "The literacy episteme, the series of theories and conjectures about the nature, significance, and implications of writing, took its modern shape in the hands of Jack Goody who proposed that writing and literacy may be one of 'the mechanisms behind sociocultural change'" (2006, 289).

Olson is an experimental social psychologist whose original research focused on the development of children's use of language. Exceptional in the breadth of his interests, Olson first extended his horizon and announced his commitment to "the Goody thesis" in his 1977 article "From Utterance to Text: The Bias of Language in Speech and Writing." In 1991, he posited "Literacy as Metalinguistic Activity," shifting his terms from metaliterate to metalinguistic and metacognitive without pausing to explain or differentiate. Despite claims to the contrary and a tendency to qualify such assertions, he argues for the relative autonomy of writing. In the shadow of Goody, he has attempted to present his work as historically based, but it is not. In Olson's work, as in Goody's, assertions stand in the place of documented and developed arguments.

Repeating the words historical, cultural, and social as mantras is a poor substitute for historical grounding.

Experimental psychologists rarely tackle such meta-issues with respect to historical development. The "consequences" or "implications" of literacy have generally been the preserve of anthropologists, classicists, philosophers, and historians. Typically, social psychologists and cognitive scientists have focused more closely on mental orientations and actions, most often with respect to the moment at hand, though occasionally framed as timeless.

Justifying his own and Goody's approach, Olson writes: "For Goody, the product of exploiting the possibilities of writing by a society over historical time was written culture." "By written culture, I, following Goody, mean a society that both assumes a particular form of psychological competence—the ability to read, interpret, and construct documents in a standard, norm-based way—and a particular form of social organization—institutions organized around constitutions, rules of order, contracts, and explicit norms set out in written documents. I, like Goody, am surprised that such a seemingly obvious claim can be widely disputed" (2006, 291).

Revealingly, Olson seems unaware of these statements' circularity and potential for contradiction and oblivious of the need to elaborate and document relationships with evidence in actual historical contexts of people, time, place, and action. Norms or traditions of "psychological competence," if that in fact is an apt term, do not describe the uses or effects of specific practices. Instead, to use his own words, they constitute one of many possibilities. As psychologist James Wertsch pointed out in a review of *The World on Paper*, Olson slips "into assuming what needs to be explained ... in much the same way he sees others doing" (1996, 127; the specific reference is to "writing as the transcription of speech"). Citing documents and repeating assumptions do not make his case beyond his own rhetoric.

Olson's *The World on Paper: The Conceptual and Cognitive Implications of Writing and Reading* (1994) is a curious book. Strangely, he fails to ask "what world?" or "whose world?"—a fundamental question—and how any world can come to be inscribed on paper, in what media and form. These are basic historical matters. Equally revealing is his subtitle, parsing

Goody. Is the conceptual not also cognitive? What, precisely, is meant by "implications"? That question escapes Olson's semantics. Tellingly, he addresses the implications *of* writing and reading rather the implications *for* reading and writing. This fundamental confusion with regard to causality is a point to which I will return.

The World on Paper attempts a grand revision of scholarly understanding of the relationships among speech, writing, and the development of modern culture. The central focus is the use of formal writing. Olson contends that writing provides an important model of the way "we" think about speech, and that in turn consciousness of language is structured by "our" writing system. In his view, historically or, perhaps, evolutionarily, writing comes to provide the dominant model for text, nature, and mind. Olson thinks that he can demonstrate this development through his own readings of a selection of major written texts. Finally, he sees this analysis as a reversal of generally accepted wisdom.

In my view, Olson attempts the impossible. His method relies on a deterministic, reductionist, circular, and ahistorical approach that can only mislead efforts to understand the theory and practice of literacy in historical context. Based on a narrow selection of examples of writing—predominantly religious texts—and narrow readings of them, this approach is a major step backward for the study and understanding of literacy. In a telling review, Venezky (1995) exposes Olson's misreading of the American Declaration of Independence.[7]

The World on Paper is characterized not only by the reassertion of dichotomies and from→to formulae but by the presumption that the texts Olson privileges are autonomous from their authors, past readers, and the times and places in which they were produced and reproduced. He interprets these writings in the context of the semantic structures of other writings, not (despite his occasional disclaimers) in relation to the history of reading. This is a textual tradition removed from the history of reading and writing, as well as that of communities of readers and writers, which are both central to any understanding of literacy. His choice of texts for analysis is also highly selective, unevenly spanning thousands of years.

Olson employs a limited view of history and uses a limited range of both primary texts and documents and secondary historical sources in order to advance his claims, which are presented as scientific and repeated as propositions or principles. It is never clear why he refuses to articulate a more interactive and dynamic approach to the relationships of writing and speech, and writing and reading, and to the historical contexts of literate production and receptions and their changes. This stance contradicts his occasional references to social organization. When he finally mentions schools and schooling, he does not consider their relationship to social organization or documentary traditions.

The construct of a literate mind does not advance our understanding of literacy, much less of its instruction and practice. Although Olson might respond that my criticism is semantic, I strongly insist that words—in historical context—matter. There is no "literate mind" per se; rather, there are literate minds that we need to understand and facilitate. They must be conceptualized, historically and cognitively, as plural and variable. To paraphrase Brian Street, Olson's literate *World on Paper* is literacy in theory rather than literacy in practice.[8]

Linguistic and educational researcher Richard Venezky summarizes Olson's basic—and, he thinks, erroneous—starting point: "Awareness of linguistic structure … is not a precondition for the development of writing but a product of writing. Writing, therefore, can be viewed not as an attempt to represent speech but as a model of speech. Through experience with writing, we become conscious of words and sentences and begin to perceive speech as a linear sequence of basic phonological units, even though their acoustical cues partially overlap in time." From this assumption, advanced with almost no attention to the actual contexts of reading and writing, historical circumstances, and sociocultural relationships, Olson next asserts that reading—or, that is, the history of reading—"can be viewed as a sequence of attempts to overcome what is not represented in scripts, which is how the speaker intended the text to be understood." Depending on a certain understanding of speech act theory (which is not accepted by many experts in the field), Olson "points to the lack of illocutionary force in writing as 'the central problem in interpreting written texts and a critical problem in composing them'" (Venezky 1995, 442).

In addition to confusing language with literacy, Olson asserts their synonymy with cognition, an illogical leap that conflates exactly what it needs to disentangle, examine, and reconnect. In his contribution to *Technology, Literacy, and the Evolution of Society*, Olson formulated the key argument this way:

> The central claim linking literacy and cognition is that the habits of reading, writing, consulting, and interpreting texts in the dominant cultural practices become routinized as modes of thinking. Further, the habits are seen as distinctive from those involved in ordinary speech. Put simply, if one learns to read and interpret a document in a unique yet standardized, culturally sanctioned way, one can begin to interpret other experiences in an analogous way. Reading the book of scripture in a certain way invited 17th-century scholars to read the book of nature in same literal way and to institutionalize that way of reading as method taught to initiates. (2006, 296)

Few scholars of religion and even fewer of science accept such a formulation. Indeed, Olson can only assert it by ignoring their historical context, debates about interpretation, and the scholarly literature. Here too Olson's readings are marked by binaries rather than exploring relationships in the texts themselves (see, for examples, his Chaps. 7 and 8). Curiously, as reviewers have mentioned, Olson does not take sufficiently into account late medieval and early modern theories of reading that complicate his singular and unified view of developments that occurred over almost a millennium (Venezky 1995). We must ask, why?

The answer lies in another set of assertions, which relate to a traditional and highly normative view of instruction and practice of reading and writing that flies in the face of almost everything linguists, educators, anthropologists, and historians have learned in almost four decades of New Literacy Studies. Olson remains a nominalist, which is itself a legacy of medieval philosophy. He points out, first: "Admittedly, literacy can give access to documents that are read outside of their appropriate institutional context." To support this contention, he cites the example of the Italian miller Menocchio as his mental world has been reconstructed by Carlo Ginzburg in a microhistorical study (1980) that allows no generalization. Olson then revealingly recognizes that "to understand the role of documents in culture and cognition it is necessary to understand at the same time the official institutions of the society that determine how and what is written and read, and the implications, sometimes severe, of reading them the 'wrong way'" (2006, 296). Moving from this recognition to a deterministic view of literacy, as Olson proceeds to do, is possible only by misconstruing both literacy and history. Indeed, if Olson's acknowledgment of the power of official social institutions were applied in this case, the story of Menocchio could never have happened. Ironically, Menocchio's story is very likely a tale of oral culture that Olson gets wrong.[9]

Olson does not understand the historical era or its culture of communicative practices in which the oral and written inseparably and mutually shaped and reshaped each other. Texts, as his own reminder about institutions and authority suggests, are never autonomous. Neither are reading and writing. Shifting unaccountably from writing to reading, Olson further asserts, "Literate competence, then, is not only the ability to read but to read in functional and institutionally sanctioned ways. Schooling is learning to deal with writing and the written tradition of a particular society in socially mandated ways" (2006, 296). Once again, we return inexplicably to the world of either/ors and binaries, not human history. Olson continues convolutedly, "special types of complex social organization rely necessarily on a documentary tradition." But practice is shaped, not by literacy by or in itself, but rather by institutions and the uses of literacy. Olson never embraces this point. Forgetting society, history, culture, he instead asserts, "In my view, learning to read and write any script is a lesson in metalinguistics that may, in certain cultural contexts, be turned into a lesson in metacognition" (297).

With respect to contemporary studies of children, Olson's original field of expertise, this idea is contested. Olson's own experimental psychology originated in research about children's development of language. In fact, a sense of human developmentalism underlies all of Olson's ostensibly historical writing.[10] By analogy, what is historically unknowable and empirically and contextually insupportable becomes an assertion owing to an implicit developmentalism of the metalinguistic, metacognitive, and metaliterate mind.

The development of the collective mind follows the development of the individual child, a fallacious notion (called recapitulation) that was popular in the nineteenth century but has been repudiated across the biological and human sciences. In his final chapter, Olson posits "the literate mind." To play on a theme central to Olson's concerns, this is more an article of faith than a restatement of theory. Allied with a view of literacy or, specifically, writing as autonomous, it obviates the need to understand the actual practices of literacy and writing and to offer systematic evidence to support that understanding.

Specialists in language and cognition have raised strong objections to Olson's arguments. Their views accord with my own: not only does he elaborate a striking version of a deterministic and relatively autonomous view of writing and its impact on the mind, but this presumption and his consequent neglect of the historical and textual contexts of literacy are deeply misleading. Olson never seems to notice that he takes writing as the evidence of speech—so that writing serves as the evidence of both speech and writing—and then deals contradictorily with its status conceptually and cognitively, to use his own tortured semantics.

Writing in *Nature*, neuropsychologist John C. Marshall declares that in claiming that "writing is largely responsible for bringing language into consciousness" or that "Cartesian mentalism 'was the by-product of a new understanding of what was in the text and was contributed by the reader'" Olson "recklessly throws himself into some very muddy theological waters" (1994, 665).

> The central (and fatal) flaw in Olson's position arises from his premise that spoken language is a perspicuous and unambiguous expression of the speaker's mental state. This error leads him to contrast the (supposed) transparency of speech with the (purported) fact that writing cannot readily represent the elocutionary force of an utterance. From this misconception, Olson argues that the reader must reflect on the written sentence in order to determine the speech act that it represents. The consciousness-raising involved therein then gives rise to the (post-medieval) distinction between the literal and the metaphysical. But once Olson's premise is seen to be false, the entire argument collapses. (665)

Marshall and other critics object strongly to both the linguistic foundations of Olson's view and the reading of theological, philosophical, and scientific texts that he provides (Unger 1994; Wertsch 1996; Venezky

1995). Most suggest that Olson (re)invents a straw figure when he argues against "those who believe that the meaning is in the text ready to be extracted by an ardent reader" (Unger 1994; see also Halverson 1991, 1992).[11]

With respect to Olson's efforts to connect Protestant scriptural readings to scientific rereadings and reinterpretations of the Book of Nature—the medieval idea that views nature as a book to be "read" for knowledge and understanding, Marshall exposes a central flaw. "The line of argument is consistent, however, with Olson's belief in a very strong form of the hypothesis that literacy facilitates precision. 'Traditional cultures,' he writes, 'treat alternative expressions of the same sense as being "the same"; literate ones use the stricter criterion of the verbatim repetition as "the same."' But the claim that preliterate people (adults or children) do not make the distinction must surely be false." Marshall finds it difficult to believe that "traditional cultures do not have fixed forms of expression for significant rites" (1994, pages). Students of traditional and oral cultures certainly concur.[12] Olson, I add, is a very literal reader, given to linear forms of causal connections, inattentive to complex relationships and the presence and uses of metaphor and analogy. That interferes greatly with notions from and about worlds on paper and books of nature.[13]

Historical linguist J. Marshall Unger returns us to the question of why Olson's views matter to the student of literacy. In a phrase, they matter because the world as we know it, live in it, and seek to understand it across diverse media and modes of comprehension and expression is only in part a world on paper. Historically, this is true for religion, government, science, and much more. As Unger puts it, "Most if not all of the logical, moral, and scholarly problems in *The World on Paper* stem, I think, from Olson's implicit assumption that all information is external and fixed, and that there is only one way in which we learn it.... Literacy is just one of many tools the use of which, as Olson's mentor Marshall McLuhan observed, affects how people relate to their environment.... Elaborate theories of literacy constraining thought are simply unnecessary: spoken and written language certainly differ, but that is a function of how they are used" (1994).

Toward New Psychologies of Literacy

Other traditions in psychology open the mind to the world beyond paper. They locate literacy in lives and in the world. Despite Olson's general dismissal or neglect of them, as broadly *social* and deeply *cultural* rather than narrowly *cognitive*, they command the attention of anyone seriously interested in literacy in practice and in theory.[14]

Based on research around the world, they are diverse and wide-ranging. They represent a far wider and richer approach to culture, cognition, and the relationships of reading and writing than Olson's. In the view of cultural psychologists, culture and environment shape thought and are in turn influenced by mental actions. To psychologists like Olson, to point to an apt example, Vygotsky and Luria, among the tradition's modern founders, "worked from the Marxist perspective which claimed that cognition and consciousness were the products of human activity, rather than the cause" (Olson 1994, 33). I ask: why must we choose one *or* the other perspective, and not consider their relationships and interactions?

Here I explicitly acknowledge Paulo Freire's seminal observation that we must read the world in order to read the word. While recognizing the priority of the world, I emphasize the dialectical relationships between the word and the world (Freire 1970; Bartlett 2010). In my view, this idea is central to the approach to a psychology of literacy along the lines sketched here.

Psychologist James Wertsch, who is a student of A. R. Luria and the author of a key critical study of Lev Vygotsky, two pioneering Soviet social-historical psychologists, helps us to bridge the gap. Criticizing the intellectual isolation of many social psychologists, he remarks that "they have tended to lose sight of the fact that their ultimate goal is to contribute to some integrated, holistic picture of human nature" (Wertsch 1985, 1; see also Vygotsky 1978; Luria 1976). He points to "the division that separates studies of individual psychology from studies of the sociocultural environment into which individuals live. In psychology we tend to view culture or society as a variable to be incorporated into models of individual functioning. This represents a kind of reductionism which assumes that sociocultural phenomena can ultimately be explained on the basis of psychological processes." An opposing tradition, which

Wertsch associates with sociologists and social theorists, is "no less naïve": it views "psychological processes as posing no special problems because they derive straightforwardly from social phenomena" (1985, 1).

Wertsch summarizes, "Keeping sight of this totality while examining particular levels of phenomena in social science is as elusive a goal today as earlier in the twentieth century." His purpose in presenting a critical appreciation of Vygotsky as an exemplar is "to explicate and extend a theoretical approach that tried to avoid that pitfall" (1985, 2). In echoing his call, I make no claim that any psychologist interested in literacy in social and psychological context has completely and persuasively achieved that ambitious goal, but rather that this tradition calls compellingly to those who wish to study and understand literacy in theory and practice. While grasping their limits, we continue to learn from Vygotsky's and Luria's studies of Uzbek and Kirghiz peasants and from Sylvia Scribner and Michael Cole's (1981a) more sophisticated research on the Vai people in Liberia. Is Wertsch's goal any less elusive in the second decade of the twenty-first century than it was three decades ago?

Taken together, the diverse approaches to literacy within social psychologies that place culture at the core of human thought and action stand as a compelling alternative or set of suggestions and exemplars. Rather than offering a potted summary of all those I consider among the most exciting and useful works, I refer to what they teach us that might advance the study and understanding of literacy.

Less well-known than Scribner and Cole, Vygotsky, and Luria are studies in Mexico, Africa, and the United States by Jean Lave (1988, 2011), Barbara Rogoff (1990,2003,2011), and Lave and Rogoff (1984), and research by Mike Rose on intelligence at work (2004).[15] Readers seeking an engaging, informed introduction should look at Michael Cole's *Cultural Psychology: A Once and Future Discipline* (1996). Let me be clear: I am not making a blanket endorsement of all that passes as cultural psychology, nor, for that matter, of everything that the authors on whom I draw here have written about literacy. I take exception, for example, to some of the assumptions and generalizations of Vygotsky and Luria about the superiority of the thinking of literate persons. It is their conceptualization, their approach to literacy in the inextricably linked contexts of practice and theory that I underscore.

Often if not always, research in cultural psychology, the cultural nature of human development, everyday cognition, cognition in practice, and the mind at work—to paraphrase the titles of key books—is characterized by its *not* leading to any direct relationship with literacy despite its central connections and relevance. That carries an important point.[16]

The following perspectives and emphases individually and collectively bear special relevance to a renewed (not "new") literacy studies. It is not accidental that they, together, parallel and extend the best of the newer literacy studies and, if attended to closely, show the way to a more grounded cross- and interdisciplinary method and understanding of theory and practice. They transcend the oppositional terms that too often define literacy, from oral to literate and either autonomous or ideological.

In contrast to common practice in social and cognitive psychologies, cultural psychologies seek out and emphasize relatively complex connections among multiple factors. They tend to draw on, and derive conclusions from, qualitative as well as quantitative traditions and approaches. The plural variables do not exist in linear, causal connections; they are overlapping and interacting, inseparable in theory and in human practices. Concretely and metaphorically, notions of dependent, or determined, and independent, or autonomous, variables are diminished. Despite occasional slips, the larger perspective is strongly committed to avoiding binaries in definition, conceptualization, and actual research exercises. I identify what I see as the most valuable distinguishing characteristics that enhance our understanding and ability to study literacy. (Notice that I do not call them propositions or principles.)

Barbara Rogoff introduces this viewpoint clearly:

> Human development is a cultural process. As a biological species, humans are defined in terms of our cultural participation. We are prepared by both our cultural and biological heritage to use language and other cultural tools and to learn from each other. Using such means as language and literacy, we can collectively remember events that we have not personally experienced—becoming involved vicariously in other people's experience over many generations. (2003, 3)

Rogoff points to patterns of constraints and possibilities that stem from historical practices, cultural adaptation, and biological heritage. She underscores the role of "the cultural practices and circumstances of their communities—which also change" (3–4).

More specifically, she has stated, "Literacy is an excellent example of the levels of relationship between the cognitive skills of the individual, the cultural technologies employed, and the societal institutions in which skill with technologies is practiced and developed." With respect to practices that must inform theory, "variations in the purposes and practices of literacy appear to be closely related to the skills that individuals using a technology gain from its use; such variations are embedded in societal arrangements of human activities" (Rogoff 1990, 54–55).

A Cultural and Social Psychology of Literacy

A revised, cultural psychology of literacy in theory and practice, together, is marked by these characteristics:

- Conceptualization of literacy is a first factor. These concepts must be flexible, multiple, and dialectical. In all studies and commentaries, literacy and literacies must be defined explicitly. That task is extremely difficult and variable, and it must be incorporated into statements of "intention" (to borrow a term from linguists and psychologists).
- Literacy must be conceptualized and interpreted comparatively and with a cross-cultural, anthropological awareness. Otherwise, it is not possible to mediate both empirically and epistemologically between theory and practice within a context that grapples with the possibilities and the limits of literacy and literacies.
- Literacy must be conceptualized critically. Most specifically, in the terms of recent literacy studies, Street's contrast between autonomous and ideological approaches to literacy must be superseded. Despite disavowals, this issue plagues psychology approaches with their continuing if qualified forms of great and lesser divides. Binaries and oppositions must be eschewed at the level of conceptualization, though not always at the level of practice. Contradictions in both theory and practice may be very real.

- Literacy, in theory and practice, is always historical.
- On one hand, both the theories and the practices of reading and writing, construed broadly across media and modes of understanding and expression, are historical products. This encompasses all modes of written expression, including the semiotic or symbolic, alphabetic, numerical, other visual, embodied, spatial, etc., and the various material and cognitive tools developed to read them.
- On the other hand, it includes the situational and environmental domains of cognition, what the tradition of Vygotsky, Luria, and cultural psychology more generally see as social historical.
- Context is among most critical elements in studying and understanding (and advancing) literacy. Researchers will differ in how they conceptualize context and perhaps even more over how they attempt to operationalize it in empirical research and how to consider it theoretically. Yet very few students continue to believe that it is possible to understand literacy outside of meaningful contexts. Those who debate "great divide" theories or a "Goody thesis" agrees on at least that much.
- Specifying definitive contexts for the transmission, acquisition, practice, use, and consideration of the "implications" or influences or literacy is absolutely critical. Literacy is never autonomous. No practice or use is totally deterministic, no matter how powerful.
- Contexts for literacy include the everyday, the practical, the informal, the vernacular, the popular, the new, and so on, as well as the formal, official, institutional, authoritative, and traditional. None exist apart from the others.
- Examining literacy (and even speech) only in the context of written texts is limited and reductive. Diverse texts—of all kinds of expression, including what we typically mean by writing—take their meaning from their own encompassing social, cultural, political, economic, and psychological contexts.
- Literacy and literacies are therefore always relational, interactive, and dialectical. What is often called activity theory, along with other cultural psychologies, can incorporate these perspectives despite the more limited and deterministic ways in which they are often represented.

- Literacy only has significance in practice, informed, clarified by and in turn clarifying theory. Practice takes place in contexts inseparably shaped by society, culture, and political economy including traditions, habits, customs, institutions, and ideologies, and their various conflicts.
- Literacy is developmental. Both literacy (and literacies) and context are developmental, as are both their individual and social dimensions. Development is diachronic and synchronic, chronological and cross-sectional. It is collective as well as individual. These dimensions differ conceptually, qualitatively, and quantitatively. Great pains must be taken to distinguish them, in part because of common metaphors of presumed or autonomous developmentalism.
- Cognition must be broadly and carefully viewed. The examples of Goody and Olson and the contrast with more cultural psychology demonstrate the difficulties and the differences. They begin with questions of attention to formal mental and logical operations versus informal operations; mind shaping culture versus culture shaping mind; schooled versus unschooled populations, learning, and practice. They end in charges of determinism, reductionism, and trivialization.
- Practices of reading and writing, new and old, never exist apart from each other, except, that is, in the words of their discussants and declared theorists. Practices are historically variable; they change over time and differ across populations.[17]
- If it is possible to distinguish reading from writing conceptually, it is much more difficult to do so practically. This point is most compelling when we recall that writing and especially reading are often collective activities and that one reader brings the contents of a written or printed or digital page to the ears of many.
- Relatedly, reading and writing, viewed literally or metaphorically, take place among the media including the oral and the spoken. The recently popular analogies and even more the uncritical metaphors about literacy acts and literacy events, derived from speech act theories and metaphors in linguistic can be very misleading.
- As a result, while recognizing the risk of viewing practice too loosely, a flexible conceptualization of practice is nonetheless essential. In this regard, I point to the groundbreaking studies on literate practices in everyday life and diverse cognitive practices, intelligences, and compe-

tencies in work, child-rearing and family, health, community life, and beyond.[18] Relevant concepts of practice always exist in interaction with elements of literacy within a broader communicative context; they never exist in isolation.

- That context, to be meaningful, includes critical elements that are too often dichotomized or separated from one another, in both theory and practice. None is autonomous.

- Among the most important critical elements for literacy are:

- the formal and informal, from the established, ideological, authoritative, traditional, and institutional, to the informal but often no less established or influential but less powerful in normative, including legal and other official terms.

- the individual and the collective, at all levels of social organization from the familial and local to the larger and more formal.

- integration and differentiation across structures, traditions and customs at all levels of social organization: community relationships, from class, race, ethnicity, gender, and other lines of social division which levels, forms, and uses of literacy both cross and separate.

- generations, literacy and age, including intergenerational relationships central to the transmission and practice, and in some cases the differences in practices of literacy.

- Central to their understanding in theory and practice are:

- Schooling in cultural, social, and historical contexts. Schooling needs to be seen as a special case of literacy, learning, and practice, not a general case. Age, organization of learning, texts and tools, community and cultural contexts all matter, and they vary in basic ways. Skills and knowledge taught and practiced also vary.

- Schools themselves, and their fundamental association with learning to read and write and with age, are relatively recent developments in the long span of human history.

- The effects of the circumstances of learning, practice, and use, taken together in all their variation and real contradictions, while the subject of debate, are central and cry out for continued study. This is where theory and practice come together in the lives of real people, young and old.

- Conceptions of literacy, again in theory and practice, are intensely and misleadingly individualistic. They require revision to take into account the prevalence and power of collaboration, cross-age, and apprenticeship relationships, formal and informal. They are collective, cultural, institutional, ideological, and practical.

I end this section with two questions whose answers should occupy us deeply and at length:

- What is the crux of the matter: is it the implications of literacy, or the implications for literacy? More than semantics are at stake in these formulations. What, indeed, is implied? And what do we mean when we write (or say?) "for literacy" or "of literacy"?
- In what are we interested: literacy in the word or in the world? It matters.

A Case Study of Literacy in Cultural Context

Sylvia Scribner and Michael Cole's *The Psychology of Literacy* (1981a) remains one of the most important books written about literacy. Along with Heath's *Ways with Words* (1983) and my own *The Literacy Myth* (1979), it anchored Street's *Literacy in Theory and Practice* (1984). The book has proved contentious, despite its empirical basis and its roots in a scientific psychology, or perhaps because of those dimensions. It is hardcore social psychology set in a sociocultural rather than a cognitive-linguistic framework. Scribner and Cole dared first to question the presumption of the relative autonomy of literacy and the cognitive power of some kinds of writing and then to test specific propositions. Working in the tradition of cross-cultural anthropological psychology, over a period of several years they studied the several literacies—in different languages and taught and practiced in different ways, with and without schooling—of the Vai people in Liberia.

Reflecting on the research, Michael Cole wrote, "Literacy has typically been seen as the great mental transforming invention underpinning the accumulation of systematic knowledge, the transformation of human thought, and the development of civilization. Institutionalized in schools and government programs, literacy has been seen as the engine of the machinery that produces the cognitive and social consequences of involvement in schooling" (1996, 227). Acknowledging experimental psychology's "severe difficulty in assessing the psychological consequences of schooling," Scribner and Cole boldly seized a chance to pursue very contentious but extremely important questions about the influence of literacy. Briefly, they conclude: "the first answer to this question is that literacy is not equivalent to schooling." They explain their rationale for this case study: "Although rare, cases where literacy is acquired independent of schooling do exist, offering an opportunity to unpackage these oft-confounded forms of activity. Equally important, the exercise of analyzing various kinds of literacy practices not only motivates a reconceptualization of the question of schooling's impact on cognition but demonstrates rather clearly the possibility of modeling local cultural practices in experiments (Scriber and Cole 1981a, 227).[19]

A tribal group residing on the northwest coast of Liberia bordering on Sierra Leone, the Vai "were remarkable because they had been using a writing system of their own invention for more than one hundred years. Most important, their literacy was acquired without any formal schooling" (Cole 1996, 228). From their initial fieldwork, Scribner and Cole learned that three distinct kind of literacy existed among the Vai. Approximately 20 per cent were literate in the Vai language, which they learned informally. About 16 per cent "had some degree of literacy" in Arabic, primarily though not exclusively the ability to read the Qur'an and commit it to memory, but not to write in Arabic. About 9 per cent were able to read and write in English, which they had learned in formal schools. About 28 per cent of adult male Vai were literate in one form or another. Few women were literate in Arabic or Vai, so the study focused on men (Scribner and Cole 1981a, 1981b).

The Vai provide an exceptional opportunity to perform experimental tests searching for the consequences of reading and writing comparatively between non-literate and literate persons and also among literates with different abilities that were also learned differently. The three literacies were acquired, practiced, and used very differently. The psychological and cognitive qualities associated with them varied as well.

The combined results of the ethnography and experimental tests are complicated. Vai literacy "involves no mastery of esoteric knowledge or new forms of institutionalized social interaction. Nor does it prepare the learner for a variety of new kinds of economic and social activity in which mediation of action through print is essential" (Cole 1996, 229). At the same time, Vai literacy is useful in traditional occupations for record-keeping and letter-writing. Both are ubiquitous among the Vai. On some tests of cognitive skills, Vai literates performed better than non-literates. Scribner and Cole showed that literacy-without-schooling is indeed related to performance on certain cognitive tasks. "This is certainly important evidence that literacy does 'count' in intellectual terms, and it is especially important in suggesting how it counts. The consequences of literacy that we identified are all highly specific and closely tied to actual practices with particular scripts; learning the Qur'an improved skills on a specific type of memory tasks, writing the Vai script improved skills in a particular communicative task" (Scribner and Cole 1981b, 85). Vai and Arabic literates and Arabic literates demonstrated different patterns of skills; neither equaled the performance of schooled literates.

Among those who acquired and practiced literacy at formal schools, Scribner and Cole were "impressed by what appeared to be the unique features of the expository or essay type text." This finding is not unexpected, of course. To them, it raises further questions that bear repeating:

> In what nonschooled settings are such texts required and produced in our own society? Although developmental models of writing place such texts at the "highest stage" of writing ability, we find it difficult to order different types of texts and writing functions to stages of development. Our evidence indicates that social organization creates the conditions for a variety of literacy activities, and that different types of text reflect different social practices. With respect to *adult* literacy, a functional approach appears more appropriate than a developmental one. The loose generalizations of developmental models developed for work with children to instructional programs to adolescents and adults are certainly questionable. (Scribner and Cole 1981b, 85)

On balance, the authors conclude, "neither Vai nor Qur'anic literacy substituted for schooling with respect to performance on psychological tests; in general those who had been to school performed better on the test battery, especially when asked to explain the basis of their performance" (Cole 1996, 229).

Scribner and Cole move the debate, in theory and in practice, beyond literacy versus non-literacy and schooling versus non-schooling. This is a major advance. Although not always admitted by critics, this shift is game-changing for literacy studies. Given that one case study cannot be conclusive and that they are also seeking to test Russian social and cultural historical theories, they focus attention on the specific influences and the relationships of context, acquisition, practice, diversity of consequences, culture, and history to an unprecedented degree. They also recognize, rather than downplay or dismiss, the collective and collaborative, the interplay between reading and writing (and other literacies), and the inseparability of the oral.

Shifting from the Vai to the contemporary United States, Cole writes:

> When technological, social, and economic conditions create many activities where reading and writing are instrumental, the range of literacy skills can be expected to broaden and increase in complexity. Under these conditions, the "context specific" and "general ability" interpretations of literacy's consequences converge. In any society where literacy practices are ubiquitous and complexly interrelated, the associated cognitive skills will also become more widespread and complexly related, giving the appearance of a general transformation of modes of thought.

In sum, "my colleagues and I, while sharing the idea of literacy as a cognitive and social tool, were focused on the context-specifics of literacy effects and its role in amplifying social inequalities it was being used to overcome (Cole 1996, 235).

In 1996, fifteen years after the publication of *The Psychology of Literacy*, Cole looked toward the future of literacy studies: "How the resulting heterogeneity should be sorted out remains a matter of dispute, but the grounds have shifted away from the 'literacy as general transformation;' view to one which takes the social organization of activity as a problematic to be worked out case by case" (Cole 1996, 235).

Literacy in Theory and Practice, Again?

Scribner and Cole's research has been very influential among many researchers, but others have raised strong objections and attempted to dismiss it. Expectedly, the first complaint was that their study focused on an exceptional population with an indigenous script and several literacies. This objection to a case study whose authors never claimed was "representative" misunderstands the point of comparative social research.

Goody and Olson have hesitated to acknowledge the importance of the research and the conclusions, or to see the common ground they share with Scribner and Cole—despite the fact that Cole and Olson coedited a festschrift dedicated to Goody (2006). Michael Cole and Jennifer Cole wrote sympathetically about "Rethinking the Goody Myth" (2006), searching for complementarity in a way that seems to me very generous.[20]

In his last major work on writing, *The Interface between the Written and the Oral* (1987), Goody spent considerable space detailing his many objections to the methods, arguments, and conclusions of *The Psychology of Literacy*, even though Chap. 9, "Writing and formal operations: A case study among the Vai," was coauthored with Scribner and Cole. To summarize a lengthy exposition, Goody was not particularly sympathetic to either their experimental procedures or their sociocultural historical theory, as opposed to his own version of historical analysis. (See the discussion in Chap. 3). He detailed his many concerns with the wording, format, and presentation of the questions that Scribner and Cole ask their subjects. To refer to this matter as "semantic" is not merely a literal description, but also an implied criticism. In my view, Goody engaged in considerable quibbling to the extent of special pleading; I suggest that interested readers decide for themselves.

The simplification and final version of his "strong" case for the "implications of writing/literacy" are presented graphically in Figures 11–12 (Goody 1987, 247–248). Goody also went to great pains to deny or minimize the status of the Vai script and language and its usefulness for rigorous social research. As a historian, I find his stance to be deeply a- or antihistorical, as well as an example of applying his own post hoc standards to sources and evidence that do not support his own views.[21] Goody paid no attention to the value of Scribner and Cole's research in raising new questions about reading, writing, and their social and cognitive correlates. His objections inconsistently cross the distinctions between what he called the sociological and the psychological.

In *The World on Paper* (1984), and to a limited extent in "The Documentary Tradition" (2006), Olson reduces the views presented in *The Psychology of Literacy* in order to dismiss them, in part by equating Scribner and Cole's approach with that of Vygotsky and Luria. Consider, for example, this representation of one of the cognitive tests on which non-literates, Vai literates, Qur'anic literates, and English schooled literates were compared: "In such cases, performance, including justifications, went almost, but not quite to the levels achieved by schooled children and was quite amenable to training. They concluded that such studies 'cast doubt on hypotheses that implicate literacy directly in the acquisition of metalinguistic knowledge about the properties of propositions' and they favor the hypothesis that such competence has more to do with learning a particular school-related mode of discourse" (Olson 1994, 40). Scribner and Cole would find this summary unsatisfactory.

Olson continues, "But suppose that the mode of discourse in question is, in fact, a literate mode of discourse, a way of setting out arguments to make that logic particularly visible and explicit primarily but not exclusively in writing" (1994, 40–41). Here Olson redefines the terms of "literate discourse" without argument or explanation--a move that Goody, too, often made.

Assertion, reductionism, and circularity do make for persuasive cases.

Indeed, Olson repeats Goody's complaints. He frames them in this way: "So Goody rejects as naïve the hypotheses regarding the consequences of literacy which Scribner and Cole test and subsequently refute" (1994, 41). Consider this rhetorical formulation:

> Scribner and Cole looked for, but failed to find, that literacy has "general cognitive effects as we have defined them," that it "profoundly change[s] what people know about their language and how they think about it," or affects "the process of thinking—how we classify, reason, remember." Their mistaken expectations, he [Goody] suggests, come from the inappropriate notion that the cognitive implications of literacy can be determined by

examining the direct impact on the individual who learns to read and write. Learning to read and write is at best a mere introduction to the world of literacy. It is not appropriate to assume that all of the things that could ever be done with literacy will immediately come into learners' minds when they first learn to read. Consider another example: Literacy, let us say, facilitates the writing of dictionaries. But it would be wrong to think that just because one learned to read and write one could give better definitions. That would depend upon learning to use a dictionary. (41–42)

This borders on *reductio ad absurdum*, but reminds us of the convictions of the literacy episteme and the literacy myth.[22]

Olson misstates Scribner and Cole's premises and conclusion. Since neither Goody nor Olson directly examined the premise that they restated, their critique is impossible to sustain. Reframing arguments in order to reject them without relevant evidence calls their own methods of reasoning into question, rather than constituting a fair criticism of Scribner and Cole's work or, indeed, a legitimate form of academic debate.

In their contribution to the festschrift for Goody (2006), Cole and Cole embrace the larger goal of bringing psychological and cultural studies closer together and accept parts of Goody's critique of Scribner and Cole's 1981 study. At the same time, they point out certain problems with his approach that demand notice here. "For various reasons" which they go on to enumerate, the set of concepts [Goody] proposed to avoid destructive dichotomies (individual/social, short-term/long-term, etc.) has not found the resonance that its well-motivated considerations deserve" (2006, 320). They explain: Goody "uses the term '*mediated/ unmediated*,' where *unmediated* refers to the short-term effects of literacy on the individual, while *mediated* refers to literacy's long-term, cumulative effects," but that formulation "is problematic." Moreover, while it "is "certainly true" "that literacy and schooling co-occur and that modern schooling would not exist without schooling," "literacy not entirely subsumed by schooling or even the many forms of school that share similar technologies of writing and reading." "In using the terms mediated and unmediated, Goody was adopting the language of cultural historical psychology but using these terms in a way that was at odds with actual cultural-historical theory. According to Vygotsky, all human thinking is mediated by culture… " (320). Cole and Cole conclude by suggesting that Goody (and now Olson) reject a view of literacy as practice and a set of findings that Scribner and Cole saw as "quite compatible with Goody's own" (321).

Caveat lector—"let the reader beware."

Notes

1. For an introduction to some of these matters, see Gardner, *Mind's new science* (1987). See also the discussion of cognitive science and literacy studies in Graff, *Undisciplining knowledge* (2015). Francois Truffaut's classic 1970 film *L'Enfant Sauvage* explores important questions with respect to literacy.
2. Nor is Wolf up to date, judging from her citations. She does not mention the critical literature in relevant fields of study or the lack of evidence for this hypothesis. She also seems to think that history is parallel to "the course of a single child's life."
3. Havelock, in fact, is ambiguous. Alphabets as symbol systems are hard to differentiate from writing systems.
4. Compare Wolf, *Proust and the Squid* (2007, 65–217); see Dehaene, *Reading in the brain* (2009). The literature is unpersuasive; see, for example, Clement and Lovat, "Neuroscience and education" (2012); Dehaene et al., "How learning to read changes cortical networks" (2010); Hruby and Gowami, "Neuroscience and reading" (2011); Mangen and Velay, "Digitizing literacy" (2010); McNamara, "Bringing cognitive science into education" (2006); Keith Oatley and Maja Djikic, "How reading transforms us," *NYT*, Dec. 21, 2014; Schrag, "Does neuroscience matter for education?" (2011); George Williams, "Students, reading and writing," *CHE*, Apr. 14, 2011; Peter Wood, "Wired to read," *CHE*, Nov. 24, 2011; Worden, Hinton, and Fischer, "What does the brain have to do with learning?" (2011).
5. For the history, compare these sweeping formulations with Yates, *Arts of memory* (1966); Ong, *Ramus, method, and the decay of dialogue* (1958); Carruthers, *Craft of thought* (1998); Spence, *Memory palace* (1984). See also Ong, *Orality and literacy* (1982).

6. For examples of ahistorical and tortured arguments, see Olson and Cole, *Technology, literacy, and the evolution of society* (2006); see also Collin, "Revisiting Jack Goody" (2013).

7. See Venezky, "Review of Olson" (1995).

8. Olson is still engaged in this pursuit, jointly with Brockmeier in "Literacy episteme" (2009) and in his own "Documentary tradition in mind and society" (2006)—a title that announces the effort at salvage. In this article, Olson introduces a further opposition between writing as expository and writing as documentary that is absent from *World on Paper*. Rather than clarifying, it only muddies matters further. Remarkably, Olson continues to argue against Scribner and Cole after more than 35 years.

9. In this case, as in other texts on which Olson draws, attention to scholarly reviews might have led him to different reading and interpretations. See Chap. 6.

10. For a specific example, see Olson, *World on paper* (2004), 260.

11. On Olson and the problem of intention, see Wertsch, "Review of Olson" (1996).

12. See Finnegan, *Orality and Literacy* (1988), discussed in Chap. 2; on religious reading, see Venezky, "Review of Olson" (1995).

13. In his 1995 review, "So far so Bletchley Park," John Ray refers to analogy with respect to mapmaking. On Olson and the history of reading, see Venezky, "Review of Olson" (1995).

14. In his chapter on "Theories of Literacy and Mind" in *World on paper* (1994, 20–44), Olson criticizes others for the kind of assertions they make and then does the same himself. In my view, he misrepresents the work of Lev Vygotsky, A. R. Luria, Sylvia Scribner, and Michael Cole. Surprisingly, Olson does not mention Jean Lave, Barbara Rogoff, or James Wertsch on Vygotsky.

15. Luria and, especially, Vygotsky have not been served well by educators who have sought to adopt their views. For examples of superficiality, misreading, and serious errors, see the anthologies edited by Moll, *Vygotsky and education* (1990), and Lee and Smagorinsky, *Vygotskian perspectives on literacy research* (2000). On appropriations of "activity learning," see Roth and Lee, "Vygotsky's neglected legacy" (2007); Russell, "Activity theory" (1995); Witte, "Research in activity" (2005). Often Vygotsky serves as little more than a source of faddish terms from "sociohistorical" to "zone of proximal development," "activity," and "collaboration," which are often taken out of context.

16. It is revealing that both Goody and Olson have attempted to criticize and dismiss the relevance of this research for literacy by branding it as trivializing; see Olson, *World on paper* (1994), esp. Chap. 2 on Scriber and Cole.

17. Reading and writing are considered in greater detail in the next chapter; non-alphabetic literacies are taken up in Chap. 6.

18. Chaiklin and Lave, *Understanding practice* (1993); Cole, *Cultural psychology* (1996); Cole and Cole, "Rethinking the Goody myth" (2006); Cole et al., *Cultural context of learning and thinking* (1971); Cole and Scribner, *Culture and thought* (1974); Lave, *Cognition in practice* (1988); Lave, *Apprenticeship in critical ethnographic practice* (2011); Lave and Wenger, *Situated learning* (1991); Rogoff, *Apprenticeship in thinking* (1990); Rogoff, *Cultural nature of human development* (2003); Rogoff, *Developing destinies* (2011); Rogoff and Lave, *Everyday cognition*, 1994; Rose, *Mind at work*, 2004; Scribner and Cole, "Cognitive consequences" (1973); Scribner and Cole, *Psychology of literacy* (1981a); Scribner and Cole, "Unpacking literacy" (1981b).

19. I refer readers interested in the details of Scribner and Cole's research to the book-length version of the study, *Psychology of Literacy* (1981a); their essay "Unpackaging Literacy" (1981b) provides a useful summary.

20. I do not agree with the reading of Goody presented by Michael Cole and Jennifer Cole. More valuable are their brief comments on the historical context of the writing and publication of "Consequences of Literacy" in the early 1960s, but they misstate the chronology of the scholarly context. Ironically, they share that problem with the viewpoint of the literacy episteme.

21. See, for example, where Goody places the Vai with respect to ancient Mesopotamian writing (1987, 211).

22. For more along these lines, see Olson, "Documentary tradition in mind and society" (2006, 296–301). Interested readers should compare it with *World on Paper* for revisions that are not explicitly acknowledged and for the continuing practice of reframing arguments and shifting terms: for example, "Literacy encourages the tendency to think not just of discourse but of documents" (2006, 299).

References

Baron, Naomi S. (2015) *Words onscreen: The fate of reading in a digital world.* New York: Oxford University Press.

Bartlett, Lesley. (2010) *The word and the world: The cultural politics of literacy in Brazil.* Creskill, N.J.: Hampton Press.

Brockmeier, Jens. (2000) Literacy as symbolic space. In Janet Wilde Astington, ed., *Minds in the making: Essays in honor of David R. Olson*, 43-61. Oxford: Blackwell.

Brockmeier, Jens. (2002) The literacy episteme: The rise and fall of a cultural discourse. In Jens Brockmeier, Min Wang, and David R. Olson, eds, *Literacy, narrative and culture*, 17–34. Richmond, England: Curzon.

Brockmeier, Jens, and David R. Olson. (2002) "Introduction: What is a culture of literacy?" In Jens Brockmeier, Min Wang, and David R. Olson, eds, *Literacy, Narrative and Culture*, 1–16. Richmond, England: Curzon.

Brockmeier, Jens, and David R. Olson. (2009) The literacy episteme: From Innis to Derrida. In David R. Olson and Nancy Torrance, eds., *The Cambridge handbook of literacy*, 3–21.

Carr, Nicholas. (2010) *The shallows: What the Internet is doing to our brains.* New York: Norton.

Carruthers, Mary. (1998) *The craft of thought: Meditation, rhetoric, and the making of images, 400–1200.* Cambridge: Cambridge University Press.

Chaiklin, Seth, and Jean Lave, eds. (1993) *Understanding practice: Perspectives on activity and context.* Cambridge: Cambridge University Press.

Clement, Neville D., and Terence Lovat. (2012) Neuroscience and education: Issues and challenges for curriculum. *Curriculum Inquiry* 42: 534–557.

Cole, Michael. (1996) *Cultural psychology: A once and future discipline.* Cambridge, Mass: Belknap Press.

Cole, Michael, and Jennifer Cole. (2006) Rethinking the Goody myth. In David R. Olson and Michael Cole, eds, *Technology, literacy, and the evolution of society: Implications of the work of Jack Goody*, 305–324. Mahwah, N.J.: Lawrence Erlbaum.

Cole, Michael, John Gay, Joseph A. Glick, and Donald W. Sharp. (1971) *The cultural context of learning and thinking: An exploration in experimental anthropology.* London: Methuen; New York: Basic Books.

Cole, Michael, and Sylvia Scribner. (1974) *Culture and thought: A psychological introduction.* New York: Wiley.

Collin, Ross. (2013) Revisiting Jack Goody to rethink determinisms in literacy studies. *Reading Research Quarterly* 48: 27–38.

Dehaene, Stanislas. (2009) *Reading in the brain: The science and evolution of a human invention.* New York: Viking.

Dehaene, Stanislas, Felipe Pegado, Lucia W. Braga, Paulo Ventura, Gilberto Nunes Filho, Antoinette Jobert, Ghislaine Dehaene-Lambertz, Régine Kolinsky, José Morais, and Laurent Cohen. (2010) How learning to read changes the cortical networks for vision and language. *Sciencexpress,* 11 November: 1–10.

Finnegan, Ruth. (1988) *Literacy and Orality: Studies in the technology of communication.* Oxford: Blackwell.

Freire, Paulo. (1970) *Pedagogy of the oppressed,* trans. Myra Ramos. New York: Continuum.

Gardner, Howard. (1987) *The mind's new science: A history of the cognitive revolution.* New York: Basic Books.

Ginzburg, Carlo. (1980) *The cheese and the worms: The cosmos of a sixteenth century miller.* Baltimore: Johns Hopkins University Press.

Goody, Jack. (1977) *The domestication of the savage mind.* Cambridge: Cambridge University Press.

Goody, Jack. (1987) *The interface between the written and the oral.* Cambridge: Cambridge University Press.

Graff, Harvey J. (1979) *The literacy myth: Literacy and social structure in the nineteenthcentury city.* New York and London: Academic Press.

Graff, Harvey J. (2015) *Undisciplining knowledge: Interdisciplinarity in the twentieth century.* Baltimore: Johns Hopkins University Press.

Halverson, John. (1991) Olson on literacy. *Language in Society* 20: 619–640.

Halverson, John. (1992) Goody and the implosion of the literacy thesis. *Man* (new series) 27: 301–317.

Havelock, Eric. (1977) The preliteracy of the Greeks. *New Literary History* 8: 369–392.

Havelock, Eric. (1980) The coming of literate communication to Western culture. *Journal of Communication* 30: 90–99.

Heath, Shirley Brice. (1983) *Ways with words: Language, life, and work in communities and classrooms.* Cambridge: Cambridge University Press; new epilogue, 1996.

Hruby, George G., and Lisa Gowami. (2011) Neuroscience and reading: A review for reading education researchers. *Reading Research Quarterly* 46: 156–172.

Lave, Jean. (1988) *Cognition in practice.* Cambridge: Cambridge University Press.

Lave, Jean. (2011) *Apprenticeship in critical ethnographic practice*. Chicago: University of Chicago Press.

Lave, Jean, and Etienne Wenger. (1991) *Situated learning: Legitimate peripheral participation*. Cambridge: Cambridge University Press.

Lee, Carol D., and Peter Smagorinsky, eds. (2000) *Vygotskian perspectives on literacy research: Constructing meaning through collaborative inquiry*. Cambridge: Cambridge University Press.

Luria, A. R. (1976) *Cognitive development: Its cultural and social foundations*, trans. Martin Lopez-Morillas and Lynn Solotaroff, ed. Michael Cole. Cambridge, Mass.: Harvard University Press.

Mangen, Anne, and Jean-Luc Velay. (2010) Digitizing literacy: Reflections on the haptics of writing. In Mehrdad Hosseini Zudeh, ed. *Advances in haptics*, 385–401. Rijeka, Croatia: Intech.

Marshall, John C. (1994) "Now read on…" *Nature* 371, Oct. 20: 665.

McNamara, Danielle S. (2006) Bringing cognitive science into education, and back again: The value of interdisciplinary research. *Cognitive Science* 30: 605–608.

Moll, Luis C., ed. (1990) *Vygotsky and education: Instructional implications and applications of sociohistorical psychology*. Cambridge: Cambridge University Press.

Olson, David R. (1977) From utterance to text: The bias of language in speech and writing. *Harvard Educational Review* 47: 257–281.

Olson, David R. (1991) Literacy as metalinguistic activity. In David R. Olson and Nancy Torrance, eds., *Literacy and Orality*, 251–270. Cambridge: Cambridge University Press.

Olson, David R. (1994) *The world on paper: The conceptual and cognitive implications of writing and reading*. Cambridge: Cambridge University Press.

Olson, David R. (2006) The documentary tradition in mind and society. In David R. Olson and Michael Cole, eds., *Technology, literacy, and the evolution of society: Implications of the work of Jack Goody*, 289–304. Mahwah, N.J.: Lawrence Erlbaum.

Olson, David R., and Michael Cole, eds. (2006) *Technology, literacy, and the evolution of society: Implications of the work of Jack Goody*. Mahwah, N.J.: Lawrence Erlbaum.

Olson, David R., and Nancy Torrance, eds. (2009) *The Cambridge handbook of literacy*. Cambridge: Cambridge University Press.

Ong, Walter J. (1958) *Ramus, method, and the decay of dialogue*. Cambridge, Mass: Harvard University Press.

Ong, Walter J. (1982) *Orality and literacy: The technologizing of the word.* London: Methuen.

Ray, John. (1995) "So far so Bletchley Park." *London Review of Books,* June 8.

Rogoff, Barbara. (1990) *Apprenticeship in thinking: Cognitive development in social context.* Oxford: Oxford University Press.

Rogoff, Barbara. (2003) *The cultural nature of human development.* Oxford: Oxford University Press.

Rogoff, Barbara. (2011) *Developing destinies: A Mayan midwife and town.* Oxford: Oxford University Press.

Rogoff, Barbara, and Jean Lave, eds. (1984) *Everyday cognition: Its development in social context.* Cambridge, Mass: Harvard University Press.

Rose, Mike. (2004) *The mind at work: Valuing the intelligence of the American worker.* New York: Viking.

Roth, Wolff-Michael, and Yew-Jin Lee. (2007) "Vygotsky's neglected legacy": Culturalhistorical activity theory. *Review of Educational Research* 77: 186–232.

Russell, David R. (1995) Activity theory and its implications for writing instruction. In Joseph Petraglia, ed., *Reconceiving writing, rethinking writing instruction,* 151–178. Hillsdale, N.J.: Lawrence Erlbaum.

Schrag, Francis. (2011) Does neuroscience matter for education? *Educational Theory* 61: 221–237.

Scribner, Sylvia, and Michael Cole. (1973) Cognitive consequences of formal and informal education. *Science* 182: 553–559.

Scribner, Sylvia, and Michael Cole. (1981a) *The psychology of literacy.* Cambridge, Mass: Harvard University Press.

Scribner, Sylvia, and Michael Cole. (1981b) Unpacking literacy. In Marcia Farr Whiteman, ed., *Variation in writing: Functional and linguistic-cultural differences,* 71–87. Hillsdale, N.J.: Lawrence Erlbaum.

Spence, Jonathan. (1984) *The memory palace of Matteo Ricci.* New York: Penguin.

Unger, J. Marshall. (1994) Writing prior to speech? *Times Higher Educational Supplement,* Dec. 2.

Venezky, Richard L. (1995) Review of Olson, *The world on paper. American Journal of Education* 103: 440–451.

Vygotsky, L. S. (1978) *Mind in society: The development of higher psychological processes.* Cambridge, Mass.: Harvard University Press.

Wertsch, James V. (1985) *Vygotsky and the social formation of mind.* Cambridge, Mass.: Harvard University Press.

Wertsch, James V. (1996) Review of Olson, *The world on paper. Language in Society* 25: 125–129.

Witte, Stephen P. (2005) Research in activity: An analysis of speed bumps as mediational means. *Written Communication* 22: 127–165.

Wolf, Maryanne. (2007) *Proust and the squid: The story and science of the reading brain*. New York: Harper.

Worden, Jennifer M., Christina Hinton, and Kurt W. Fischer. (2011) What does the brain have to do with learning? *Phi Delta Kappan* 92: 8–13.

Yates, Frances. (1966) *The arts of memory*. London: Routledge.

5

Literature and Composition: Reading and Writing Revised

Brazilian educational reformer and philosopher Paulo Freire underscored the importance of reading and deplored the limits of our uncritical contrasts and often denigration of reading in comparison with writing: "Like any act of study, reading is not just a pastime but a serous task in which readers attempt to clarify the opaque dimensions of their study. To read is to rewrite, not memorize, the contents of what is being read. We need to dispense with the naïve idea of 'consuming' what we read" (Freire 1985, 100).

Freire posited a renewal of reading—of both the "words" and the "world" which gives them meaning and which they inform. Explaining his well-known critique of the "banking concept" of education, Freire reiterated, "This static artificial concept currently informs educational practice in which 'empty vessels' are to be filled by the educators' deposits. Hence learners don't have to ask questions or offer any challenge, since their position cannot be other than to receive passively the knowledge their educators deposit." For him as for others who revision literacy and the relationships between reading and writing, "in humanistic terms, knowledge involves a constant unity between action and reflection upon reality. Like our presence in the world, our consciousness transforms knowledge, acting on and thinking about what enables us to reach the stage of reflection. This is precisely why we must take our presence in the world as the focus of our critical analysis" (Freire 1985, 100–101).

In this chapter, I ask how reading and writing, by themselves and together, speak to these issues.

A fundamental issue of theory and practice, key questions speak to disjunctures and contradictions in schooling at different levels and the relationships between reading and writing in different media and modes of expression.

Many Literacies, from Reading to Writing and All Things Digital

Moving from *The World on Paper* to the worlds of reading *and* writing requires a large step.

Reading is no less important than writing and is connected with it in a myriad of ways. Recall Olson's and Goody's hierarchical and circular claim that "the product of exploiting the possibilities of writing by a society over historical time was written culture." Olson reduced "written culture" to "a society that both assumes a particular form of psychological competence—the ability to read, interpret, and construct documents in a standard, norm-based way—and a particular form of social organization—institutions organized around constitutions, rules of order, contracts, and explicit norms set out in written documents." Dismissing a wide variety of richly human literate practices, institutions, and forms of social organization, across different modes of expression and media, he was surprised that this "seemingly obvious claim can be widely disputed" (Olson 1994, 291; see Graff 2016). It is widely disputed because, among many complications, it reifies any differential and variable, sociocultural understanding and practices of writing, and distracts attention from the mutually defining roles of reading and writing. It also excludes most writing and its sociocultural and political economic contexts. These contradictions play out in education and in our understanding of the cultures of reading and writing.

Despite recognized fields of study in reading and in writing, how casually and unreflectingly we refer to each of them. And, despite their reflexive coupling, beyond the elementary school where reading has been primary, specialists, teachers, and curricula speedily separate and sometimes oppose the two. Reading typically falls within the departmental domain of education, but also within the purview of special education for those with learning disabilities and those in need of "reading recovery" or lacking in "reading readiness." Writing—or composition, in higher-order rhetoric—is a subject over which education and English programs have battled. In one form of another, it has been part of the curriculum for several centuries. College-level writing instruction is usually located in English departments. On some campuses, writing, especially lower-level or remedial, is supervised by a university writing program or center. Creative writing, which now includes "creative non-fiction," constitutes a special, often privileged preserve of English departments. Status and support are matters of struggle and controversy. Despite their high, and often mandatory, enrollments and their dependence the cheap labor of adjunct faculty, graduate students, and even undergraduates, composition courses remain the stepchild within departments of English and literature. In composition, the relationships between writing and reading are uneven and unequal, although they have shifted over time.

Specialists in writing are loath to consider its relationships with reading, and vice versa. Reading is easier or less complicated, regarded as of lesser value intellectually and economically, and distracting in an overly full curriculum. Professor of composition Deborah Brandt declares categorically, "writing over reading" (2009a; see also 2015). Fortunately, these kinds of assertions, which border on the axiomatic and irresponsible, are rarely developed or applied; they are regularly violated by the best practices of writing instructors and by acts of writing themselves.

I do not exaggerate when I state unequivocally that *reading is the missing link in understanding, teaching, and practicing writing.* It is possible that the converse is also true, but I will not argue that here. This declaration is analogous to my conviction that *orality is the missing link in understanding literacy.* Any perceived contradictions are necessary ones. They are rooted in the limits of our received wisdom and our repetition of assumptions that I seek to challenge.[1]

Ironically, as concerns shift to the effects of new media, on the one hand, and of the brain, on the other, on both reading and writing, interest in the relationships between reading—understanding and comprehension—and writing—expression and communication—seems to diminish rather than increase. Those who are persuaded (without direct evidence) that "reading changes the brain" or concerned about what "reading does to the brain" (rather than what the brain does with reading) have little if anything to say about writing (Baron 2015; Carr 2010; Clement and Lovat 2012; Dehaene 2009; Dehaene et al. 2010; Hruby and Gowami 2011; Mangen and Velay 2010; McNamara 2006; Keith Oatley and Maja Djikic, "How reading transforms us," *NYT*, Dec. 21, 2014; Schrag 2011; George Williams, "Students, reading and writing," *CHE*, Apr. 14, 2011; Wolf 2007; Peter Wood, "Wired to read," *CHE*, Nov. 24, 2011; Worden et al. 2011).[2] Those who fear that reading online will harm reading ability or understanding, and even the quality of scholarly research, do not seem to communicate with either those who fear or those who celebrate "digital writing." Few who participate in these declarations pause to talk with each other. Literacy studies, as a field, has been removed from them.

Consistent with the literacy episteme and the literacy myth, the view that writing is more important than reading often remains implicit but is nonetheless dominant. This conviction rests in part on a logical fallacy: writing (when preserved, which is itself a biased process) necessarily leaves evidence of itself; reading is (to use an awkward term) ephemeral. We know about and study reading through written records. In other words, writing provides the evidence of reading. That allows us to study *what* people read, but not *how* they did so and with what impact or influence. Relatedly, this complication includes educators and cognitive psychologists who study reading instruction and theories of reading, and not reading and both its affects and effects.[3]

Studies of reading lead to many conclusions, not all of them warranted. Among the strongest are that writing is more important and more powerful than reading, that writing is more valuable in dollars as well as sense, and that writing should be privileged in theory and often in practice. It is more than ironic or paradoxical that schools do not teach basic expository writing very well, and that many people—certainly in the United

States—have negative associations with writing. (See interviews excerpted or referenced in Brandt 2001.) This situation is often haughtily deplored by writers and scholars who look down at others who do not write well according to the standards of the school or writerly traditions. But non-academic writing, including collective writing, is seldom studied seriously.[4]

The most severe instance is the issue of academic or "school" writing, especially the formal (and often formulaic) essay. In other words, there are presumptions about writing—its nature, form, value, signification—within the promotion and understanding of writing itself. More than three decades of criticism, New Literacy Studies, and ethnographies of writing have led to a greater recognition of this problem. But at the same time, what passes for academic writing—the three- or five-part or point essay—continues to be granted superior status. Promising beginnings in "writing across the curriculum" can confuse writing within disciplines with campus- and schoolwide initiatives. Too often they compete with each other institutionally and pedagogically. Regardless of institutional arrangements, the essay remains the lens through which many other forms of writing, for worse or better, are viewed. The larger impacts are palpable, when student abilities, limited conceptions of writing practices, and both workplace and cultural demands come together.[5]

Images of Writing and Reading

Images of writing, from paintings, portraits, and photographs to biographies, memoirs, and fiction, are more active, evocative, and powerful than images of reading (Baron 2001; Kertész 1971; Stewart 2006). They seem more consequential, even momentous, despite the surprisingly large number of images of readers across media. Consider for example, the drafting and signing of great documents. The signature is a special case, often taken out of the context of the history of conferring agreement or certifying identity, as Clanchy's *From Memory to Written Record* (1993) shows so well. One such moment is Bertrande de Rols's surprising signing of her own name to her legal testimony at the trial of her erstwhile husband Martin Guerre in Daniel Vigne's 1982 historical drama *The*

Return of Martin Guerre, an act based on historian Natalie Zemon Davis's interpretation of literacy among women (Davis 1983). In the United States, John Hancock's dominating signature on the Declaration of Independence is canonical and defining.

The act of signing itself becomes adding one's own "John Hancock" to a document. Yet, closer observation of images of readers through the lens, for example, of *The Reader Revealed* by Sabrina Baron (2001), *On Reading* by André Kertész (1971), or *The Look of Reading* by Garrett Stewart (2006) tells different stories about the presence of readers and the power of reading. Literacy studies has privileged writing, but a range of sources suggest that reading is also of great cultural significance.

Writing's importance over reading plays powerfully in other spheres of understanding. They constitute images—word pictures and symbols of power—that acquire cultural, even political power. An influential example in writing and print studies is Jennifer Monaghan's argument in "Reading for the Enslaved, Writing for the Free: Reflections on Liberty and Literacy." She proposes to "clear up the discrepancies between these views—between literacy as empowering, on the one hand, and literacy as a means of social control, on the other—if we make sharper distinctions between which literacy skill we are talking about, and how each skill, at any given moment, has been defined" (1998, 310–311). Ironically, Monaghan deepens rather than clarifies the dichotomies by articulating a hierarchy and separates just what she should seek to connect: reading and writing, literacy and liberty. Neglecting historical context and scholarship, this reading instruction researcher turns historical relationships into a formula. Monaghan pushes reading versus writing and writing over reading to an extreme. In the process, she leaves the actual history of literacy among the enslaved far behind, misunderstanding the histories of reading and writing, slavery, and African American culture. In fact, there is no basic reason to associate reading by itself with a conservative or social control emphasis or writing by itself with power or liberation.

Inquiring instead about the place of both reading and writing in colonial and antebellum American culture helps to understand the acquisition of literacy (whether taught by white mistress, white children, black or white preacher, teachers, fellow slaves, and so on, for example) and the practice of literacy in the formation of regional and then national African American culture, based in part on religious foundations.

Reading was often collective: one reader informing many more auditors, reading together, or reading in sequence. African American religious forms were a product of the slave experience for which reading *and* hearing the Bible were central. They were also collective. Slave owners construed literacy as a form of control; they recognized both reading and writing's conservative and subversive purposes. For African Americans it was a powerful source of liberatory action and movements for equality. For formerly enslaved persons worldwide (and countless others), too, literacy's link to social movements is profound and continuing. Of course, this is not to argue that desire or actions for liberty is the only or the major impact of any form of literacy; that would be ahistorical and uncritical (Cornelius 1983, 1991; Williams 2002, 2005).

Searching for "reading for the enslaved, writing for the free" also looks for the power of writing in a social world in which writing was much less common than reading for all people, free or slave. Monaghan has a narrow view of the acquisition and practice of both reading and writing. The dichotomy of religious versus secular is a poor guide. Culture and action, moreover, are never limited to literacy. The lengthy discussion of David Walker's famous *Appeal to the Colored Citizens of the World* (1829) mentions without appropriate emphasis that Walker *writes about his readings* of Thomas Jefferson, Genesis, and Exodus, among other texts. Frederick Douglass, whose canonical *Autobiography* she also quotes, was even more keenly aware, and expressive, of the interdependence of reading and writing. That is a basic lesson from this historical experience: the contexts for the acquisition, valuation, and uses of reading and writing are joined together in lived experience. The social, cultural, political and economic dimensions form critical elements that span past, present, and future.

The experiences of other marginalized and subordinated groups parallel that of the enslaved in some ways. Compare the historical experiences of racial, ethnic, and age groups; women; the working class; and other minority and oppressed groups over the centuries and even recently. The place of reading and writing is complicated and contradictory. They are both central to social control and to self-expression and self-determination (which are not equivalent). Reading and writing never stand or serve separately, so opposing them is an error. The connections are shown superbly in the classic work of Edward P. Thompson (1968) on the English working class and more recently in David Vincent's (1979, 1989) studies of English working-class literacy.

The all too common separation between reading and writing results in the negation of the importance of reading, whether regarded as religious or merely frivolous, and the failure to consider the significance of the spoken or the sung. Monaghan's final words are, in my view, shockingly ahistorical and inhumane: "Today, literacy—particularly the ability to compose—still marks a boundary between full involvement with one's own humanity and a feeling of exclusion from the human race. In free society, to be fully literate is also to be fully human" (1998, 141).

Conclusions like this, which occur frequently in writing studies, supposedly recognize oppression and exclusion. In fact, they amount to statements that the enslaved and other oppressed peoples were dehumanized, not that slave owners treated them as less than fully human beings. The presumption is repeated today, sometimes in the context of human rights as well as in descriptions of non-readers and non-writers.

This use of writing is far from liberatory. These are the words of a professor of English and education. Where is the human voice? Where is the group's own perspective on this matter, much less its sense of itself? Where are alternative and supplementary forms of expression from voice and recording to dictation and voice-activated software? Where is the interplay of opportunity and constraint? Those are among the contexts for literacy in theory and practice.

A different, although no less contradictory take on writing over reading comes from writing scholar Deborah Brandt, whose arguments are considered more fully below. In a 2009 preview of her 2015 book *The Rise of Writing: Redefining Mass Literacy*, Brandt states that in proclaiming "Writing over Reading, I wish to bring attention to the rivalry between writing and reading as discrete literate practices, their different social, economic, and legal statuses, and the growing ascendancy of writing due to recent changes in forms of labor for many developed societies" (2009a, 56). In calling attention to "the rivalry between reading and writing," Brandt reinforces a dichotomy and advances an opposition when clearer historical, critical, and practical understanding all mandate exploring interrelations. Her reasoning is not clear, and in any case this move rests on other dichotomies. As she states in her important earlier book, *Literacy in American Lives* (2001), she separates the history of literacy and its dominant practices firmly into an eighteenth- and nineteenth-century era of "mass reading literacy," sponsored by church and state, and a more recent era of the ascendancy of "mass writing literacy."

The rise of writing "does not diminish reading, necessarily, but it does re-position it," Brandt asserts. Today "more people read at the screen, from the position of the writer.... Increasingly people read to inform their own writing" (2001, 57). This misstates the multiplicity of types of screens and other venues for reading, and their novelty, as well as the positioning of the human body.

Brandt's understanding of the twentieth and twenty-first centuries rests on an unsustainable, dichotomous view of the history of reading and writing. She reduces reading to its early association "with proper conduct and right belief as well as the exercise of civic rights and duties," which "still enjoys a nearly sacred status in many societies." In other oppositions, she reduces the role of writing in "doctrines of salvation or assimilation," where she emphasizes reading. Therefore, "compared to reading, writing has been regarded alternatively as crass and mercantile or rebellious and suspect, and the democratization of writing has been far less promoted or sanctioned" (Brandt 2001, 57).

Confessional and devotional writing is an epochal and dominant tradition. The history of popular culture teaches us about both reading and writing. We need to listen to and read the prose and poetry of "A woman writing a letter" (1999) and "Poetical maids and cooks who wrote" (2005) to whom Carolyn Steedman introduced us. Brandt and others should study the history of writing, from women's writing to spiritual autobiographies, working-class stories, confessional testimonies, personal narratives, letters, and much more.

Brandt is convinced that "until now writing has played second fiddle to reading" (2001). That is a very hard case to make, given the body of research on writing in literacy studies and the bias toward writing in the evidence and the so-called episteme. Why does Brandt, who is herself among those she calls "sponsors" of writing, feel the need to assert "writing over reading" in order to make a case for a new "prominence" for writing that she associates with economic and technological determinants? It seems that this ascendance is rather defensive and derivative.

The future of literacy studies, and of literacy, lies in the reconnection of reading and writing and their movement together. This is one form of translation across media and modes of understanding and expression that is central to both images and practices of literacy. We identify a number of lines to follow.

Reading Reviewed and Renewed

Imagine reading. What images come to mind? How are they written? How do we read them?

There are entire books of paintings, drawings, and photographs of readers. Major artists from the Renaissance through and beyond Picasso's abstractions have depicted people reading. Many of these powerful images are laden with symbolism, calling out for us to read them and put them into visual historical context. Books, manuscript and printed, have always been works of art and centers of attention. Readers are illuminated by illustrations as well as words. Digital graphical literature partakes of strong traditions. None is ephemeral. Indeed the practices of book arts, book artists, and art books are still compelling.

Learning to read is often regarded as a problem, not only by specialists in reading difficulties and professors of literature but also by new parents who are worried about the development of their young children's language and reading abilities. This concern is a separate issue from the current anxiety about what and how much adults and young people read (Moje et al. 2008; Dyson 2003). Consider, to take one example, the relatively simplistic policy research brief, "Reading Instruction for *All* Students," issued by the National Council of Teachers of English (2012). The alarmist title of the U.S. National Endowment for the Arts 2004 report, *Reading at Risk*, deliberately echoed the United States Department of Education's "open letter to the American people," *A Nation At Risk*, subtitled "The Imperative for Educational Reform" (1983).[6] The general failure to problematize reading is reflected in too often sterile debate about the Common Core curriculum in the United States. If students (and others) will just read, and read the right stuff, all else will follow. Ironically, research in cognitive or neuroscience is used and misused by some writers in the humanities in a self-serving quest for the authority enjoyed by science to support this normalism and developmentalism (Graff 2015, Chap. 4).

Despite perennial fears, alarmist proclamations, and proposals for reform, study after study reports that young people, as well as adults, are still reading. More books are being published.

The *Chronicle of Higher Education* trumpets that "For Many Students, Print is Still King" (Jan 27, 2013). This report refers in passing to "the 'comfort' of print." More and more people, of all ages, are reading on screens and remote devices, about whose effects we still know too little but whose deleterious influence cannot be presumed.

The promotion of reading, a very ambiguous gauge of progress or decline, knows no bounds.

English professors dominate the genre, but they have lots of company. While *The Future of the Book*, a phrase that recurs in the titles of many volumes (Nunberg 1996; Darnton 2009), is debated, it seems to be secure in one form or another. At the same time, communication professor Ted Striphas refers to *The Late Age of Print* (2009). Historians of reading and publishing note that that description actually applies over centuries. Andrew Piper tells us that books (in academic parlance, "the book") have a "past, present, and future" (*CHE*, Nov. 5, 2012). Some might draw a different conclusion from the title of his own *Book Was There: Reading in Electronic Times*, "a meditative look at what books are, what they have been, and what they may be." To Piper, reading is "an integral part of our lived experience, our sense of being in the world" (2012). Alan Jacobs discourses on *The Pleasures of Reading in an Age of Distraction* (2011), though of course he never asks what era was *not* an age of distraction.

As they should, "reading fast" and "reading slow," "close reading" and "distant reading," skimming and scanning, reading singly and silently or together and out loud, all have their own detractors and adherents.[7] Reading has, in the words of one professor who seeks to find it, a "Lost, Secret History" (Arthur Melzer, *CHE*, May 4, 2015). David Mikics makes a case for *Slow Reading in a Hurried Age* (2013), a "practical guide for anyone who yearns for a more meaningful and satisfying reading experience, and who wants to sharpen reading skills and improve concentration" (see also his "The Slowness of a Good Book," *CHE*, Nov. 6, 2013).

Does yearning imply nostalgia? Perhaps *Slow Reading* should come with a video, if not a reading guide.

Even more prescriptive, almost doctrinal, is Philip Davis's *Reading and the Reader* (2013). This slim book "offers a defense of the value of reading serious literature." For instance, it promotes "an awakened sense of being." The publisher's blurb declares: "Literature provides a holding ground for the exploration of human experience …to think thoughts that customarily may be unadmitted or felt as anomalous." Publishers seem to perceive that this is an open, unfillable market. Indeed, the genre of writing advice about how-to read is almost as old as books themselves and has been a staple of print for more than two centuries.

Consider the vast array of aids to reading (Aubry 2011; Dolby 2005; Smith 2015), many now available online. The most recent study of *Reading as Therapy* attempts to ascertain *What Contemporary Fiction Does for Middle-Class Americans* by reading such novels as *Divine Secrets of the Ya-Ya Sisterhood, Infinite Jest, A Million Little Pieces, The Pilot's Wife*, and *The Kite Runner*. Such works ask texts to bear more weight than they can carry (Aubry 2011). Next we will have a prescription drug to stimulate that satisfying, slow experience …if we do not already.

In the meantime, we have an occasionally playful but often ponderous discourse about reading that sounds like declarations of faith. In the *New York Times Book Review*, Diane Ackerman rhapsodizes about "Romanticizing the Reader" which differs, it seems, from "romancing the reader" (Apr 25, 2015; see Radway 1984a, 1984b). It is hardly news that readers have secret lives of which books are a part and to which books "invite" readers.[8] Reading is linked, although not very clearly, to "habits of the mind: lessons for the long term" (Dan Berrett, *CHE*, Oct. 8, 2012). Writing in the *Chronicle of Higher Education*, Ian Desai assures us that a "renewed passion for print is not just talk." Noticing community book sales, he remarks, "If this is what death looks like for the world of books, we may be in heaven." Alas, Larry McMurtry's famed warehouse of books, which was proudly mentioned, is no more; it was sold, and the store closed several months before this praise appeared in print (Desai, "Shelf

Life," *CHE*, Jan. 14, 2013; McMurtry's books were auctioned in August 2012). The look of death may bear reexamination.

Is this slow reading or slow writing in an age of acceleration?

Books deserve better. I notice that in a digitally assisted world of "social reading," books "become places to meet" (*CHE*, Nov. 30, 2012). When we recall nineteenth-century lyceums, lecture circuits, community bookstores, and especially book clubs of all kinds, we realize that social reading is not so new (Long 2013).

More complicated and thought-provoking is the fact that soldiers took books with them, which is documented in Molly Guptill Manning's *When Books Went to War* (2014). But there is no way for her to do more than assert her subtitle, *The Stories That Helped Us Win World War II*. Only in fiction does the former necessarily lead to the latter. Argument by listing books is a well-worn device in making a case, to borrow a phrase, that "book was there." We want books—that is, some books—to make a difference. Showing that they can and sometimes do, however, requires evidence and argument, rather than a leap of faith.

Reading, sound artists remind us, is also an "interior performance art." As reported by Jennifer Schuessler, during final exams at New York University in 2013, in a Bobst Library reading room, "for three pairs of readers scattered around among the laptop-laden tables, wearing special headphones hooked up to iPod Nanos and shuffling through a pile of suspiciously literary books, the act of reading was transformed into a strange—and sometimes very loud—drama of turning pages, pointing fingers and eerily drifting thoughts." The record began: "The first thing you notice is that for a place dedicated to silence, there's not really that much silence at all…. After a while you start to think it might be better considered as a place dedicated to the collection of sounds." The readers, who had registered, were "both the audience and the stars of 'The Quiet Volume,' a 55-minute stealth performance piece" by British artists Ant Hampton and Tim Etchells. The piece prompted readers' interactions between literary books, a photography book, audio sounds of reading from the books, and readers' responses. In the words of one student, "The whole thing made you think about the nature of your sensory experience while reading, the relationship between the voice in your head and the words on the page" (Schuessler, "The Interior Performance Art," *NYT*, May 2, 2013).[9]

We face a paradox, or perhaps an outright contradiction, when we take reading seriously in breadth, depth, time, and space. Reading demands actions to complicate, problematize, and consider in context. That context always includes reading's relationship to other modes of communication and aspects of literacy, including writing and speech. The nascent, still undeveloped ethnography or anthropology of reading makes for a beginning. So too do efforts in the history of reading and literacy to examine readers and reading as practiced and lives in addition to an ideology or opportunity (Boyarin 1992; Livingston 1995; Radway 1984a, 1984b).

A renewed understanding and appreciation of reading must move between typical studies of the availability of print or other reading material and ideologies in support of certain kinds of reading and censure of others, on the one hand, and actual practices, valuations, and influences of reading, on the other. All kinds of reading of all kinds of materials must be recognized and valued. No less important, the interrelationships among reading and writing must be appreciated. The traditions of dichotomizing, opposing, and devaluing one in favor of the other need to be criticized and revised. Just as "the reader" and "the author" have not died, neither reading nor writing can be understood or practiced without a role for the other.[10]

Similarly, the old but inconsistent and contradictory tradition of seeing reading as easier, more natural and less problematic than writing is contradicted both by empirical studies and by personal accounts of actual reading and readers and by criticism. Reading is vast and variable. Serious reading of all kinds of material is hard work. The practices of reading defy simple description or summary. Reading, as we regularly rediscover and then forget, is not only individual, private, and silent. It is often collective, social, and aloud. It is indescribably complex in any of its forms.

And it is interactive across forms of literacies at the levels both of individuals and of groups.[11]

Rereading

Reading well and usefully is a set of competencies and practices that requires continuous development throughout education, as well as in occupations and other non-school activities.

Systems of schooling that do not facilitate developing reading (and writing) well and usefully are a massive problem. This situation is widely deplored, but what reading well entails is seldom studied. Among writings aimed at high school and college teachers, literary historian and critic John Guillory is a rare voice when he discusses "On the Presumption of Knowing How to Read" (2008a), "How Scholars Read" (2008b), and "Close Reading" (2010).

As English professors are wont to do, Guillory addresses the problem of "*articulation*, or the way in which the exit stage of the school system relates to the entry stage of the next," a persistent concern of instructors in higher education (2008a, 8). Rather than simply complaining or blaming students and school teachers, Guillory essays a fresh opening: "I mean to suggest first that it is presumptuous to assume that one ever knows how to read, that reading is a skill that can be acquired finally and completely." From that admittedly modest first step, he continues: "Clearly my colleagues don't mean that students are unable to decode written language or to give a reasonably accurate summary of what they've read. What is meant by this complaint is that students lack skill in a more sophisticated practice of reading, beyond the ability to comprehend basic meaning or even respond effectively to a text" (2008a, 8).[12]

These are not "special education" students or those unfortunately labeled in need of "reading recovery." The problem is more acute at other institutions. National surveys estimate that 40 percent of first-year students "are directed to remedial classes of some kind" at an estimated annual cost of $7 billion. Guillory remarks, "Although the task of remediation is usually oriented toward writing, the difficulty students have with writing often reflects an underlying and much more prevalent difficulty with reading" (2008a, 8). Correctly, he observes that these complaints have persisted over more than a century; they are not correlates of the Internet or electronic age.

Addressing one broad kind of reading, Guillory reiterates that the issue is not the standard and tested "interpretation" that students are meant to learn in primary and secondary schooling.

"Comprehension is only the first stage of interpretation," he stresses.

> The skill or tacit knowledge of which I am speaking might even be described as a conceptual break with the level of comprehension. With this break, reading begins anew. The text that was thought to be comprehended remains still to be understood. Only at this point, in which reading reverses itself, in which the text at hand becomes suddenly unfamiliar and strange, does interpretation begin. Only when the longtime reader can say "I don't yet know how to read" or "I don't know how to read this text," does it become possible. (2008a, 9)

Guillory introduces two related concepts that push the analysis forward: translation and misreading. Translation is a concept that I find relevant to literacy and literacies at every point. Guillory explains "By *interpretation*, I mean the capacity of a reader to re-understand the world of a text by translating these words into a new frame of reference or intelligibility. How does this happen? Interpretation in this sense means that the reader must first return to the *words of the text*, ultimately to undertake a translation of these words into a new interpretative frame." In turn, Guillory defines this act as a "conceptual break," when "interpretation asserts the possibility of multiple frames of reference, with no one final correct interpretation." The consequences for reading and readers are complicated. Guillory asks: "What does it mean, then, to say that comprehension fails in order to enable interpretation?" He responds that it means "something at once familiar and strange: the process of interpretive reading is self-corrective and implies the necessity or inevitability or misreading or misinterpretation. I suggest that this necessary misreading, and the correction of misreading, is the key to understanding the gap between the reading produced at the secondary level and the reading demanded at the college level" (2008a, 9).

If this conceptualization seems esoteric and unnecessarily complex, let me say that when I have my own first and second year students read Guillory's short article and ask them to reflect together about their own ways of reading, they light up with an exciting, even liberating new understanding of its travails. They also grasp its clear relevance to their writing practices.

Elsewhere, Guillory (2008b, 2010) considers differences and historical shifts in scholarly and lay reading practices. In terms that David Olson and others interested in literacy would do well to ponder, Guillory outlines how scholarly reading has changed over five or more centuries. Scholarly and non-scholarly have never been simple opposites. Moreover, "scholarly reading and lay reading have both intensive and extensive modalities, depending on the task of pleasure in view. For the modern scholar, reading in the conduct of research can be pleasurable, but it might also be painful, intensive because laborious." Yet "in the discipline of literary study, scholarly reading is also complicated by a certain historical irony precipitated by the emergence of lay reading: the object of study for literary scholars is often the very kind of text intended mainly to give pleasure" (Guillory 2008b, 12). Novels are the primary example.

Guillory offers a neat, more or less historical sociology of the reading as well as the production of scholarly texts that is too often missing in studies of other textual forms—that is, reading materials and the act of reading—which is too often called "consumption," as if reading were a passive process. Students of literary reading and popular reading, as well as of cultural studies, and of gender, race-ethnicity, and class would do well to take notice of it. Paying close attention to practices of reading would improve upon the well-known studies of British working-class readers, from Richard Hoggart's sympathetic, sensitive, yet critical *The Uses of Literacy* (1961), a classic that long served those seeking to set working-class and popular culture in a broad cultural context, to Jonathan Rose's unsympathetic *The Intellectual Life of the British Working Classes* (2001). Intensive and extensive, slow and fast, close and more distant reading techniques and modes of understanding do not constitute single transitions or "reading revolutions." They exist among and across different classes of readers, from scholarly to lay, and those in other specialties. How different is writing?[13]

Toward a New Future for Reading Studies

A brief review of some of the principal findings of historical research advances our understanding. Many of these works illustrate the interrelationships of reading and writing, even when that is not the author's main theme.

Both the history and, in part by extrapolation, contemporary understandings of reading have been limited and misled by a fundamental and recurring dependence on dichotomies and an epistemology or trajectory of shifts from one set of oppositions to another. Often these are summarily generalized into relatively vague notions of a reading revolution or revolutions (Chartier 1989; Darnton 1990; Eisenstein 1979; Hall 1992, 1996; Lyons 2010). These formulations parallel and more or less follow notions of writing and printing revolutions (Grafton 1980; Grafton et al. 2002; Baron et al. 2007). Relationships are presumed, instead of examined; reading tends to follow from other changes as a more or less dependent variable. Recent research tells a more interesting and richly human story.

To take some major examples, Michael Clanchy's *From Memory to Written Record: England, 1066–1307* (1993) reveals the dangers of relying on such traditional categories as *litteratus* and *illiteratus*, which describe expectations and prescriptions rather than reading and writing abilities. Clanchy illustrates the richly complicated mix of Latin, Hebrew, and variants of emerging French and English vernaculars in medieval England. At the same time, he sensitively identifies the power and the limits of both writing and reading, while documenting the continuing importance of visual literacy.

Carlo Ginzburg's classic microhistory, *The Cheese and the Worms* (1980), follows the record of a sixteenth-century trial for heresy which brought to light a provincial grain miller who read widely, curiously, critically, and idiosyncratically. He also talked about what he read—in the end, fatally so. While he had little formal education, Menocchio also wrote. Often cited but seldom read contextually or critically, this study has major implications for how we conceptualize and investigate reading, speaking, and writing in the past.

In her evocative essay, "Printing and the People" (1975), Natalie Zemon Davis surveys rural and urban regions of sixteenth-century France. Although levels of individual literacy were not especially high, print was ubiquitous and reading aloud was widespread. Just as orality and literacy built upon each other, specialized and more popular cultures and bodies of print also intersected and influenced each other across rural and urban places, gender, social classes, age groups, and occupations. Popular literacy and literatures did not wait for putative revolutions.

The reading practices of enslaved and free African Americans and the effects of print on their self-consciousness is a significant subject of research and debate among historians. No testimony, perhaps, speaks louder than Frederick Douglass's *Autobiography* to the constraints and the possibilities, the challenges of learning to read and to write, the opportunities to use both reading and writing, and the lasting consequences these skills had, not only in his own life but in the antislavery movement.[14]

No less evocative but less heralded are the stories of women's reading. Barbara Sicherman's studies of nineteenth-century American women are especially illuminating. Consider, for example, the inseparably intertwined individual and collective reading practices of the sisters and female cousins in the Hamilton family, who resided in Fort Wayne, Indiana in the late nineteenth century (Sicherman 1989). Educated by tutors and then sent to elite private schools and, in some cases, universities, they had the exceptional advantages of family wealth, encouragement, and their grandfather's substantial private library. They talked and wrote to one another frequently about what they were reading. Their letters document not only the wide range of what they read but also the interactions that took place around reading, as well as its role in shaping their imagination, experience, and aspirations. These young women were extraordinary; several became intellectuals and professionals in public health. But their powerful tales belie facile generalizations about the cultural limitations to which middle-class women were subject. Relatedly, although historians Sicherman (1993) and Helen Horowitz (1992) differ about many things in their studies of women's higher education pioneer M. Carey Thomas, they agree that Thomas was "made" in significant part by her reading. Indeed, their differences in emphasis and interpretation are instructive about the powers and multiple influences of reading.

The collective is tied to the social and the personal in another classic, although controversial study of women's reading, Janice Radway's *Reading the Romance: Women, Patriarchy, and Popular Literature* (1984b). Radway's work was innovative in a number of ways. She took women's reading of popular novels seriously and studied it directly with ethnographic methods, focusing on a group of women in Baltimore. Their culture of romance novel reading formed "an interpretive community," a concept she borrowed from literary criticism (Radway 1984a). She argues not only that this literary genre and reading practices is legitimate, but that these women found personal psychological and practical value in reading within an organized, ongoing setting. For these women, reading popular romances was educational, Radway concludes. She insists "that books and reading serve myriad purposes and functions for a wide variety of individuals" (1984a, page).

Writing over Reading Revisited and Revised

I begin with a serious question. Recent and current studies of writing emphasize "writing as social and cultural practice" and refer to "writing acts." David Barton and Uta Papen use these terms in explicit reference to "the anthropology of writing" (2010). This formulation parallels recent emphases in discussions of reading and of literacy more generally. Yet the refrain, "writing over reading," continues its steady beat and dominance. Why?

This construction of the anthropology of writing properly celebrates writing as "an everyday communicative practice" beyond the "world on paper" of the literacy episteme. Barton and Papen explain: "Given the omnipresence of the written word, research into the role of written language in everyday communication is at the heart of understanding contemporary forms of social interaction, between institutions and communities as well as between individuals." In contrast to observers who oppose new technologies, especially digital and electronic modes, to more familiar means of writing, they posit their connection: "These new ways of writing are central to how we work and live, to how governments communicate and how economies operate" (2010, 3). Writing appears more present and prominent, it seems.

Like most writing and communication researchers, they do not probe the specific relationships of writing in different modes. Thus, the field misses a larger and, I argue, important subject of inquiry. As a result, implications for the socialization of the young, intergenerational relationships, education at all levels, the impact of new media on specialized professions, and popular culture do not attract the attention they require.

No less importantly for our purposes, reading is almost totally excluded from their concerns. (The term appears only twice in Barton and Papen's index.) This is more than ironic. They repeatedly make such assertions as "Examining written texts is essential for understanding how societies operate and are organized, how institutions communicate with the public, how work is being done, how individuals and social groups organize their lives and make sense of their experiences and how cultures in all their variations are produced and reproduced" (Barton and Papen 2010, 5). Two large questions loom: first, how do we interact with, work with, or make sense of writing if not through reading of one kind of another; second, what if anything changes if we refer to reading rather than writing in statements like this one? Why is reading neglected if not necessarily resisted? How did literacy studies become an incomplete approach based a presumption of the dominance of writing? (See Brandt 2015.)

This neglect or devaluation of reading is long-standing, we have seen. This is not necessary or determinant in itself, to be sure. On one level, it is deeply if incompletely rooted in hegemonic notions of civilization and progress, especially but not only in Western civilization. Herein lies the reflexive acceptance and endorsement of "great divide" and "strong theories" of literacy, the literacy myth, and the literacy episteme. It is reinforced by the assumptions and acceptance as persuasive of cognitive or brain science. This is not a necessary conclusion, but it is hard to study writing in action and thus easier to make sweeping assumptions on limited, ambiguous evidence. Despite the older and recent celebration of the good things that follow from (at least some kinds of) reading and "what reading does to" the mind or the brain, reading remains ephemeral compared to writing. Literacy is assumed to be superior not only to orality but also to reading, both evolutionarily and developmentally.

Perhaps the major symbols of the contradictions surrounding the dominance of writing are the fissures and dichotomies within studies and interpretations of writing itself. They are longstanding and have been powerfully influential. I point to two. One that ebbs and flows in explicit recognition but shapes institutions and notions of written culture is the formal normative and declarative writing tradition. In some formulations, this is the educated, scholarly, proper "literate"; in David Olson's "world on paper," it is "documentary." This is the hypothetical story of the "implications" of unspecified forms of writing. The second complication is more commonly recognized: the related category of school or essay writing. Indicative of another, reinforcing dichotomy, in reaction to the dominant models of writing and their institutional and broad cultural endorsement, *The Anthropology of Writing* almost total excludes school writing. The exception is school notebooks "as model for personal record keeping" (Barton and Papen 2010, 158). The pendulum swings to the other side, but without consideration of the connections and associations of school writing with other forms of writing. Writing in popular culture, a vast and still unstudied domain, is also absent.

It is now several decades since the air was abuzz with proclamations of a "writing crisis." Closely related was a heated debate over the usefulness of much required and traditionally valued formal essay writing. Is it a limited use of writing or a requirement for the development of rational thought and intellectual development? Scribner and Cole, as well as Heath, Farr, Gee, and others, expressed serious reservations about "the restricted model of the writing process from which hypotheses about cognitive consequences tend to be generated" (Scribner and Cole 1981b, 72). Scribner and Cole elaborate:

> Most of our notions of what writing is about, the skills it entails and generates, are almost wholly tied up with school-based writing. Centrality of the expository text and wellcrafted story in models of the writing process accurately reflects the emphasis in most school curricula.... Since such writing skills are both the aim of pedagogy and the enabling tools which sustain many of the educational tasks of the school, their preeminence in current research does not seem inappropriate. But we believe that nearexclusive preoccupation with school-based writing practices has some unfortunate

consequences. The assumption that logicality is in the text and that the text is in school can lead to a serious underestimation of the cognitive skills involved in non-school, nonessay writing, and, reciprocally, to an overestimation of the intellectual skills that the essayist text "necessarily" entails. This approach binds the intellectual and social significance of writing too closely to the image of the academic and the professional member of society, writ large. It tends to promote the notion that writing outside of the school is of little importance and has no significant consequences for the individual. The writing crisis presents itself as purely a pedagogical problem, a problem located in the schools to be solved in the schools. (1981b, 75–76)

Debates continue over the dominance, value, and transferability of the rhetoric and intellectual benefits of the essay form. Digital modes of writing only complicate the issues. The outlines of both school and non-school writing are contested. But has much changed since the outcries and openings of the 1970s and 1980s? I am not convinced that we have made needed progress. Slighting reading and elevating writing over reading has not significantly advanced our understanding, even of writing. Ironically, studies from Olson to Brandt unintentionally demonstrate this point.

Writing *and* Reading

To conclude this discussion, I identify several aspects of literacy that should be interrelated and whose connection may prove beneficial, in schools and outside them. They are aspects of what composition and rhetoric scholar Michael Harker terms *The Lure of Literacy* (2015). Harker's own emphasis is on the long debate over college-level compulsory composition requirements.[15] In instructive ways, the issue of whether all college students should be required to complete a course of some kind in composition defines the field. Unintentionally but predictably, this question has proved to be divisive both within and beyond English departments and writing programs. It has limited the scope and significance of writing across university degree requirements and areas of study.

Ranking high among the rationales and justifications for writing, past and present, in Harker's argument, is the attachment of "compulsory composition" to a "lure of literacy." By this, he means that proposals and arguments in support of writing requirement have typically allied themselves to broad conceptions of literacy. At the same time, they have seldom considered critically what they mean by reference to literacy and the implications, for better or for worse, of this view. The failure to explore and probe the meanings and uses of literacy in discourse and in practice limits the debate and the field. Harker "challenges teacher-researchers who presume that the topic of literacy is 'well-traveled' ground in rhetoric and composition and composition scholarship." He argues that the unresolved place of literacy constitutes the "most compelling reason for renewed interest in literacy studies, specifically the ways in which the literacy myth intersects with the day-to-day work of teaching composition" (2015, 4–5) Suggestively, Harker ends his book by proposing a literacy studies curriculum for first year writing. Reading ranks high among the salient elements in a newly recognized and developed conception of literacy in composition and composition in literacy studies.[16]

The overarching issues compel us to locate writing in the larger culture, especially but not only in the United States. On the one hand, we are well aware that writing instruction in schools so often has a negative impact on students, and future adults' interests in writing of almost any kind, though why that happens is seldom studied (Brandt 2001; Moje et al. 2008; Dyson 1989, 2003, 2013). Today's renewed interest in the economic value of writing (over reading) seldom takes this problem into account.

The current renewal of interest in handwriting is a curious but understandable phenomenon in an electronic age. Alongside advertising that links cheap ballpoint pens to the promotion of communication and individuality is the recent explosion in the sales of very expensive "writing instruments" intended as symbols of status. The marketing of literacy, and its many implements and accoutrements, calls out for serious study.[17] So too does the question of the relationships among fears about the presumed decline of literacy, the rise of digital devices for reading and writing, and a resurgence of interest in handwriting. Today many of us add our handwritten signatures to documents digitally, a form of facsimile.

Tamara Plakins Thornton's *Handwriting in America: A Cultural History* (1996) explores the social, cultural, and economic dimensions of handwriting. Her publisher unwittingly echoes the advertisement for BIC pens in the blurb, which describes Thornton's work as evoking a "lost world, in which people looked to handwriting as both a lesson in conformity and a talisman of individuality." The fact that the book appeared just as handwriting attracted interest from marketers, educators, and expressive young people is hardly coincidental. In diverse, sometimes bizarre ways, script and self are seen as interconnected. In the past, or so the story goes, handwriting represented character and learning. Young people required training and practice; handwriting disciplined them and prepared them for work and life. Signatures were celebrated and collected—perhaps now replaced by selfies.[18]

Today handwriting remains a sign of character, discipline, and preparation, not just of selfexpression. A coalition between manufacturers of writing implements and instruments and traditionalists promotes a return to required instruction in cursive writing is promoted, especially at the elementary school level. The campaign against the Common Core Curriculum Standards points to nonexistent scientific research to buttress its claims: "Experts recommend at least 15 minutes of handwriting instruction each day for students. Research has shown that improved handwriting skills has benefits for cognitive development and motor skills and can lead to improved writing skills and reading comprehension."[19]

Educators also tangle over the value of note-taking: not whether or not to have students take notes, but whether they should be handwritten or electronic and in what textual form. Sometimes students' intellectual future would seem to depend on the claims made for and against handwritten versus laptop, complete words or text-speak.[20]

In a new book based in part on interviews with a small number of students toward the end of high school and then at the beginning of college, composition professor Daniel Keller gives us a rare breath of fresh air by "locating reading in composition studies," suggesting that writing and reading are related, and positing the interdependence of reading with writing development and instruction. Keller observes that "composition scholars have recognized how the proliferation of interactive and multimodal communication technologies has changed what it means to write in the twenty-first century. However, the counterpart to this phenomenon, changes in the purposes and forms of reading practices, has been largely unexamined by the field." He proposes "relocating reading's place in composition" by examining "the opportunities and challenges of contemporary literacy contexts: navigating various technologies, shifting among genres and media, making meaning from a wealth of information, and alternating between reading and writing practices. These reading practices require new approaches to literacy education" (2013, 1).

Unfortunately, these advances struggle amidst a sea of currently fashionable metaphors and softfocus images. In entitling his 2013 book *Chasing Literacy and Reading and Writing in an Age of Acceleration*, Keller follows Brandt (2001). "Accumulation," or the "piling up" of new literacy material and expectations, is a weak, unhelpful descriptor masquerading as a concept, and its relationship with "acceleration" is undefined except by alliterative association. How do literacies "accumulate"? What is new and what is not? Where are human choice, agency, and practices? The task of "relocating reading's place in composition" remains incomplete. For that, we need a broader familiarity with work about reading outside the context of rhetoric and composition.

Reading in the Rise of Writing

These questions take us back to Deborah Brandt, especially her emphatic new book *The Rise of Writing: Redefining Mass Literacy* (2015).[21] In this culminating work, Brandt takes the strongest stand I have seen in pronouncing the "rise of writing" over reading, and the value of writing in eclipsing reading in virtually all respects, from individual to societal, intellectual or spiritual to economic. As a teacher and scholar of composition, she is convinced that reading has received too much attention and that its time has passed. Succinctly, "mass writing has been implicated in the making of goods and services. To understand the development of writing literacy is to understand how it has been organized around production processes. This gives it a distinctive character, particularly in the way that writing literacy has been an object of private and not just public investment" (Brandt 2009b, 63).[22]

Overall, Brandt's most sweeping claims about the significance of writing form bookends for the presentation of interviews of sixty persons who make a living ghost-writing political speeches and doing other forms of mid-level bureaucratic, professional, and technical writing. She followed the same method of interviewing a non-random and non-stratified group of subjects as she did in *Literacy in American Lives* (2001), which begs the same questions about the sample population. As with *Literacy*, I underscore her lack of familiarity with the literature on the structure and requirements of today's economy and the relationships between education, jobs, and their rewards, although she makes stronger claims in her 2015 book than in her previous study.

Some of the many kinds of writing have demonstrable economic value, some carry social and collective significance and utility, and others are more personal and individual. Many types of writing may add value for employers; some add value to employees, personally and economically. "Value," economists and philosophers of all stripes teach us, is seldom selfevident. The fastest growing area of "writing on the job" is electronic data entry, which increasingly demands credentials or certification. Although data entry is perhaps the purest example of writing as production or manufacturing, Brandt never mentions it. In contrast to some of the occupations she did study, it is neither well paid nor likely to lead to better opportunities, and it is neither intellectual nor expressive.[23]

Brandt's work attests to the danger of failing to make critical distinctions and differentiations in forms and levels and relationships of writing. That should have been among the greatest mandates of the New Literacy Studies and an anthropology or ethnography of writing, but it is often lost in the rise of *some kinds* of writing.

Denigrating reading by incomplete, often misleading, and even metaphorical comparisons with writing is another problem. Brandt's pool of interviewees and her questioning of them seem to be biased in the direction of "writing over reading." Yet, the descriptions of the content of interviewers and the work of interviewees often speak clearly of the presence and centrality of reading in relationship to writing. Reading is valuable and has value, in both economic and other terms. Brandt shows but does not explicitly recognize that this is true. Incorporating reading fully and interactively into her notion of literacy and mass literacy would strengthen, rather than weaken, Brandt's arguments.

Underlying these complications is another, partly theoretical and partly ideological problem.

Brandt uncritically accepts the currently fashionable—partly descriptive and partly ideological— notion, or metaphor of a "knowledge" or "information" economy. This line of thinking, propounded with particular emphasis by neoliberal economists and the World Bank, has in fair measure replaced earlier, more avowedly conservative human capital approaches and more mixed modernization theories and policies. Part of its ideological appeal lies in its sense that it is both necessary and inevitable. Both rest on notions of "investment in human capital," "human resources," and "brain power" as signified by certification from educational institutions. Brandt adopted this as both description and explanation in *Literacy in American Lives* (2001). To some degree, she is critical of, and uncomfortable with, the course of economic and social change and rising inequality in the United States.

But in most other ways she accepts incomplete and contradictory descriptions of the economy and the workplace, as well as the theories and ideologies that support them. She attempts to mold her explanation of the "rise of writing" and the triumph of "writing over reading" to the rise of the so-called information or knowledge economy. It is a neat fit for her purposes. These theories and ideologies value literacy, coupled with institutional certification and credentialism, as providing the inputs of human capital, the resources of formerly raw human materials polished to fill the needs of a well-functioning economy. Thus, we read of "the toil of writing," "writers as mediators," "mediational means in production," the "transactional value of writing," "high stakes writing," "private and public investment in writing," and "writing as a manufacturing process." Brandt never addresses the theoretical or ideological nature of this account, the extensive criticism of this viewpoint and its ramifications, or the incomplete and contradictory evidence about these formations and processes.

While a full-scale critique of these theories and the assumptions on which they are is beyond the scope of this chapter, we must recognize that they are self-fulfilling prophecies, often logically circular. They are incomplete and, at best, only partly descriptive of the economy, its needs, and functioning. They fail to describe accurately the economy or its workings. In that, they depend to a considerable extent on metaphors.[24] *The Rise of Writing* (2015) and the articles that preceded it are awash in discourse that does not suffice to serve as evidence or argument.

In sum, writing itself has become a manufacturing process. Failure to criticize such terminology and the assumptions on which it rests ideologically undergirds the strong case for the rise of writing, even if it does not describe the economy very well or help us to understand actual writing practices. Repeating the words "write for pay" conflates and confuses very different kinds of writing, levels of work, degrees of worker preparation, and their disparate rewards.

Emphasizing the rise of writing ignores the greatest number of workers, the many rapidly growing occupations that require lesser levels of education and offer fewer rewards. It ignores the recent widening of socioeconomic inequality, the various skill, education, opportunity, and pay divides that structure national economies and "economic participation" today. An ideological premise of this theory is that access to education and more advanced literacies—not the ability to write by itself—is the route around structural and social "imperfections" in markets. Among the many lies that educators and politicians do not refute publically is that neither a high level of literacy nor completion of a certain amount of schooling and certification guarantee paid work, let alone a commensurate level of work and appropriate reward.

Notions of the "rise of writing" and "writing over reading" are incomplete and fallacious. Indeed, they are central to the literacy myth and the literacy episteme. Brandt's subjects represent a minority of workers in a minority of vocations and a minority of writers. Some, but not all, succeed. Most employees do not "write for pay." Brandt does not listen closely enough to how her interviewees speak of the human and literary effects of manufacturing words and texts, as well as the mixture of satisfactions and frustrations they express. As in *Literacy in American Lives* (2001), the examples she presents sometimes suggest more complicated and contradictory stories than she emphasizes. That is to her credit. At the same time, many of Brandt's descriptions speak to the interaction of reading and writing, and thus contradict her claims. I venture to suggest that this is in fact a matter of (mis)reading spoken words and their transcriptions.[25]

Brandt ends her book by advocating "deep writing." By this, she means "a literacy practiced primarily through writing. Writing as a productive imperative can only be expected to spread," she avers. "Most people will dwell for longer periods of time within deeply interactive networks and in immersive mental states that consequential writing demands" (2015, 15). If I follow her, she alludes implicitly to notions of "deep reading" despite her general disavowal of attention to reading. Deep reading is synonymous with slow reading, to use another term of the moment. But on-the-job writing, especially that associated with internet and network writing, is necessarily fast. In making her case for deep writing, she often suggests, not depth, but rather system or regular process.

It may well be that the future of literacy—and to an unappreciated extent its past—is captured in the contradictions that arise from failing to acknowledge the relationships between reading and writing and their metaphorical and real value. If that is true, it underscores the necessity of building our understanding of contemporary literacies and contemplation of future literacies on the foundation of the dynamic interrelations of reading and writing. In the terms of this book, we must clarify in part by reducing dichotomies and probing relationships. Carolyn Steedman's (1999, 2005) eighteenth- and nineteenth-century "poetical maids and cooks who wrote" certainly knew this. So should we.[26]

Reading, Writing, and Renewing Literacy Studies

Reading remains the missing link in the place of writing in literacy studies. However ironic, paradoxical, or contradictory, this absence to some degree or another marks composition studies, ethnographies, popular culture studies, New Literacy Studies, multimodal studies, and vocational projects. What is most remarkable is how simple and obvious the point is. That, too, is a sign of the continuing divides in literacy and literacy studies.[27]

How we construe and construct "written culture" is a major cause and consequence of this set of failings. It spreads out widely to influence how we understand literacy and the place of writing within it. Far too often, the concept rests on the myth that there is distinctive cultural formation that may be characterized as written culture. That misconception rests on notions of its opposite, another, almost always inferior non-written or oral culture. Seen as in a distorted mirror, these kindred images are part and parcel of what I have called the literacy myth. They limit scholarship and do a disservice to humanity past and present. Even recent reconceptualizations that attempt to take into account new media and popular practices are ahistorical and dichotomous. The recognition that media have changed, that forms of texts are diverse, and that cultures are plural are only first steps.

Almost all conceptions of written culture rest on inherited and limiting notions of both writing and culture and an uncritical coupling that exaggerates their power. They are hegemonic and deeply embedded in theories, ideologies, policies, institutions, expectations. They are inseparable from structures of power and authority—inequalities in the past and present.

We who are deeply committed to the preservation of the widest range of social practices of literacy and literacies, new and old, must become, at least in part, the critics of both past and present assumptions and modes of expression and understanding. But that demands a far wider and deeper conception of historical and comparative criticism than our usual efforts that stress inequalities, on the one hand, and diversity, on the other hand, bring to bear. Nor, despite many efforts, can we relegate them to the past.

Consider, toward a new beginning:

- *Deconstructing "written culture"* with respect to a dynamic, dialectical literacy studies perspective. What do we signify by reference to "written culture" in critical, historical, comparative, and interactive contexts?
- *Reconceptualizing and redefining "written culture."* Is that in itself a redundancy? When do we *not* equate writing and culture? In so doing:

What is left out? Why does it matter? In what directions does that realization take us?

- *Reconstructing "written culture."* Can we reconceptualize both writing and culture, following Freire in dialectically "reading the word and reading the world"? In other words, can we understand reading and writing in relationship to each other, reconstructing writing as modes of expression and communication, composition and performance across media, and the means of their access; and culture as different formations with a different basis and operation? How does this relate to our new awareness of "new media," many of them not so very new? And to "multimedia" and "multimodal" media? We must begin to explore relationships rather than opposition and dichotomies.

This approach means seeing written culture as historical and contradictory; as dynamic and developmental; as founded in reading and writing broadly construed; as constituted and conducted as oral and written; as collective and individual; as variable and based in both continuities and changes; and as constituted by contradictions and resistance, and conflicting structures of authority. Otherwise, we continue repeating myths of the past; reinforcing myths of the present; and turning them into myths of the future, as do prevailing notions of "written culture" *qua* "civilization."

Notes

1. Fabian, "Keep listening" (1993), discusses the neglect of reading in the study of literacy.
2. For the latest set of fallacies, see Colleen Murphy, "One College's Method to Prove Its Value: Scanning Students' Brains," *CHE*, June 4, 2015.
3. Among the studies in the new field of the history of reading, see: Ablow, *Feeling of reading* (2010); Brophy, *Popular culture and the public sphere* (2007); Cavallo and Chartier, *History of reading in the West* (1999); Crone and Towheed, *History of reading: Methods, strategies, tactics* (2011); Dane, *What is a book?* 2012; Darnton, *Case for books* (2009); Davidson, *Reading in America* (1989); Finkelstein and McCleery, *Introduction to*

book history (2013); Fischer, *History of writing* (2001); Halsey and Owens, *History of reading* (2011); Howard, *Book* (2009); Jack, *Woman reader* (2012); Lyons, *Readers and society* (2001); Lyons, *Reading culture and writing practices* (2008); Lyons, *History of reading and writing* (2010); Lyons, *Writing culture of ordinary people* (2013); Manguel, *History of reading* (1996); Manguel, *Library at night* (2006); Manguel, *Reader on reading* (2010); Manguel, *Traveler* (2015); Raven, Small, and Tadmor, *Practice and representation of reading* (1996); Sedo, *Reading communities* (2011); Towheed, Crone, and Halsey, *History of reading* (2010); Towheed and Owens, *History of reading: International Perspectives* (2011).

4. Recent literacy studies, especially small group and community research, is making a start.

5. For instructive comparisons, see Scribner and Cole, "Cognitive consequences" (1973); Scribner and Cole, *Psychology of literacy* (1981a); Scribner and Cole, "Unpacking literacy" (1981b); Farr, "Essayist literacy" (1993); Heath, "Protean shapes in literacy events" (1982); Heath, *Ways with words* (1983); Olson, *World on paper* (1994). See also Brandt, *Rise of writing* (2015); Bazerman, "Theories of the middle range" (2008).

6. See Motoko Rich, "Pediatricians Group to Recommend Reading Aloud to Children from Birth," *NYT*, June 24, 2014.

7. Among the large literature, see Elfenbein, "Cognitive science and the history of reading" (2006); Gallop, "Historicization of literary studies" (2007); Gang, "Behaviorism and the beginnings of close reading" (2011); Guillory, "Ethical practice of modernity" (2000); Guillory, "Close reading" (2010); Hayles, "Hyper and deep attention" (2007); Hoggart, *Uses of literacy* (1961); Jenkins and Kelley, *Reading in a participatory culture* (2013); Mikics, *Slow reading in a hurried age* (2013); Piper, "Novel devotions" (2015); Slaughter, "Only Reading" (2013); Dennie Palmer Wolf, "Becoming literate: One reader reading," *Academic Connections* (Fall 1988): 1–4.

8. Jennifer Howard, "Secret Lives of Readers," *CHE*, Dec. 17, 2013, on Price 2012.

9. See also Dwight Garner, "The Reader as Artist, Intuitively Plumbing a Psychic Well," reviewing *What We See When We Read* by Peter Mendeldund, *NYT*, July 31, 2014.

10. The history and practice of note-taking and letter writing is eye-opening.

11. None of the work on reading embraces this comprehensive view, including Chartier, *Culture of print* (1989); Littau, *Theories of Reading* (2006); Lyons, *History of reading and writing* (2010). Our understanding of reading must also sharply differentiate between the dominance of metaphors and readers' practices in reading studies. For example, see Kress, *Multimodality* (2010), 37–43, 175–178.

12. Compare to Radway, "Interpretive communities" (1984a); Radway, *Reading the romance* (1984b); Sicherman "Sense and sensibility" (1989); Sicherman, "Reading and ambition" (1993); Sicherman, "Reading *Little Women*" (1995); Sicherman, "Connecting lives" (2006); Sicherman, "Ideologies and practices of reading" (2007).

13. Recent appeals to neuroscience or cognitive science substitute for interpretations of reading, generally presuming that some kinds of reading have direct effects on the brain. There is very little relevant data, but that does not prevent both scientists and nonscientists from making grandiose claims; misleading cognitive metaphors dominate. See for example Lisa Zunshine, "Why Fiction Does it Better," *CHE*, Dec. 9, 2013; Keith Oatley and Maja Djikic, "How Reading Transforms Us," *NYT*, Dec. 21, 2014.

14. Frederick Douglass's *Autobiography* was written and published in numerous versions during his lifetime. See especially Cornelius, "'We slipped and learned to read'" (1983); Cornelius, *When I can read my title clear* (1991); Hager, *Word by word* (2013); Logan, *Liberating language* (2008); McHenry, *Forgotten readers* (2002); McHenry and Heath, "The literate and the literary" (1994); Monaghan, "Reading for the enslaved, writing for the free" (1998); Royster, *Traces of a stream*, 2000; Williams, "Clothing themselves in intelligence" (2002); Williams, *Self-taught* (2005).

15. This book includes references on the history of composition. Disclosure: Harker was my doctoral student.

16. The new online journal *Literacy in Composition Studies* promises to move in this direction.

17. A personal testimony: after years of buying BICs pens in quantity and losing them, more than 25 years ago I bought myself a Mont Blanc ballpoint pen, which I have not lost and continue to use.

18. See Heath, *Ways with words* (1983); Robert J. Bliwise, "Our Handwriting, Ourselves," *CHE*, May 6, 2013; Dan Berrett, "An Old-School Norton: Writing Required," *CHE*, Oct 15, 2012.

19. BIC's website cites Hanover Research, "The Importance of Teaching Handwriting in the 21st Century" (2012), with footnotes mainly to newspaper articles.

20. See, among a virtual sea on texting, Jennifer Schuessler, "Note-Taking's Past, Deciphered Today," *NYT*, Nov. 6, 2012; Geoffrey Nunberg, "Noted," *CHE*, Jan. 7, 2013; David Greenstein, "The Pre-digital Arts of Crafting Notes," Letter to the Editor, *CHE*, Jan 28, 2013. These questions are also central to debates about the use of electronic and other technologies in classrooms more broadly.

21. Brandt's conclusion are foreshadowed in *Literacy in American Lives* (2001) and *Literacy and Learning* (2009b); see also Brandt, "Writing over reading" (2009a).

22. Disclaimer: Brandt is my good friend and colleague. I nominated *Literacy in American Lives* for the Grawemeyer Award in Education, which it won. For earlier criticisms, see my "Epilogue: Literacy Studies and Interdisciplinary Studies with Notes on the Place of Deborah Brandt," in *Literacy, Economy, and Power: Writing and Research after Literacy in American Lives* (2014).

23. See Jeff Madrick, "Goodbye Horatio Alger," *The Nation*, Feb. 5, 2007, 20–24; Henwood, *After the new economy* (2003); Andrew Hacker, "Where Will We Find the Jobs?" *NYRB*, Feb. 24, 2011, 39–41; Hacker, "The Frenzy About High Tech Talent," *NYRB*, July 9, 2015; Katz and Stern, *One nation divisible* (2006); Michael Hiltzik, "Tech industry's persistent claim of worker shortage may be phony," *LA Times*, Aug. 1, 2015. See also Watkins, *Literacy work*, 2015.

24. For a range of views, I refer readers to the many works of David Harvey, the more popular writing of Alan Krugman, and Brown, *Undoing the demos* (2015), as well as the literature cited in the preceding note.

25. Brandt's use of Carr's *Shallows* in her conclusion is a sign of her tendency to turn uncritically to such sources, as with her approach to economics, and use them more as metaphors than bases of information or understanding. It implicitly reminds us of the imperatives of critical reading. The statement that "the effects of writing on the writer—positive or deleterious—go largely unexplored" (Brandt, 2015, 163) ignores much of literary criticism and all of literary biography.

26. On writing, see Camille, "Book of signs" (1985); Dierks, *In my power*, 2009; Eldred and Mortenson, *Imagining rhetoric* (2002); Goodman, "L'Ortografe des dames" (2002); Hilliard, *To exercise our talents* (2006);

Hobbs, *Nineteenth-century women* (1995); Hunter, *How young ladies became girls* (2002); Miller, *Assuming the positions* (1998); Moylan and Stiles, *Reading books* (1996). More generally, see Barton and Papen, *Anthropology of writing* (2010); Gnanadesikan, *Writing revolution* (2009); Harris, *Rethinking writing* (2000); Lorenzen-Schmidt and Poulsen, *Writing peasants* (2002); Lyons, *Reading culture* (2008); Lyons, *History of reading* (2010); Lyons, *Writing culture of ordinary people* (2013); Martin, *History and power of writing* (1994); McNeely, *Emancipation of writing* (2003); Standage, *Writing on the wall* (2013); Tribble and Trubek, *Writing material,* 2003.

27. This section draws on my "Searching for Literacy: The Social and Intellectual Origins of Literacy Studies," *Revista Brasileira de História da Educação* (2016), in Portuguese translation.

References

Ablow, Rachel, ed. (2010) *The feeling of reading: Affective experience and Victorian literature.* Ann Arbor: University of Michigan Press.

Aubry, Timothy. (2011) *Reading as therapy: What contemporary fiction does for middle-class Americans.* Iowa City: University of Iowa Press.

Baron, Naomi S. (2015) *Words onscreen: The fate of reading in a digital world.* New York: Oxford University Press.

Baron, Sabrina Alcorn, with Elizabeth Walsh and Susan Scola, eds. (2001) *The reader revealed.* Washington, D.C.: Folger Shakespeare Library.

Baron, Sabrina Alcorn, Eric N. Lindquist, and Eleanor F. Shevlin, eds. (2007) *Agent of change: Print culture studies after Elizabeth L. Eisenstein.* Amherst: University of Massachusetts Press.

Barton, David, and Uta Papen, eds. (2010) *The anthropology of writing: Understanding textually mediated worlds.* London: Routledge.

Bazerman, Charles. (2008) Theories of the middle range in historical studies of writing practice. *Written Communication* 25: 298–328.

Boyarin, Jonathan, ed. (1992) *The ethnography of reading.* Berkeley: University of California Press.

Brandt, Deborah. (2001) *Literacy in American lives.* Cambridge: Cambridge University Press.

Brandt, Deborah. (2009a) Writing over reading: New directions in mass literacy. In Mike Baynham and Mastin Prinsloo, eds., *The future of literacy studies*, 54–74. London: Palgrave Macmillan.

Brandt, Deborah. (2009b) *Literacy and learning: Reflections on writing, reading, and society.* San Francisco: Jossey-Bass.

Brandt, Deborah. (2015) *The rise of writing: Redefining mass literacy.* Cambridge: Cambridge University Press.

Brophy, James M. (2007) *Popular culture and the public sphere in the Rhineland, 1800–1850.* Cambridge: Cambridge University Press.

Brown, Wendy. (2015) *Undoing the demos: Neoliberalism's stealth revolution.* New York: Zone Books.

Camille, Michael. (1985) The book of signs: Writing and visual difference in Gothic manuscript illumination. *Word & Image* 1: 133–148.

Carr, Nicholas. (2010) *The shallows: What the Internet is doing to our brains.* New York: Norton.

Cavallo, Guglielmo, and Roger Chartier, eds. (1999) *A history of reading in the West*, trans. Lydia G. Cochrane. Amherst: University of Massachusetts Press.

Chartier, Roger, ed. (1989) *The culture of print.* Princeton: Princeton University Press.

Clanchy, Michael T. (1993) *From memory to written record: England, 1066–1307.* Rev. ed. Oxford: Blackwell.

Clement, Neville D., and Terence Lovat. (2012) Neuroscience and education: Issues and challenges for curriculum. *Curriculum Inquiry* 42: 534–557.

Cornelius, Janet. (1983) "We slipped and learned to read": Slave accounts of the literacy process, 1830–1860. *Phylon* 44: 171–186.

Cornelius, Janet. (1991) *When I can read my title clear: Literacy, slavery, and religion in the antebellum South.* Columbia: University of South Carolina Press.

Crone, Rosalind, and Shafquat Towheed, eds. (2011) *The history of reading*, vol. 3, *Methods, strategies, tactics.* London: Palgrave Macmillan.

Dane, Joseph. (2012) *What is a book? The study of early printed books.* Notre Dame: University of Notre Dame Press.

Darnton, Robert. (1990) *The Kiss of Lamourette: Reflections in cultural history.* New York: Norton.

Darnton, Robert. (2009) *The case for books: Past, present, and future.* New York: PublicAffairs.

Davidson, Cathy N., ed. (1989) *Reading in America: Literature and social history.* Baltimore: Johns Hopkins University Press.

Davis, Natalie Zemon. (1975) Printing and the people: Early modern France. In Natalie Z. Davis, *Society and culture in early modern France*, 189–226. Stanford: Stanford University Press.

Davis, Natalie Zemon. (1983) *The return of Martin Guerre.* Cambridge, Mass: Harvard University Press.

Davis, Phil. (2013) *Reading and the reader: The literary agenda.* New York: Oxford University Press.

Dehaene, Stanislas. (2009) *Reading in the brain: The science and evolution of a human invention.* New York: Viking.

Dehaene, Stanislas, Felipe Pegado, Lucia W. Braga, Paulo Ventura, Gilberto Nunes Filho, Antoinette Jobert, Ghislaine Dehaene-Lambertz, Régine Kolinsky, José Morais, and Laurent Cohen. (2010) How learning to read changes the cortical networks for vision and language. *Sciencexpress,* 11 November: 1–10.

Dierks, Konstantin. (2009) *In my power: Letter writing and communications in early America.* Philadelphia: University of Pennsylvania Press.

Dolby, Sandra K. (2005) *Self-help books: Why Americans keep reading them.* Champaign: University of Illinois Press.

Dyson, Anne Haas. 1989. *Multiple worlds of child writers: Friends learning to write.* New York: Teachers College Press.

Dyson, Anne Haas. (2003) "Welcome to the jam": Popular culture, school literacy, and the making of childhoods. *Harvard Educational Review* 79: 328–361.

Dyson, Anne Hass. (2013) *Rewriting the basics: Literacy learning in children's cultures.* New York: Teachers College Press.

Eisenstein, Elizabeth L. (1979) *The printing press as an agent of change.* 2 vols. Cambridge: Cambridge University Press.

Eldred, Janet Carey, and Peter Mortensen. (2002) *Imagining rhetoric: Composing women of the early United States.* Pittsburgh: University of Pittsburgh Press.

Elfenbein, Andrew. (2006) Cognitive science and the history of reading. *PMLA* 121: 484–502.

Fabian, Johannes. (1993) Keep listening: Ethnography and reading. In Jonathan Boyarin, ed., *The ethnography of reading*, 80–97. Berkeley: University of California Press.

Farr, Marcia. (1993) Essayist literacy and other verbal performances. *Written Communication* 10: 4–38.

Finkelstein, David, and Alistair McCleery. (2013) *An introduction to book history.* 2d ed. London and New York: Routledge.

Fischer, Steven Roger. (2001) *A history of writing*. 2 vols. London: Reaktion Books.

Freire, Paulo. (1985) *The politics of education: Culture, power, and liberation*, trans. Donaldo Macedo. Boston: Bergin and Garvey.

Gallop, Jane. (2007) The historicization of literary studies and the fate of close reading. *Profession*: 181–186.

Gang, Joshua. (2011) Behaviorism and the beginnings of close reading. *ELH* 78: 1–25.

Ginzburg, Carlo. (1980) *The cheese and the worms: The cosmos of a sixteenth century miller*. Baltimore: Johns Hopkins University Press.

Gnanadesikan, Amalia E. (2009) *The writing revolution: Cuneiform to the Internet*. New York: Wiley-Blackwell.

Goodman, Dena. (2002) L'Ortografe des dames: Gender and language in the Old Regime. *French Historical Studies* 25: 191–223.

Graff, Harvey J. (2014) Epilogue: Literacy studies and interdisciplinary studies with notes on the place of Deborah Brandt. In Julie Nelson Christoph, John Duffy, Eli Goldblatt, Nelson Graff, Rebecca Nowacek, and Bryan Trabold, eds., *Literacy, economy, and power: Writing and research after Literacy in American lives*, 202–226. Carbondale: Southern Illinois University Press.

Graff, Harvey J. (2015) *Undisciplining knowledge: Interdisciplinarity in the twentieth century*. Baltimore: Johns Hopkins University Press.

Graff, Harvey J. (2016) "Searching for literacy: The social and intellectual origins of literacy studies" (in Portuguese translation). *Revista Brasileira de História da Educação*.

Grafton, Anthony T. (1980) The importance of being printed. *Journal of Interdisciplinary History* 11: 265–286.

Grafton, Anthony T., Elizabeth L. Eisenstein, and Adrian Johns. (2002) How revolutionary was the print revolution? *American Historical Review* 107: 84–128.

Guillory, John. (2000) The ethical practice of modernity: The example of reading. In Marjorie Garber, Beatrice Hanssen, and Rebecca L. Walkowitz, eds., *The turn to ethics*, 29–46. New York and London: Routledge.

Guillory, John. (2008a) On the presumption of knowing how to read. *ADE Bulletin* 145: 8–11.

Guillory, John. (2008b) How scholars read. *ADE Bulletin* 146: 8–17.

Guillory, John. (2010) Close reading: Prologue and epilogue. *ADE Bulletin* 149: 8–14.

Hager, Christopher. (2013) *Word by word: Emancipation and the act of writing*. Cambridge, Mass.: Harvard University Press.

Hall, David D. (1992) *Worlds of wonder, days of judgment: Popular religious belief in early New England.* Cambridge, Mass: Harvard University Press.

Hall, David D. (1996) *Cultures of print: Essays in the history of the book.* Amherst: University of Massachusetts Press.

Halsey, Katie, and W. R. Owens, eds. (2011) *The history of reading,* vol. 2, *Evidence from the British Isles, c. 1750–1950.* London: Palgrave Macmillan.

Harker, Michael. (2015) *The lure of literacy: A critical reception of the compulsory composition debate.* Albany: State University of New York Press.

Harris, Roy. 2000. *Rethinking writing.* Bloomington: Indiana University Press.

Hayles, N. Katherine. (2007) Hyper and deep attention: The generational divide in cognitive modes. *Profession:* 187–199.

Heath, Shirley Brice. (1982) Protean shapes in literacy events: Ever-shifting oral and literate traditions. In Deborah Tannen, ed., *Spoken and written language: Exploring orality and literacy,* 91–117. Norwood, N.J.: Ablex.

Heath, Shirley Brice. (1983) *Ways with words: Language, life, and work in communities and classrooms.* Cambridge: Cambridge University Press, 1983; new epilogue, 1996.

Henwood, Doug. (2003) *After the new economy: The binge …and the hangover that won't go away.* New York: New Press.

Hilliard, Christopher. (2006). *To exercise our talents: The democratization of writing in Britain.* Cambridge, Mass.: Harvard University Press.

Hobbs, Catherine, ed. (1995) *Nineteenth-century women learn to write.* Charlottesville: University of Virginia Press.

Hoggart, Richard. (1961) *The uses of literacy: Changing patterns in English mass culture.* Boston: Beacon.

Horowitz, Helen Lefkowitz. (1992) "Nous autres": Reading, passion, and the creation of M. Carey Thomas. *Journal of American History* 79: 68–95.

Howard, Nicole. (2009) *The book: The life story of a technology.* Baltimore: Johns Hopkins University Press.

Hruby, George G., and Lisa Gowami. (2011) Neuroscience and reading: A review for reading education researchers. *Reading Research Quarterly* 46: 156–172.

Hunter, Jane. (2002) *How young ladies became girls: The Victorian origins of American girlhood.* New Haven: Yale University Press.

Jack, Belinda. (2012) *The woman reader.* New Haven: Yale University Press.

Jacobs, Alan. (2011) *The pleasures of reading in an age of distraction.* New York: Oxford University Press.

Jenkins, Henry, and Wyn Kelley, with Katie Clinton, Jenna McWilliams, and Ricardo PittsWiley, eds. (2013) *Reading in a participatory culture: Remixing Moby Dick in the English classroom.* New York: Teachers College Press.

Katz, Michael B., and Mark J. Stern. (2006) *One nation divisible: What America was and what it is becoming.* New York: Russell Sage.

Keller, Daniel. (2013) *Chasing literacy and reading and writing in an age of acceleration.* Logan: Utah State University Press.

Kertész, André. (1971) *On reading.* London: Penguin.

Kress, Gunther. (2010) *Multimodalilty: A social semiotic approach to contemporary communication.* London: Routledge.

Littau, Karin. (2006) *Theories of reading: Books, bodies and bibliomania.* Cambridge: Polity Press.

Livingston, Eric. (1995) *An anthropology of reading.* Bloomington: Indiana University Press.

Logan, Shirley Wilson. (2008) *Liberating language: Sites of rhetorical education in nineteenthcentury Black America.* Carbondale: Southern Illinois University Press.

Long, Elizabeth. (2013) *Book clubs: Women and the uses of reading in everyday life.* Chicago: University of Chicago Press.

Lorenzen-Schmidt, Klaus-Joachim, and Bjørn Poulsen, eds. (2002) *Writing peasants: Studies in peasant literacy in early modern northern Europe.* Kerteminde, Denmark: Landbohistorisk Selskab.

Lyons, Martyn. (2001) *Readers and society in nineteenth-century France: Workers, women, peasants.* Basingstoke: Palgrave.

Lyons, Martyn. (2008) *Reading culture and writing practices in nineteenth-century France.* Toronto: University of Toronto Press.

Lyons, Martyn. (2010) *A history of reading and writing in the Western world.* London: Palgrave Macmillan.

Lyons, Martyn. (2013) *The writing culture of ordinary people in Europe, c. 1860–1920.* Cambridge: Cambridge University Press.

Mangen, Anne, and Jean-Luc Velay. (2010) Digitizing literacy: Reflections on the haptics of writing. In Mehrdad Hosseini Zudeh, ed. *Advances in haptics*, 385–401. Rijeka, Croatia: Intech.

Manguel, Alberto. (1996) *A history of reading.* New York: Harper Collins.

Manguel, Alberto. (2006) *The library at night.* New Haven: Yale University Press.

Manguel, Alberto. (2010) *A reader on reading.* New Haven: Yale University Press.

Manguel, Alberto. 2015. *The traveler, the power, and the worm: The reader as metaphor.* Philadelphia: University of Pennsylvania Press.

Manning, Molly Guptill. (2014) *When books went to war: The stories that helped us win World War II*. Boston: Houghton Mifflin.

Martin, Henri-Jean. (1994) *The history and power of writing*, trans. Lydia G. Cochrane. Chicago: University of Chicago Press.

McHenry, Elizabeth. (2002) *Forgotten readers: Recovering the lost history of African American literary societies*. Durham, N.C.: Duke University Press.

McHenry, Elizabeth, and Shirley Brice Heath. (1994) The literate and the literary: African Americans as writers and readers—1830–1940. *Written Communication* 11: 419–444.

McNamara, Danielle S. (2006) Bringing cognitive science into education, and back again: The value of interdisciplinary research. *Cognitive Science* 30: 605–608.

McNeely, Ian F. 2003. *The emancipation of writing: German civil society in the making, 1790s–1820s*. Berkeley: University of California Press.

Mikics, David. (2013) *Slow reading in a hurried age*. Cambridge, Mass: Harvard University Press.

Miller, Susan. (1998) *Assuming the positions: Cultural pedagogy and the politics of commonplace writing*. Pittsburgh: University of Pittsburgh Press.

Moje, Elizabeth Birr, Melanie Overby, Nicole Tysvaer, and Karen Morris. (2008) The complex world of adolescent literacy: Myths, motivations, and mysteries. *Harvard Educational Review* 78: 107–154.

Monaghan, E. Jennifer. (1998) Reading for the enslaved, writing for the free: Reflections on liberty and literacy. *Proceedings, American Antiquarian Society* 108: 309–341.

Moylan, Michele, and Lane Stiles, eds. (1996) *Reading books: Essays on the material text and literature in America*. Amherst: University of Massachusetts Press.

National Council of Teachers of English, Policy Research Brief. (2012) Reading Instruction for *All* Students. *NCTE Council Chronicle*, Sept.: 15–18.

National Endowment for the Arts. (2004) *Reading at Risk*. Washington, D.C.: National Endowment for the Arts.

Nunberg, Geoffrey, ed. (1996) *The future of the book*. Berkeley: University of California Press.

Olson, David R. (1994) *The world on paper: The conceptual and cognitive implications of writing and reading*. Cambridge: Cambridge University Press.

Piper, Andrew. (2012) *Book was there: Reading in electronic times*. Chicago: University of Chicago Press.

Piper, Andrew. (2015) Novel devotions: Conversional reading, computational modeling, and the modern novel. *New Literary History* 46: 63–98.

Price, Leah. (2012) *How to do things with books in Victorian Britain.* Princeton: Princeton University Press.

Radway, Janice. (1984a) Interpretive communities and variable literacies. *Daedalus* 113: 49–73.

Radway, Janice A. (1984b) *Reading the romance: Women, patriarchy, and popular literature.* Chapel Hill: University of North Carolina Press.

Raven, James, Helen Small, and Naomi Tadmor, eds. (1996) *The practice and representation of reading in England.* Cambridge: Cambridge University Press.

Rose, Jonathan. (2001) *The intellectual life of the British working classes.* New Haven: Yale University Press.

Royster, Jacqueline Jones. (2000) *Traces of a stream: Literacy and social change among African American women.* Pittsburgh: University of Pittsburgh Press.

Schrag, Francis. (2011) Does neuroscience matter for education? *Educational Theory* 61: 221–237.

Scribner, Sylvia, and Michael Cole. (1973) Cognitive consequences of formal and informal education. *Science* 182: 553–559.

Scribner, Sylvia, and Michael Cole. (1981a) *The psychology of literacy.* Cambridge, Mass.: Harvard University Press.

Scribner, Sylvia, and Michael Cole. (1981b) Unpacking literacy. In Marcia Farr Whiteman, ed., *Variation in writing: Functional and linguistic-cultural differences,* 71–87. Hillsdale, N.J.: Lawrence Erlbaum.

Sedo, DeNel Rehberg, ed. (2011) *Reading communities from salons to cyberspace.* London: Palgrave Macmillan.

Sicherman, Barbara. (1989) Sense and sensibility: A case study of women's reading in late Victorian America. In Cathy Davidson, ed., *Reading in America,* 201–225. Baltimore: Johns Hopkins University Press.

Sicherman, Barbara. (1993) Reading and ambition: M. Carey Thomas and female heroism. *American Quarterly* 45: 73–103.

Sicherman, Barbara. (1995) Reading *Little Women*: The many lives of a text. In Linda K. Kerber, Alice Kessler Harris, and Kathryn Kish Sklar, eds, *U.S. history as women's history,* 245– 266. Chapel Hill: University of North Carolina Press.

Sicherman, Barbara. (2006). Connecting lives: Women and reading, then and now. In James P. Danky and Wayne A. Wiegand, eds., *Women in print: Essays on the print culture of American women from the nineteenth and twentieth centuries,* 3–24. Madison: University of Wisconsin Press.

Sicherman, Barbara. (2007) Ideologies and practices of reading. In Scott E. Casper, Jeffrey D. Groves, Stephen W. Nissenbaum, and Michael Winship, eds, *The Industrial Book, 1840– 1880*, 279–302. Chapel Hill: University of North Carolina Press, in association with the American Antiquarian Society.

Slaughter, Joseph R. (2013) "Only Reading: An Introduction." *New Literary History* 80: 317–321.

Smith, Erin. (2015) *What would Jesus read? Popular religious books and everyday life in twentieth-century America.* Chapel Hill: University of North Carolina Press.

Standage, Tom. (2013) *Writing on the wall: Social media—the first two thousand years.* New York: Bloomsbury.

Steedman, Carolyn. (1999) A woman writing a letter. In Rebecca Earle, ed., *Epistolary selves: Letters and letter writers, 1600–1945*, 111–133. Farnham, Surrey: Ashgate.

Steedman, Carolyn. (2005) Poetical maids and cooks who write. *Eighteenth-Century Studies* 39: 1–27.

Stewart, Garrett. (2006) *The look of reading: Book, painting, text.* Chicago: University of Chicago Press.

Striphas, Ted. (2009) *The late age of print: Everyday book culture from consumerism to control.* New York: Columbia University Press.

Thompson, E. P. (1968) *The making of the English working class.* New York: Vintage.

Thornton, Tamara Plakins. (1996) *Handwriting in America: A cultural history.* New Haven: Yale University Press.

Towheed, Shafquat, Rosalind Crone, and Katie Halsey, eds. (2010) *The history of reading.* London: Routledge.

Towheed, Shafquat, and W. R. Owens, eds. (2011) *The history of reading*, vol. 1, *International Perspectives, c. 1500–1990.* Basingstoke: Palgrave Macmillan.

Tribble, Evelyn B., and Anne Trubek, eds. (2003) *Writing material: Readings from Plato to the digital age.* London: Longman.

United States Department of Education (U.S. DoE). (1983) *A nation at risk: The imperative for educational reform.* Washington, D.C.: U.S. Department of Education.

Vincent, David. (1979) *Bread, knowledge, and freedom. A study of nineteenth century working class autobiography.* London: Europa.

Vincent, David. (1989) *Literacy and popular culture: England 1750–1914.* Cambridge: Cambridge University Press.

Watkins, Evan. (2015) *Literacy work in the reign of human capital.* New York: Fordham University Press.

Williams, Heather Andrea. (2002) "Clothing themselves in intelligence": The freedpeople, schooling, and northern teachers, 1861–1871. *Journal of African American History* 87: 372–389.

Williams, Heather Andrea. (2005) *Self-taught: African American education in slavery and freedom.* Chapel Hill: University of North Carolina Press.

Wolf, Maryanne. 2007. *Proust and the squid: The story and science of the reading brain.* New York: Harper.

Worden, Jennifer M., Christina Hinton, and Kurt W. Fischer. (2011) What does the brain have to do with learning? *Phi Delta Kappan* 92: 8–13.

6

Many Literacies, Other Visions: Digital, Visual, Science, Numbers, Performance

Digital literacy. New media literacy. Cyber literacies. Computer literacy. Screen literacies. Visual literacies. Videogame literacy. Teleliteracy. Text literacy. Cartographic literacy. Spatial literacy (graphicacy). Math literacy (numeracy). Science literacy. Dance literacy. Performance literacies. Reading and writing (with) the body.

These are among the many new literacies that are mentioned in print and other media. They are among the literally hundreds of disconnected, usually topical and often fabulous and faddish if not facetious purported literacies. Some of them are raw marketing ploys, some more sophisticated commercial enterprises. Many are laughable, a few dangerous. Together they demonstrate both the endless appeal of literacy and literacies and the lack of meaning and coherence. They range from health and financial literacy through cultural and religious literacy to sexual, emotional, and even depression literacy. My own list of almost five hundred terms that I have seen in print includes advertising, apocalypse, food, ironic, palpatory, and vegetable literacy, plus cliteracy, letteracy, and transliteracy (Graff 2011).

We often hear of financial or health literacy. In fact, financial literacy is confused with financial "wellness." Among the many limits of the common notion of financial wellness is that it does not mean having *enough*

© The Author(s), under exclusive license to Springer Nature Switzerland AG 2022
H. J. Graff, *Searching for Literacy*, https://doi.org/10.1007/978-3-030-96981-3_6

money; it merely means being able to manage money, for example, use credit cards, take out a student loan, and so on. This is neither literacy nor wellness.

Health literacy, in one version or another, has been defined as the ability of medical providers to communicate understandably to their patients and their families (and to each other), and the ability of patients and their families to understand caregivers, health providers, and medical, insurance, and civic institutions in any media. The complicated, intersecting problems include different languages, levels of education, technical and specialized terminology, questions of interpersonal psychology and communications, modes of written and spoken communication, power and authority relationships, and matters involving of choices about medical treatment, not to mention matters of the law and legal liability. Oral, written, and audiovisual, individual and collective, intergenerational, socioeconomic and institutional relationships inseparably intertwine (Zarcadoolas et al. 2006; Berkman et al. 2010; Peterson et al. 2011).

Financial issues are no less problematic. Health and finance are ever more integrated. The resort to literacy for such matters confusingly elevates the term and simultaneously reduces it to the lowest common denominator.[1]

Calling all forms of communication, disclosure, and education literacy obscures what literacy is and also obfuscates the real problems in the healthcare system and financial institutions that result in uninformed patients, defrauded customers, and overly indebted college graduates or dropouts. Among the many problems is the extent to which much of what passes as "content knowledge" at any moment is confused with literacy and literacies that may have a lasting value. Instead, providing "knowledge" that will be obsolete and superseded by new information and tools within students' lifetimes substitutes for the teaching critical and adaptable "skills" or "competencies" needed to understand the subject or master the tools necessary for effective understanding, expression, and development.

While I have long supported the concept of multiple literacies and recognize that knowledge about health and finances (and many other subjects) is extremely important, I think that more may be lost than gained in lumping together so many disparate things under the rubric of literacy. Trivialization is among the lesser cost. The debasement of a distinctive and recognizable conception and set of practices of reading and writing is a much greater loss. The result is a farreaching and, I fear, long-lasting incoherency in both language and thinking.

Amidst their contradictions, literacy and literacy studies are at a crossroads today. On the one hand, the last few decades have witnessed the increased recognition, or even the proclamation, of a multitude of literacies, ostensibly to meet the growing needs of the future, and also the presumed legacies of the past. Let a thousand literacies bloom! To some, we have a proliferation of literacies; at times, it seems more like an explosion. On the other hand, while the field embraces multiple and multimodal literacies, the embrace is loose and limited. For example, the recent collection of essays, *The Future of Literacy Studies* (Baynham and Prinsloo 2009), has remarkably little to say about visual literacy, numeracy, scientific literacies, or performance literacies. The field is also characterized by the absence of a serious consideration of *relationships* among even major forms of literacy and a sustained effort to understand them in a broadly contextualized way. Too much is made of digital media and presumptions of their distinct literacies, as well as new worlds of social design in learning and communication, without probing and articulating the critical connections among them and their relationships with other literacies. As the explosion of literacies and modalities threatens recognition and understanding, literacies and literacy studies risk implosion. Everything a literacy; everyone a literacy student. But whither literacy? What, I insist on asking, *is* the place of reading and writing in digital and other literacies, new and old?

Most of the endless literacies are not literacies, if by that term, we mean forms of reading—comprehending and making meaning—and writing—expressing or communicating meaning—across media and modes of communication, and their analogies and analogs. Many are metaphors of and for literacy and must be recognized as such. They are dominated by an endless proliferation of subject areas and undefined abilities. Many are objects for sale or training, consumer durables, and real or imagined needs to be fulfilled by purchases (Graff and Duffy 2007).

Yet the questions of their relationships, first, to fundamental literacies, and, second, to each other, are seldom addressed. This neglect, tellingly, is shared by educationists, literacy theorists, popular pundits, policy makers, and politicians. Indeed, this neglect and the need to confront it is the culmination of the literacy myth and the literacy episteme.

Digital Literacy or Digital Media?

By the late twentieth and early twenty-first centuries, discussions about literacy and literacies focused on digital literacy or literacies. The image of the reader and the writer is beautifully and lovingly portrayed by Garrett Stewart (2006) in *The Look of Reading: Book, Painting, Text*. In an effervescent blurb, Terry Castle commented: "A picture of someone reading: who would have imagined that this seemingly commonplace subject in Western arts could take us so far into the enigmatic relations between word and image, self and other, life and death, the sacred and profane?" With its self-consciously ambiguous title, *The Look of Reading* looks at art's "compulsive 'scenes' of *reading* … to see far and deep into literacy itself and to appreciate anew the astonishing impact the written has had." Castle could easily have added "the astonishing impact the visual has had."

Is the image of the writer and the reader, with all its ambivalences, from the Old Masters to Expressionist and Abstract artists, rapidly becoming an element of the past?[2] These developments are intertwined with the omnipresence of computers from mainframes to desktops, laptops, tablets, and minis. The smartphone, which seemingly so often leads to not-so-smart behaviors from texting while driving to obsessive fixations on video games and endless photographs of selves and other things, encapsulates the present moment. We have Google, Facebook, and Twitter in our hands and pockets. The ubiquitous cellphone has become the symbol for our era. But do we have information or the ability to use it or the technology critically or meaningfully? The answer is clearly no, and that has become a market itself for publishers, universities, and training institutes. This trend, along with a window into the sociology of professional development, may be seen in the move from computer literacy to cyber and then digital literacy (Selber 2004).

Part of a major economic engine, the effort to shift the focus on literacy or even redefine literacy as digital has implications for social, cultural, political, cultural, and economic life. In the tradition of writing and printing, although seldom appreciated, the digital world is extremely divisive. Just how new is a realm of mixed modes of reading and writing? The visual and spatial dimensions of literacy are not new. They are age-old, and readers and writers have always conducted their practice across media, long before the advent of electronic or digital mixed media and multimodality. Block printed images were the most popular products and objects of consumption and personal value in early printing. Literacy is often confused or conflated with the media in which the information is presented.

Moreover, the gap between what passes for critical analysis of new media and the literacies they require, on the one hand, and critical studies of these contemporary cultural trends and the political-economic changes that underlie them, on the other, is disturbing, because it allows many assertions to escape analysis or explanation. As one consequence, utopian dreams and apocalyptic nightmares of the impact of technological change coexist, and perhaps even generate one another. They do not substitute for serious analysis.

In a well-known essay, "Expanding the Concept of Literacy," Elizabeth Daley presumes and asserts the great novelty of things digital without pausing to demonstrate it. She also writes interchangeably about language, text, and screen. No less seriously, she makes no effort to learn the history of literacy in relation to print or other media. Instead, she declares that "print supports linear argument" but "deals inadequately with nonverbal modes of thought and nonlinear construction" (2003, 34) and does not support "nonlinear construction." Screen literacy, by contrast, is collaborative and public. These clichés are serious exaggerations, or even outright errors. They surprise many readers and writers and ignore the myriad of mass-produced, even printed images that appear across media. To Daley, "screen literacy" has become a prerequisite for "true literacy," which differs from the "full literacy" of reading and writing. That print and screen reading and writing may well bear important relationships is never considered.[3]

Similarly, when computer literacy was new and all the rage, it sparked an informative series of debates. As packaged software programs rapidly replaced the need for almost all users to learn programming languages (which did involve a certain kind of literacy), the discussion began with the question: did computer literacy mean much more than knowing how to turn on the machines and open the programs? In *Multiliteracies for a New World*, Stuart Selber contrasts three levels of computer literacy: the technical; the contextual, including the historical and cultural; and the critical, including the ideological, political, and economic dimensions. Expanding them into "multiliteracies" or digital literacies, he frames them as functional, critical, and rhetorical literacies. Selber's "metaphors" for the three are computers as tools, cultural artifacts, and hypertextual media. He argues for a curriculum based on the latter. "There is one sweeping statement I am prepared to make. Students who are not adequately exposed to all three literacy categories will find it difficult to participate fully and meaningfully in technological activities" (2004, 24).[4]

Alongside its neglect of ideology and power, the critical and contextual is by far the least common model; it is seldom put into practice. "Critical" does not appear in the index of *The Future of Literacy Studies*. These important concerns are relegated to a subfield of "critical media studies" or "critical literacy," although the meaning of either critical or critique is rarely made clear. Too often they stand as undeveloped adjectives and slogans rather than intellectual or action-oriented programs.[5]

These concerns culminated, at least temporarily, in the move toward a computer literacy requirement of some kind for college undergraduates. More recently, the question is becoming whether knowing how to code for data entry is a necessary part of literacy. "Boot camps" in coding are the new wave to prepare people in search of jobs, full of grandiose promises of financial rewards.[6]

Digital Literacy to Save the World?

To some, digital literacy or media literacy (typically used synonymously) is a cultural and political savior, linking citizens in democratizing and equalizing political and cultural participation. These efforts, which are sometimes directed at particular subgroups deemed to be underrepresented, are promoted by philanthropic foundations, some of them rooted in the media. *Confronting the Challenges of Participatory Culture: Media*

Education for the 21ˢᵗ Century (Jenkins 2009) is one of many such reports. The concern—and the almost universally assumed digital link (pun intended)—is to the young, new and future citizens. That is the focus of Shakuntala Banaji and David Buckingham's *The Civic Web: Young People, the Internet and Civic Participation* (2013). Another hopeful MacArthur Foundation report on Digital Media and Learning, it focuses on "producing" the civic web, young people "online and offline," "the young civilians," "politics online," and "making civic identities." Herein lies the remedy for the decline in civic engagement and electoral politics and the rise in apathy—or so it is asserted. The young, who were formerly the target of alphabetic literacy and mass education, are supposed to become caught up in the civic web for a more secure future.

The pervasive assumption in this camp is that the internet, the web, and networking—terms that are more often used metaphorically than literally—have the potential to save us. The better studies admit the limits and advise caution. But just how the digital represents an improvement in literacy or in the human condition is seldom made clear. That lack of specificity is itself part of the problem. While many possibilities are promoted, digital determinism has become a new myth, cresting on the wave of another great divide.[7]

Much of the writing on digital and media literacy takes the form of textbooks and general interest journalistic articles (among numerous examples, see Tyner 1998; Hartley 2009). James Paul Gee attempts to remix the academic with the more popular profits of new media with his *What Video Games Have to Teach Us about Learning and Literacy* (2003).[8] In *Confronting the Challenges of Participatory Culture*, Jenkins and his collaborators, like many others, cast the problem explicitly with respect to teaching media literacy inside and outside schools and necessarily, even reflexively, "rethinking literacy." Yet, what they call "core literacy skills" are not novel, nor do they have a distinctive or particular foundation in a digital world. They endorse the importance of play, games, real world problem solving, role playing and adapting identities, much as do educators and others without the same avowed commitment to "media education for the 21ˢᵗ century." They also advocate learning to "remix" and "repurpose" in arts and creative writing classes. In a reprise of current buzzwords and controversies in psychology, they promote multitasking, carefully defining it as different from "distraction"; "distributed cognition, the ability to interact meaningfully with tools that expand mental capacities" (Jenkins 2009, 65); and "collective intelligence." They emphasize the ability to evaluate information and collaborate in a "media landscape." (See also Davidson and Goldberg 2010; Davidson 2011.)[9]

As the media and information technologies change, so too must learning at all levels. At the same time, I must ask: does this constitute "digital or media literacy" or "rethinking literacy"? Or does it suggest instead an expansion and relative shift in emphasis? There is a significant difference, I think. Jenkins and his colleagues write: "It becomes increasingly critical to help students acquire skills in understanding multiple perspectives, respecting and even embracing diversity of views, understanding a variety of social norms, and negotiating between conflicting opinions" (2009, 100). No doubt those abilities are crucial in enabling young people to navigate a diverse social world, both locally and globally. But when they equate those skills with the mastery of specific technologies, they are on dubious ground. They continue: "Literacy skills for the 21st century are skills that enable participation in the new communities emerging within a networked activity. They enable students to exploit new simulation tools, information appliances, and social networks; they facilitate the exchange of information among diverse communities, and the ability to move more easily across different media platforms and social networks" (103). In my view, this does not constitute a rethinking of literacy. What is its relationship to its foundations in reading and writing in letters and words and other forms, including the visual, numerical, and spatial? Why not propose truly integrative learning that places digital and other media in a larger social, cultural, communicative, and educational context? An adequate understanding of literacy lies in probing the relationships.

Digital Divides or Cultural Integration?

Is the neglect of relationships, cultural contexts, and historical foundations a signs of the major implications of digital culture? The omnipresence and presumption of transformation are accepted so readily. An understanding of the reasons why this shift is promoted as sweepingly innovative lies in the consumer economy, which is now inseparable from the digital economy, the sociology of expertise and the professions, and the larger culture of late capitalism. To explicate that demands a different book. Here, I consider some works that critically analyze this tendency.

I have long found it curious and problematic that supposedly critical approaches to new media and all things digital, especially in the realm of literacy, remain fundamentally disconnected from the mounting critical studies of digital media in cultural studies, media and journalism studies, and political economy. In a field that touts its multi-, cross-, and interdisciplinarity, this absence is a serious matter. Among the major studies are Dan Schiller's *Digital Capitalism: Networking the Global Market System* (1999) and his *Digital Depression: Information Technology and Economic Crisis* (2014), and Robert McChesney's *The Problem of the Media: U.S. Communication Politics in the 21st Century* (2004). Schiller examines higher education as digital industry and digital media as crucial elements in national and global economies. So much of this important research argues against the assumptions on which today's emphasis on digital literacy for networking, participation, and democracy rest. This disjunction is deeply contradictory.[10]

Despite this burgeoning critical scholarship, the dominant view follows the lead of Jonathan Alexander's *Digital Youth: Emerging Literacies in the World Wide Web* (2006) and has been developed in foundation-sponsored and media-related research, including *Living and Learning with New Media* (Ito et al. 2009), *Hanging Out, Messing Around, and Geeking Out* (Ito et al. 2010), and *It's Complicated: The Lives of Networked Teens* (Boyd 2014). The message is that "the kids are alright," more or less. The goal is to allay adults' and educators' fears about youth who are growing up today, as such titles as *Born Digital: Understanding the First Generation of Digital Natives* (Palfrey and Gasser 2010) indicate. For me, as for many others, these works stimulate ambivalence and some foreboding.

These positive reports compete with the testimony of those who worry about a new "lost generation" on one of the multiple sides of the shifting digital divides. Principally, that group includes both the boundless young digital natives *and* the digital have-nots. Beyond the concerns of political economists and cultural critics, the evidence is mixed at best. Popular opinion, never a clear guide, includes many voices convinced of a "digital decline." Strong views of rise and fall, hope and fear clash but seldom meet.

For example, prominent voices, claiming empirical evidence, pronounce that digital media ruin reading and writing and distort learning. In sharp contrast to Stanislas Dehaene's *Reading in the Brain: The Science and Evolution of a Human Invention* (2009) and Maryanne Wolf's *Proust and the Squid: The Story and Science of the Reading Brain* (2007), Nicholas Carr raises questions about "what the Internet is doing to our brains" (2010) and linguist Naomi Baron worries about "the fate of reading in a digital world" (2015; see also Baron 2008).

In his widely publicized *The Shallows*, Carr asked the leading question, "Is Google making us stupid?" and answered it without hesitation. He makes sweeping, undocumented generalizations about how human thought has been shaped for centuries by "tools of the mind," principally the alphabet and print, while leavening them with a selective sprinkling of recent neuroscience. In his view, centuries of mental habits are threatened by the recent rise of the internet and Google's online tools. Calling the assumptions of dominant technologies an "ethic" and confusing them with those tools' actual effects and specific influences vitiates his argument, rendering his portrayal comedic. Neither thinking, nor the contributions of reading and writing, in print or online, is uniform, singular, or determinative.

I am not persuaded by Carr or by Baron, who presents digital technologies as a serious threat to scholarship and knowledge. Their arguments are not well supported; but overstated and intentionally provocative. That does not mean, of course, that new media have no impacts and cannot be deployed or employed poorly so as to have negative impacts. Teachers, researchers, writers, and many others understand that new media are powerful and can be employed effectively or misused. We are becoming familiar with their advantages, limitations, potential distortions and biases, and their abuses as well as uses. But none of this accumulated experience is an adequate substitute for systematic investigation. At present, the evidence remains unclear, limited, and problematic. The concerns that are expressed on both sides of the issue are symbolic and culturally relative, testifying to pervasive hopes and fears rather than representing careful analysis of these changes.

Voices decrying the negative influence of new media have emerged in direct opposition to widespread celebrations of the rise of digital media, digital culture, and digital literacy. Longstanding dichotomies that mark the history of literacy persist in new forms and formats, discourses and ideologies. Oppositional formulations about the meaning of transformations, divides, and determinisms continue to mark the field.

Sociologist Judy Wajcman explored how we are *Pressed for Time: The Acceleration of Life in Digital Capitalism* (2015). To her credit, Wajcman maintains that contemporary culture's acceptance of the inescapable and inexorable press of an "accelerating everyday life" is not a necessity or a given. To the contrary, she suggests that the sense of a population held hostage to digital technology in a commodified world has been valorized. She argues, sensibly, that speed has become synonymous with progress. In her interesting book, she shows that the impacts vary by social groups and among different aspects of life, from work to family. Technology, values, and contemporary practices are of a piece. In my terms, the digital and its "culture of acceleration" have become hegemonic and are fundamentally if not completely ideological. That does not diminish the reality of its influence.[11]

Digital Culture, Literacy, and Ideology

The conflicting responses prompted by the new digital world speak to the ideological bases of many recent developments and the complicated ways that digitalization affects media, culture, and literacy. That literacy is seen as central and complicit, however unclearly, is another element of the present moment. Each of the opposing sides expresses a heightened and exaggerated sense of the value or harm of the activity. Digital culture, media, and literacy, as a symbol and sign, is also a site of struggle.

In his Parisian-inflected *Digital Cultures*, first published in French as *La grande conversion numérique* (of which the English title is not a literal translation), University of Laval professor Milad Doueihi defines digital literacy in essentialist, circular, and reductive terms. In his prefatory note to the American edition, he states that his objective "is to articulate, through the diversity of digital practices, the need for a rich understanding of digital literacy and the emergence of a literate environment that is essentially founded on an anthological practice." Seemingly unaware of the centrality of "anthological practice" throughout the history of writing and print, from early sacred, philosophical, and scientific-medical writings through the middle ages and the eighteenth and nineteenth-century makings of modern literature," the professor, who styles himself "an accidental digitician," can only see novelty and difference, despite referring to similarities. "Digital literacy embodies the radical changes brought about by the socioeconomic impact of the new technology. While it is useful to think of it through an analogy with the literacy associated with print and the culture of the book, it is equally important to take into account the full power of their differences. With the digital, it is not sufficient, at least in my opinion, to reduce literacy to a minimalist familiarity with the tools and their exploitation." Instead, "we need to rethink some of our received models, so embedded within print and its powerful heritage (both cultural and legal), in order to better appreciate the new dimensions of digital culture" (Doueihi 2008, ix–x).

Thus, while "digital tools disrupt our received ideas about authorship and reading, digital literacy invites a new look and an evaluation of what it means to be literate," Doueihi presumes that "in the digital environment, more so than at any other moment in the past, literacy is the agency not only of communication and the production and exchange of knowledge, it also the site of the deployment of a new iteration of individual and collective identities. In this fashion, it is also the site of a conflict, one opposing our inherited practices and their powerful history and the emerging new world of digital culture" (2009, x). But neither evidence nor explication or explanation accompanies the claims.

Doueihi asserts "the emergence of a *new literacy*—a digital literacy—that is not simply a numeracy, nor is it a set of norms for manipulating a technology." In contrast to this exaggerated minimalism, he pronounces expansively, "This digital literacy is not only defining new socioeconomic realities but is also articulating critical if not radical modifications of a set of abstractions and concepts operative in our broad social, cultural, and political horizons—identity, location, territory and jurisdiction, presence and location, community and individuality, ownership, archives, and so on" (2009, xiv–xv).

This discourse is familiar, but so abstract and speculative as to become devoid of meaning. Doueihi is not interested in literacy per se, which he never defines, but simply equates it with print. By analogy, that differs from digital literacy. But his analogy rests on opposition, and the twain will never meet. He seems unaware that the same discourse and assertions of novelty and difference have been applied to print in contrast with orality.[12]

Doueihi unselfconsciously applies to digital culture the same terms that have been used to celebrate print, describing it as "a civilizing process and "the *only* rival to religion as a universal presence" (2009, 2–3). But the book is not about literacy or rethinking literacy. Its overarching concern is with the law and intellectual and literary property and usage rights, rather than literacy or culture as lived or practiced. Thus, concern with "concepts" overwhelms practice or experience.

One inescapable conclusion is that digital literacy, to Doueihi and others who hail its advent, has much less to do with literacy than with their appropriation of the name and, occasionally, justification by association with its historical provenance yet mediated by the immediate assertion of difference. Revising the literacy myth for the twenty-first century, it is an interesting set of moves that bears further scrutiny.

Other books fail to define digital literacy or simply equate it with digital media. Kathleen Tyner's textbook, *Literacy in the Digital World: Teaching and Learning in the Age of Information* (1998), and her edited collection, *Media Literacy: New Agendas in Communication* (2010), never define literacy, whether digital or otherwise. Digital and media appear to be synonymous, and lists of literacies substitute for conceptualizations. In *The Uses of Digital Literacy*, John Hartley, former dean of the Creative Industries Faculty at Queensland Institute of Technology in Australia, can only define digital literacy by asserting a contrast with print literacy, which he does not develop (2009, 104–107). This is not "repurposing literacy," which his first chapter promises.

New literacies. New media. Digital literacy. Digital media. A mantra for the future? A return to great divides and transformative literacies? The claims are many and strong, but clarity and evidence lag behind. We need to make better sense of the new literacy myths. To do this, we should probe the relationships between and among the major forms of literacy without succumbing to the temptations of endless literacies.[13]

New or Old Literacies?

One way of beginning that crucial task, I suggest, lies in identifying a small number of major forms of literacy that extend beyond traditional alphabetic literacy and may include some digital forms. Here I briefly consider visual, numerical, scientific, performance, and dance-movement literacies. In calling for their recognition, I argue for sustained study and exploration of their relationships to other forms of literacy. Herein lies the foundation for new, cross- and intermedial and modal forms of reading and writing, literally, metaphorically, and analogically. And therein lies the future of literacy and literacy studies, of education and communication, both digital and analog.

Visual

Although the digital and onscreen worlds heighten awareness of the visual, the gaps between literacy studies and visual studies remain large and exist on both sides. In part, this stems from the disciplinary roots and development of visual studies, which reflects in large part in a resistance to embrace the concept or language of literacy in contrast to a rhetoric of culture.

More apparent among art historians and theorists than art educators, this preference bespeaks a sense that literacy marks the endeavor as elementary and lowers its intellectual, aesthetic, and academic status (indeed, its cultural capital). Visual literacy is typically more closely associated with pedagogy than with artistic expression or aesthetic understanding. Representative works include Eileen Landay and Kurt Wootton's *A Reason to Read: Linking Literacy and the Arts* (2012); James Elkins's collection, *Visual Literacy* (2008); Brian Goldfarb's *Visual Pedagogy: Media Cultures in and beyond the Classroom* (2002); Paul Messaris's *Visual Literacy: Image, Mind, and Reality* (1994); and Donis A. Dondis's *A Primer of Visual Literacy* (1973). Reading and writing instructors and literacy studies scholars pay little attention to visual literacy, except by noting its affinity in the digital realm.[14]

Goldfarb's *Visual Pedagogy* opens with a striking assertion: "The second half of the twentieth century was marked by the global expansion of communications media and a burgeoning visual culture." For him and many others, this radical "expansion alter[ed] the dissemination and production of information and knowledge." As a direct result, "education, widely espoused as the principal instrument of social change, was fundamentally changed and transfigured." Related to our concerns, Goldfarb further states, "Visual media culture was perceived as a threat to literacy, but also touted as a potentially powerful tool for educators. Behind those variously phobic and euphoric reactions to communication technology was an increasingly undeniable apprehension that any stable conception of literacy was being eroded" (2002, 1).

Literacy is entirely undefined, and forms of media and communication effects are unspecified. Equally problematic is the failure to distinguish perceptions from actualities. This problem pervades media studies. So, too, does the dichotomizing of print and visual forms. Equating literacy with language, Goldfarb writes, "To focus exclusively on language literacy and speech is to overlook the visual and graphic means of knowledge production and reproduction that played a major role in strategies of resistance and social transformation" (2002, 2). When we so commonly refer to reading and writing across media, prominently with respect to reading visual images and to visual languages, this statement shows only how badly informed he is.[15]

Introducing a collection of essays stemming from a 2005 conference, art historian James Elkins comments: "A tremendous force of rhetoric has been brought to bear on the notion that ours is a predominantly visual culture. Theories concerning the visual nature of experience have been proposed in art history, cognitive psychology, psychoanalytic criticism, anthropology, artificial intelligence, women's studies, neurobiology, neurology, linguistics, and various branches of philosophy" (Elkins 2008, vii).

Elkins's collection raises important issues, some by omission. Is it significant that he does not include history and literature? In his generalization about "our" culture, there is no hint of historical perspective or either chronological or cross-cultural comparisons. He answers part of the question himself when he explains that he chose to title the collection *Visual Literacy* "because its two words compress the common and unavoidable contradiction involved in saying that we 'read' images." The book "does not avoid that contradiction, or try to improve on it, but starts with the most succinct form of the contradiction itself" (2008, 1).

In his essay, W. J. T. Mitchell argues that "visual literacy," in Elkins's words, "has the virtue of not trying to solve that structural problem," an opening that the book does not that take up.

Elkins remarks that "visual literacy" "has been in uncommon but intermittent use" for more than a century and a half "to denote low-level, secondary school appreciation," as in identifying Michelangelo's *David*. Is this either literacy or visual literacy? That Elkins is basically unconcerned with clarifying his appropriation of literacy is further confirmed when he adds, "A third and last reason for choosing *visual literacy* is that it is convenient in the absence of anything better." He explains: "It might be possible to speak of *visual competence*, or *visual competencies*, but that sounds awkward, utilitarian, and prescriptive. *Visual practices* is common but vague. *Visual languages* is so freighted with inappropriate precedents, from Umberto Eco to Nelson Goodman, that it is practically useless. *Visual skills* is too narrow, because much of what matters here is politics, ideology, and history, as well as skills." Yet, he hopes that "*visual literacy*, paradoxical and old-fashioned as it is, can be a useful expression for a very pressing problem" (Elkins 2008, 1–3). Here, too, are openings that Elkins does not follow.

Recently, the language of literacy has begun to seep or creep its way into the arts in general—museums and galleries, schools, and across the disciplines. Even when not that language is not used explicitly, the concepts and conceptualization are evident. Discussions and programs are short on definitions, historical foundations, and familiarity with the literature on literacy and literacies—and their debates. They rest often primarily on metaphors.

In contrast, Johanna Drucker's *Graphesis: Visual Forms of Knowledge Production* (2014) is a revealing new beginning. Drucker, a visual and bibliographic scholar and a book artist who is well aware of research and debates around literacy, does not depend on inexact and partial appropriation of a rhetoric or ideology of literacy and its divides. Her notion of "graphesis" is founded on the graphic production of knowledge that parallels and is closely related to reading and writing as modes of understanding or comprehending and means of expression or communication. Her concern, at base, is with the generation as well as the representation of knowledge graphically, and the ability to "read" it, a word she uses. She is also unusually aware of historical continuities and transformations in visual domain of writing, books, and other graphic representations.

Without summarizing *Graphesis*, I call attention to those elements that compare most directly to other forms of literacy, new and old. Prominent in the vocabulary and epistemology from which Drucker works are these elements: information graphics, graphical user interface, visual epistemology, and languages of form (visual or graphic languages). These are clear parallels to what we might call the language and epistemology of reading and writing, and are especially reminiscent of John Guillory's critical exegesis of reading. Visual epistemology, for example, "refers to ways of knowing that are presented and processed visually," while language of form "suggests a systematic approach to graphic expression as a means as well as an object of study." Drucker, whose own concerns are primarily with nonalphabetic imagic or visual graphic forms, focuses on representations rather than cognition. She wishes to bring the uses and demands of visual representations to a wider audience. "Visual expressions of knowledge are integral to many disciplines of the natural sciences but language-oriented humanities traditions have only barely engaged with visual forms of knowledge," she comments (2014, 8–9).

Drucker provides basic terms and methods to be elaborated, tested, and perhaps followed across the chasms that are presumed to separate old and new media, alphabetic and visual, traditional and new literacy. Letters and words, as well as the graphical signs that preceded and accompany them, are visual. Her agenda remains close to the basics of reading and writing. She suggests that "our task is three fold. First to study information graphics and begin to understand how they operate; to denaturalize the increasingly familiar interface that has become so habitual in daily use; and finally, to consider how to serve a humanizing agenda by thinking about ways to visualize interpretation" (2014, 9). She continues, articulating connections:

> The task of making knowledge visible does not depend on an assumption that images represent things in the world. Graphics make and construct knowledge in a direct and primary way. *Most information visualizations are acts of interpretation masquerading as presentation.* In other words, they are images that act as if they are just showing us *what is*, but in actuality, they are *arguments made in graphical form.*

But paradoxically, the primary effect of visual forms of knowledge production in any medium—the codex book, digital interface, information visualizations, virtual renderings or screen displays—is to mask the very fact of their visuality, to render invisible the very means through which they function as argument. (9–10)

Recognizing the import and the power of the relationships between graphic representations and acts of interpretation in the visual realm calls attention immediately to the parallels within alphabetic literacy and, even more consequentially, to the relationships between Drucker's graphesis and more traditional notions of literacy. They are visual. Therein lie "new literacies" that are not new at all. They have been fundamental to human cultures historically.

Throughout her work, Drucker shows how visual language and its graphical representation incorporate time, space, hierarchy, rhetoric, and ideology, among other forms of experience. That is their provenance, and their challenge. In this, they compare instructively to other forms of writing and reading, and their demands. There is no contradiction in recognizing that what Drucker teaches about visuality enhances our understanding of so-called traditional or alphabetic reading and writing. They are all, to use her words, "knowledge generators." Drucker's discussion of different forms of graphs and diagrams, for example, tree-diagrams, is eyeopening. It merits a place in any understanding of digital or media literacy, and in the necessary pursuit of relationships between and among forms of literacy.[16]

What is striking is how many of the visual forms also use or incorporate alphabetic expressions, among the plethora of graphical representations including numbers, symbols, and pictures. No less central to digital forms, here is a concrete display of what was once commonly called mixed media and now multimodality that prompts calls for multiliteracies. Drucker, for example, has studied the history of the visual representation of the alphabet.

In one of her many examples, Drucker points to another of today's hot topics in both literacy and visual studies: what was once called comics or comic books, recently elevated to graphic literature. "The study of visual elements and systems in formal terms gets augmented when it meets the analysis of narrative sequences and editing practices" (2014, 45). She turns to comics artist Scott McCloud's groundbreaking *Understanding Comics: The Invisible Art* (1993).

Although neither the promotional nor the critical literature has emphasized the point, graphic literature is among the most dynamic grounds on which words and pictures speak together and to each other, to put it simply but evocatively. (For a recent, interesting but not successful attempt, see Sousanis 2015.) Their mutual shaping and reshaping are clearly exposed if not always clearly expressed and understood. That comics and other graphic literature are not brand new or unprecedented is well-established but not yet assimilated into considerations of media literacy or new media. Drucker summarizes, "McCloud's approach focuses on the ways graphical frames organize story elements into sense and narrative.... The transitions that McCloud outlines establish relations between frames (character, place, event, time, story, point of view, detail, and jump) and find their echo in the description of film and video-editing" (Drucker 2014, 45–46).

The use of the words reading and writing by McCloud, as well as Drucker and Elkins, is more than an echo. Anyone interested in literacy would do well to ponder McCloud's *Understanding Comics*.[17] Ending his book, McCloud writes provocatively: "**Comics is a great balancing act. An art as subtractive as it is additive.** But nowhere is the balance between the *visible* and the *invisible* more conspicuous than in **pictures** and **words**" (1993, 206–207; emphasis in original).

He then equates "the will to learn" with "the ability to **see**" (213).

Education

Elementary education and non-school-based programs have recently been attempting to integrate reading, writing, the visual, and the digital, or at least to bring them more closely together.

Although there are parallels in other countries, the ArtsLiteracy Project is best known in the United States. Touted as "exploring the rich possibilities at the intersection of arts and literacy developments for deep learning and teaching," it "remind[s] us that the 'reason to read'—truly the desire to learn anything well—springs from the same ineffable emotions summoned by the arts." Its summa, *A Reason to Read: Linking Literacy and the Arts* (Landay and Wootton 2012), addresses arts education. That reading promotes the arts and the arts may promote reading is certainly important. But the program's goals stop short of exploring reading and writing across different media and modes of expression and understanding.

Another approach has the potential to come closer to that goal. In a series of books and articles over more than three decades, English education scholar Anne Haas Dyson (1989, 2003, 2013) reports on pioneering research on how elementary school students, especially African American and other inner-city youngsters in Oakland, California, learn to write. Closely observing the students in their classroom and also investigating their out-of-school and family lives, Dyson followed groups of children for periods of one or more school years, paying the closest attention to kindergarten and first grade. Her studies innovate by understanding elementary writing as collective. Groups of self-identified "friends" who call themselves "the brothers and the sisters" learn to write by actively adapting elements from popular culture, ranging from sports to videos. Dyson explores the extended example of "Space Jam" to illustrate how the youngsters participate in the "making of childhoods," their own childhoods—that is, culture and experience—as they began to learn to write and practice writing within elementary school. As she puts it, the children "made use of familiar media-influenced practices and symbolic materials to take intellectual and social action in the official school world" (2003, 328). They select from media genres such as sounds, images, and ways of talking, and adapt them to their own childhood practices, including storytelling, drawing, dramatic play, group singing, and informational display.

Dyson's term for the children's learning process and practice is "recontextualization." She also refers to "composing" across different technologies (video, radio, animation, and writing). These practices shaped the children's entries into school literacy. Emphasizing their agency, she says: "Literacy itself can be seen as entailing the *deliberate* manipulation of symbolic material within social organized practices. Unlike more spontaneous casual conversation, literacy is viewed more 'volitional', involving a conscious choice of signs to render meaning" (2003, 332–333; she cites Vygotsky).

For me, it is also a matter of translation and negotiation across media and contexts. Dyson's observations detail this step-by-step. Needless to say, this is complicated. But it reflects, indeed underscores, the interconnections among modes of reading and writing across alphabetic and visual, popular and school cultures. Conceptions, studies, instruction, and practices of literacy need to reflect that to a much greater extent. Therein, I believe, lies a foundation for new literacies and a radical reduction of oppositions.[18]

Science and Numeracy

Equally briefly, I turn to numeracy and scientific literacies. These are large, legitimate, and compelling domains within the pursuit of distinctive and interrelated modes of reading and writing across media and modes of communication and understanding. Despite their age-old historical provenance, they are gaining new recognition, in part from recent attention to multiple literacies, on the one hand, and perceptions of mass education's failure to meet the literacy needs of citizens, present or future, on the other. Fears of a crisis resulting from a presumed decline in the United States' and Western Europe's education and production of skilled workers in STEM(M) fields (science, technology, engineering, mathematics, and sometimes medicine) fuels the fires and, too often, yields a distorted view of both priorities for education and forms of literacy.[19]

But that is not the only fear. The current concern about "science denial," such as the alarming proportions of Americans, for example, who do not think that evolution is valid or that human activities have contributed to climate change, is directly relevant. The inadequacy of science education in schools that restricts young people's understanding of scientific findings, and the basic elements of science themselves, is primarily responsible for these views. They are reinforced by the religious strictures placed on science teaching in the United States. Consequently, the public is unprepared to read, much less evaluate, research-based scientific findings and is likely to gullibly accept or ignorantly dismiss whatever is announced as what "science says." Science and numerical literacy is not solely or even primarily a question of training specialists.

This is parcel and fuel of today's discourse of literacy crises. Science literacy and numeracy, which are not precisely the same, take their place in the *Dictionary of Cultural Literacy*.[20] These literacies bear little relationship to literacy as recognized in this book. Instead, literacy is a metaphor, reaching out widely, even wildly to encompass great expanses of ground. Many writings about science and math literacy lack definitions; too often the word "literacy" does not appear in indexes of books with literacy in their titles. More critically, writers in this vein are not familiar with standard and critical works in literacy studies.

To take one example, skeptical readers might well compare the sound, contextualized, and knowledgeable approach of Robert P. Moses and Charles E. Cobb, Jr.'s *Radical Equations: Civil Rights from Mississippi to the Algebra Project* (2001) with the wide-eyed academic text by Wolff-Michael Roth and Angela Calabrese Barton, *Rethinking Scientific Literacy* (2004). The latter book seems bent on using as many trendy terms as it can include. Linking itself to the "science for all" movement (sometimes identified with "science for the people"), but not conversant with its actual development and operations, it claims the equally fashionable motif of "rethinking literacy." Seldom defining its terms, it moves from "science as collective practice" to "literacy, power, and struggle for a better world," "scientific literacy as emergent feature of collective praxis," "scientific literacy, hegemony, and struggle," and "politics, power, and science in inner-city communities" before concluding with "dangerous teaching: using science as tool and context to work for social justice." Why they wrap their overwrought and faddish rhetoric around literacy is a question worth raising.

Here we confront the problem of literacy and literacy studies today. With hundreds of others, science literacy and numeracy take their places in the list of the interminable, many literacies. By and large, divisions reign. They are separate, too often dichotomized from alphabetic literacy on which they draw. They are erroneously cast as new as opposed to more traditional literacies.

Their appropriation is too often self-serving, exaggerated, uncritical, faddish, and metaphorical.

Like writing, they often elevate science and numeracy over alphabetic reading and writing. Digital media and today's movement for boot camps to provide "coding literacy" reflect this push. They do not reflect science or literacy.

Much more is lost than gained. Science literacy and numeracy cry out for a larger, encompassing, contextualized, and critical understanding and practice. The reasons why that is necessary are many and obvious. Uncritical, often exaggerated claims for and approaches to literacy are increasingly marketed commercially, especially by the purveyors of watered-down vocational training with false promises of jobs and compensation. The reasons for action include the need to combat the increasingly documented consequences of "science deniers" and disregard of firm scientific evidence and knowledge (recently dubbed "merchants of doubt"). While science literacy and numeracy do not guarantee sound attention and ensure understanding of the results of scientific research, they certainly help to promote a greater awareness, interest, and concern about veracity and caution against misunderstanding and abuse. And they certainly include recognition of the imperative to accept, teach, and practice the multiple literacies of science together, principally alphabetic, visual, and mathematical.

The history of scientific discovery and understanding depends on visual literacies, both for understanding and comprehension and for expression and communication. In addition to the works of practicing scientists through the ages, landmark studies in the history of science are unanimous in their views (although, understandably, they differ as to details). To begin, I refer specifically to Daniel Calhoun's *The Intelligence of a People* (1973); Eugene S. Ferguson's "The mind's eye: Nonverbal thought in technology" (1977) and his *Engineering and the Mind's Eye* (1992); Arthur L. Miller's *Insights of Genius: Imagery and Creativity in Science and Art* (2000); and Luc Pauwels's collection, *Visual Cultures of Science: Rethinking Representational Practices in Knowledge Building and Science Communication* (2006). Some of this work reflects an awareness that visual and alphabetic literacies have complicated relationships. This work should be required reading for students of literacy and literacy studies scholars.

In *Graphesis*, Johanna Drucker considers tables, graphs, and presentations of numbers both as representations of information and as "knowledge generators." Like some but not all scientists and science educators, she warns against the false realism of numbers and supposedly objective representations of data. To the contrary, she explains how they operate in ways that demand a practice of critical visual literacy as part of science literacy and numeracy:

Knowledge generators are graphical forms that support combinatoric calcu-
lation. Their spatial organization may be static or mobile, but their spatial
features allow their components to be combined in a multiplicity of ways.
They make use of position, sequence, order, and comparison across aligned
fields as fundamental spatial properties…. So is … a list of numbers to be
added up, or a problem of long division. The outcome is determined by a
set of operations, but the result is a product, generated through the combination of spatial organization and a set of rules for its use. (2014, 104)

Taking a step backward, as we must, Drucker reflexively warns nonscientists that they must understand and read the writings of scientists and
mathematicians critically and contextually. She speaks to humanities
scholars who may be overly impressed by graphic representations and
what is called digital humanities. I extend her cautions more broadly.
Drucker criticizes "graphical tools" as "a kind of intellectual Trojan horse,
a vehicle through which assumptions about what constitutes information
swarm with potent force." Central to those assumptions is that these
graphical and numerical representations purport to be realistic. She continues: "These assumptions are cloaked in a rhetoric taken wholesale from
the technologies of the empirical sciences that conceals their epistemological biases under a guise of familiarity. So naturalized are the maps and
bar charts generated from spread sheets that they pass as unquestioned
representations of 'what is'" (2014, 125).

Reiterating the basis for a critical literacy, Drucker explains that this
"hallmark" of a realist model of knowledge "needs to be subjected to a radical critique to return the humanistic tenets of constructedness and interpretation to the fore." Consequently, "Rendering *observation* (the act of
creating a statistical, empirical, or subjective account or image) as if it were
the same as the phenomena observed collapses the critical distance between
the phenomenal world and its interpretation, undoing the concept of
interpretation on which humanistic knowledge production is based"
(Drucker 2014, 125). She reminds today's humanities and social science
students that most, if not all, of the popular visualization tools, such as
GIS mapping, graphs, and charts, were developed in other disciplines.

This understanding stands among the tenets of a serious science and
mathematics literacy as it is of traditional reading and writing. It is certainly not news to serious scientists, but it may be a revelation to many

who write about visual, science, math, and digital literacies as if they are necessarily different and opposed. Chemist Henry Bauer sees this, at least in part, when he entitles his critique of the so-called traditional scientific method *Scientific Literacy and the Myth of the Scientific Method* (1992). Bauer recasts general concerns about popular understanding of science and the problems of science education in terms of revising long-standing but dated and inaccurate notions of a singular, universal conception and practice of science and a scientific method. Writing more than two decades ago, but like others today, he was not familiar with the criticisms developed in literacy studies. He refers causally and unquestioning to the "science literate" and "literate citizens," seeing no need to problematize concept or language.

The situation is changing, but slowly and incompletely. In science education, for example, the critical discourse has begun to change. But the discourse is often undeveloped. Stephen Norris and Linda Phillips (2003, 2009) strenuously argue that "literacy in its fundamental sense"—that is, reading and writing—"is central to scientific literacy."[21] "Scientific literacy is a good that educators, scientists, and politicians want for citizens and society," Norris and Phillips begin (2009, 271). Reading is "intrinsic to science" and reading texts is complicated, they conclude (2009, 276–277). That is a beginning. It demands development into both theory and practice in science and beyond.

Curiously, science literacy and to a comparable decree numeracy remain disconnected to both literacy studies and science studies, let along visual studies and mathematics (Whitin and Whitin 2011). When references are made to those fields they are often dated and limited. Government and national science association calls for action of the 1980s and 1990s continue to be cited and quoted without updating. But there are some hopeful openings for more critical and intermediating approaches. A new, exciting, and fundamental set of fields demand attention across criticism, research, teaching, and popular applications. Beyond all clichés, I urge that the imperative to develop new literacies of words, number, visual images, and beyond is not merely academic or scholarly. Dare literacy studies take the lead? Can science and mathematics be exemplars? Can they learn from their own histories and from the arts?[22]

Performance and Dance

A final area that mandates attention today is the new area field of performance studies, including dance. Aside from oral poetry and other forms of oral culture discussed in Chap. 2, performance literacies are even farther afield from the other modes of literacy reviewed in this chapter (Bauman and Briggs 1990; Finnegan 1988). Performance is almost never mentioned even in discussions of new literacies, multiliteracies, and multimodal literacies. Perhaps most commonly identified with oration and reciting from memory or by reading from written or print texts or, more challengingly, with oral composition, the notion of performance literacies requires additional steps. They move into music, song, and dance, or movement, across many genres and styles.

Dance, although seldom included among discussions of art literacies, is an unusually attractive area of interest for reading and writing across media and modes of understanding and expression. For example, French choreographer Boris Charmatz composed his "Flip Book" from his reading of a book about the American modern dancer Merce Cunningham. "From looking at it with a little distance, I could suddenly see, this is a dance," Charmatz recalled. As a *New York Times* the reporter put it, "Mr. Charmatz has created a work animating the photographs in that 1997 book, David Vaughan's 'Merce Cunningham: Fifty Years.'"[23] In an act of translation, Charmatz recontextualized his understanding across media and modes of expression, achieving a new level of comprehension and communication in the process.

This vision of literacy goes beyond what is slowly becoming more common in the arts. Dance has been more receptive to appropriating the term than other studio or performance art forms. Dance, it seems, finds grounds to elevate its status and distinguish itself by reference to literacy, compared, for example, to the visual arts or theatre where literacy is still identified with schools and elementary levels of understanding and practice.

Dance educator Ann Dils reports on the use of student writing about dance as part of high school language arts classes. She constructs "dance literacy" in association with "dance appreciation." In surveying student writing, she observes that "students attend to the kinesthetic properties of dance—bodily position, deployment of weight, sense of tension or freedom in the muscles—and retell their experience of the movement in evocative verbs." In addition, "They describe the images called up by the dance through metaphors, venture their own opinions, and form meaning by drawing on their past experiences of motion, everyday life, and other subject areas." In sum, as concludes, "they are learning about dance while sharpening their language skills and beginning to engage in the cross-disciplinary, cross-experience thinking that builds understanding and sparks creativity" (2007, 96). Is this dance literacy, or is it writing about dance? There is a difference.

Along with many arts educators, Dils is not familiar with the literature or debates among either literacy studies scholars or literacy educators, a continuing problem in the use of the term across fields. Partly as a result, she exaggerates what may be gained in such language arts classes and programs from their appropriations of and appeals to literacy. Consequently, she fails to grapple with the important questions of understanding and expression across major media and modes of communication.

Despite these typical, although revealing limits, dance remains a compelling and instructive field for anyone interested in reading and writing across media and modes of understanding and expression. Recent studies underscore the relationships of diverse modes of reading and writing in building a broader, dynamically integrated conception and practice of literacy and literacies.

Rachael Riggs Leyva's groundbreaking new doctoral dissertation, "Dance Literacy in the Studio: Partnering Movement Texts and Residual Texts" (2015) is a distinctive exemplar.[24] A dancer and dance teacher, as well as proficient in Laban notation, one of several writing systems used to record choreographic compositions, Riggs Leyva explores "both *dance literacy* and interactions between *dance and literacy*." Through qualitative case studies, she examines the forms and practices of literacy in creating dances, teaching and practicing dance, and recording dance. Avoiding dichotomies and exaggerated claims, she asks "'how are dancers literate across different kinds of studio activities (teaching and learning technique, making choreographic works, re-staging repertory, documenting artistic practices) and how these dance literacies contribute to creating dance specific knowledge." This practice includes the active use of written texts in the creation of dances, the use of alphabetic and other symbolic writing or notational systems in composing and recording dance, and what feminist and movement theorists have called writing with the body.

Toward an answer, she works with the concept of multimodality, which typically has not considered literacies across the arts. Viewing dance literacy with respect to reading, writing, and uses of written scripts, she suggests that "through multimodality—visual, kinesthetic, aural/oral, tactile, verbal/linguistic, alphabetic/textual modes of communication—dancers produce sensate information about what they see, feel, hear, and sense" (Riggs Leyva 2015). She also explores dancers' production of notational and alphabetic residual texts that support or extend movement texts.

To an unusual degree, Riggs Leyva demonstrates the possibilities of a new approach to literacies, old and new, that is rooted in relationships and eschews opposition and dichotomies and that broadly crosses distinct media and modes of comprehension and communication. Reading and writing across textural, embodied, graphical, spatial, and other symbolic literacies, expressed and understood in multiple media and modes, represents a promising new beginning.

Notes

1. On financial literacy, a Google Search finds 13.4 million items, including Financial Literacy days, months, institutes, academies, courses, requirements, programs. There is a very small critical literature, but enormous marketing. See LiteracyStudies@OSU Interdisciplinary Seminar for Graduate Students financial and health literacy case books, OSU, April 2015: https://literacystudies.osu.edu/sites/literacystudies.osu.edu/files/GradSem%20Financial%20Literacy%20Casebook.pdf and https://literacystudies.osu.edu/sites/literacystudies.osu.edu/files/GradSem%20Health%20Literacy%20Casebook_1.pdf
2. See also Baron, *Reader revealed* (2001); Kertész, *On reading* (1971).
3. Daley is representative of much of the writing about new digital literacies. Nothing seems to have improved in the ensuing decade; Apkon, *Age of the image* (2013), makes similar assertions but is even more lacking in foundation.

4. The notion or discourse—I hesitate to say concept—of multiliteracies has been popularized especially by the New London Group, "A Pedagogy of Multiliteracies: Designing Social Futures," first published in *Harvard Educational Review* (1996) and reprinted in Bill Cope and Mary Kalantzis, *Multiliteracies* (2000) and Kress, *Multimodality* (2010). "Pedagogy of Multiliteracies" has much more to say about design than about literacies or social futures.

5. On critical literacy, see for example Wikipedia entries for "critical literacy" and the online *Critical Literacy Journal*: www.criticalliteracyjournal. org/ and http://teacher.scholastic.com/products/scholasticprofessional/ authors/pdfs/Sample_pages_Critical_literacy.pdf. See also Lankshear and McLaren, *Critical literacy* (1993); Shor, *Empowering education* (1992); Shor, "What is critical literacy?" (1999).

6. Compare Tasneem Raja, "We Can Code It! Why Computer Literacy is Key to Winning the Twenty-First Century," http://www.motherjones. com/meida/2014/06/computer-scienceprogramming-code-diversity-sexism-education, with Chris Granger, "Why Coding is Not the New Literacy," http://www.chris-granger.com/2015/01/26/coding-is-not-the-new-literacy.

7. For critiques, see Hindman, *Myth of digital democracy* (2009); Schiller, *Digital capitalism* (1999).

8. Their notions about literacy are surprisingly limited; consider, for example, Gee, *What video games have to teach us* (2003), Chap. 2.

9. Compare with Wajcman, *Pressed for time* (2015). Cognitive psychologists and others raise objections to educators' approach to "attention" and their use of research results. Many of these works acknowledge a debt to the ahistorical but influential work of Brown and Duguid, *Social life of information* (2000).

10. In addition, see Castells et al., *Mobile communications and society*, 2007; Powers and Jablonski, *Real cyber war*, 2015; Hindman, *Myth of digital democracy* (2009); Brown, *Undoing the demos* (2015), esp. Chap. 6.

11. For the presumption of "acceleration" in literacy studies, see Brandt, *Literacy in American Lives* (2001); Keller, *Chasing literacy*, 2014.

12. *Digital Culture*'s text and notes are marked by a conspicuous absence of references to the huge volume of writings about literacy in any of its forms, as a close look at Chap. 2, "Digital Divides and the Emerging Digital Literacy," indicates. References to Bill Gates, Steve Jobs, technology and the law, and the URLs of online sources dominate, a pattern

that is appropriate to its contents but indicates that he has been captured by the view Doueihi studies.

13. See also diSessa, *Changing minds* (2000); Nunberg, *Future of the book* (1996); Bloch and Hesse, *Future libraries* (1993); Baron, *Better pencil* (2009); Welch, *Electric rhetoric* (1999).

14. Dondis, *Primer of visual literacy* (1973), and Messaris, *Visual literacy* (1994).

15. Dondis, *Primer of visual literacy* (1973), and Messaris, *Visual literacy* (1994) are missing from Goldfarb's bibliography.

16. Useful discussions of visual forms of presenting information in the past for studies of literacy include Carruthers, *Craft of thought* (1998); Carruthers, *Book of memory* (2008); Ong, *Ramus, method, and the decay of dialogue* (1958); Yates, *Arts of memory* (1966); Esrock, *Reader's eye* (1994); Major, *Prints and people* (1971). For the present, see Allwein and Barwise, *Logical reasoning with diagrams* (1966); Bender and Marrinan, *Culture of diagram* (2010); Michael Benson, with reply by Privamvada Nataragan, "What Astro Images Do," *NYRB*, July 9, 2015; Benedict T. Carey, "Learning to See Data," *NYT*, March 29, 2015; Klapisch-Zuber, "Tree," (2007); Larkin and Simon, "Why a diagram" (1987); Lima, *Book of trees* (2014); Pettersson, "Information design theories" (2014); Tufte, *Visual display* (1983); Tufte, *Envisioning information* (1990); Tufte, *Visual explanations* (1997); Tufte, *Beautiful evidence* (2006).

17. See also McCloud, *Reinventing comics* (2000); McCloud, *Making comics* (2006); and the underdeveloped although forward-looking Sousanis, *Unflattening* (2015). McCloud's *Understanding Comics* is a much smarter book than *Unflattening*.

18. See also Moje et al., "The complex world of adolescent literacy" (2008).

19. There are major debates about actual supply and demand, and needs, quality, and quantity of students and trained workers. See the brief discussion and references in Chap. 5.

20. Trefil, *Why science?* (2008), by a coeditor of the *Dictionary of Cultural Literacy*; Mooney and Kirshenbaum, *Unscientific America* (2009).

21. See also Laugksch, "Scientific literacy" (2000); Linder et al., *Exploring the landscape of scientific literacy* (2011).

22. On numeracy, see Crump, *Anthropology of numbers* (1990); Colleen Flaherty, "Just how much math, and what kind, is enough for life sciences majors?" *CHE*, April 24, 2015; Hallett, "Role of the mathematics

course" (2002); Moses and Cobb, *Radical equations* (2001); Samson, "From writing to doing" (2014); Steen, "Numeracy" (1999); Steen, *Achieving quantitative literacy* (2004); Van Dyke, Malloy, and Stallings, "An activity to encourage writing in mathematics" (2014); Whitin and Whitin, *Learning to read the numbers* (2011). On science education with respect to the environment, see Golley, *Primer for environmental literacy* (1998); Stone and Barlow, *Ecological literacy* (2005).On science education more generally, see Michael Anft, "The STEM Crisis: Reality or Myth?" *CHE*, Nov. 11, 2013; NRC, *From analysis to action* (1996); Nelson, "Science literacy" (1999); Privamvada Natarajan, "What scientists really do," *NYRB*, Oct. 5, 2014; Samson, "From writing to doing" (2014); Thomas and Kondo, *Towards scientific literacy*, 1978.

23. Gia Kourlas, "Life a Blizzard of Dance Fragments," *NYT*, Oct 29, 2013.
24. Disclaimer: I was a member of Riggs Leyva's dissertation committee, and she completed the Graduate Interdisciplinary Specialization in Literacy Studies, which I direct.

References

Alexander, Jonathan. (2006) *Digital youth: Emerging literacies in the World Wide Web*. Cresskill, N.J.: Hampton Press.

Allwein, Gerard, and Jon Barwise, eds. (1966) *Logical reasoning with diagrams*. New York: Oxford University Press.

Apkon, Stephen. (2013) *The age of the image: Redefining literacy in a world of screens*. New York: Farrar, Straus, and Giroux.

Banaji, Shakuntala, and David Buckingham. (2013) *The civic web: Young people, the Internet and civic participation*. John D. and Catharine T. MacArthur Foundation Series on Digital Media and Learning. Cambridge, Mass.: MIT Press.

Baron, Dennis. (2009) *A better pencil: Readers, writers, and the digital revolution*. New York: Oxford University Press.

Baron, Naomi S. (2008) *Always on: Language in an online and digital world*. New York: Oxford University Press.

Baron, Naomi S. (2015) *Words onscreen: The fate of reading in a digital world*. New York: Oxford University Press.

Baron, Sabrina Alcorn, with Elizabeth Walsh and Susan Scola, eds. (2001) *The reader revealed*. Washington, D.C.: Folger Shakespeare Library.

Bauer, Henry H. (1992) *Scientific literacy and the myth of the scientific method.* Champaign: University of Illinois Press.

Bauman, Richard, and Charles L. Briggs. (1990) Poetics and performance as critical perspectives on language and social life. *Annual Review of Anthropology* 19: 59–88.

Baynham, Mike, and Mastin Prinsloo, eds. (2009) *The future of literacy studies.* London: Palgrave Macmillan.

Bender, John, and Michael Marrinan. (2010) *The culture of diagram.* Stanford: Stanford University Press.

Berkman, Nancy D., Terry C. Davis, and Lauren McCormack. (2010) Health literacy: What is it? *Journal of Health Communication* 15, suppl. 2: 9–19.

Bloch, R. Howard, and Carla Hesse, eds. (1993) *Future libraries.* Berkeley: University of California Press. Boyd, Danah. (2014). *It's complicated: The lives of networked teens.* New Haven: Yale University Press.

Brandt, Deborah. (2001) *Literacy in American lives.* Cambridge: Cambridge University Press.

Brown, John Seeley, and Paul Duguid. (2000) *The social life of information.* Boston: Harvard Business School Press.

Brown, Wendy. (2015) *Undoing the demos: Neoliberalism's stealth revolution.* New York: Zone Books.

Calhoun, Daniel. (1973) *The intelligence of a people.* Princeton: Princeton University Press.

Carr, Nicholas. (2010) *The shallows: What the Internet is doing to our brains.* New York: Norton.

Carruthers, Mary. (1998) *The craft of thought: Meditation, rhetoric, and the making of images, 400–1200.* Cambridge: Cambridge University Press.

Carruthers, Mary. (2008) *The book of memory: A study of memory in Medieval culture.* 2d ed. Cambridge: Cambridge University Press.

Castells, Manuel, Mireia Fernández-Ardèvol, Jack Linchuan Qui, and Araba Sey. (2007) *Mobile communications and society: A global perspective.* Cambridge, Mass.: MIT Press.

Center for Science, Mathematics, and Engineering Education, National Research Council (NRC). (1996). *From analysis to action: Undergraduate education in science, mathematics, engineering, and technology.* Washington D.C.: National Academy Press.

Cope, Bill, and Mary Kalantzis, eds. (2000) *Multiliteracies: Literacy learning and the design of social futures.* London: Routledge.

Crump, Thomas. (1990) *The anthropology of numbers*. Cambridge: Cambridge University Press.

Daley, Elizabeth. (2003) Expanding the concept of literacy. *EDUCAUSE Review*: 32–40.

Davidson, Cathy N. (2011) *Now you see it: How the brain science of attention will change how we live, work and learn*. New York: Viking.

Davidson, Cathy N., and David Theo Goldberg, with Zoë Marie Jones. (2010) *The future of thinking: Learning institutions in a digital age*. John T. and Catherine D. MacArthur Foundation Reports on Digital Media and Learning. Cambridge, Mass.: MIT Press.

Dehaene, Stanislas. (2009) *Reading in the brain: The science and evolution of a human invention*. New York: Viking.

Dils, Ann. (2007) Why dance literacy? *Journal of the Canadian Association for Curriculum Studies* 5: 95–113.

diSessa, Andrea A. (2000) *Changing minds: Computers, learning, and literacy*. Cambridge, Mass: MIT Press.

Dondis, Donis A. (1973) *A primer of visual literacy*. Cambridge, Mass: MIT Press.

Drucker, Johanna. (2014) *Graphesis: Visual forms of knowledge production*. Cambridge, Mass: Harvard University Press.

Dyson, Anne Haas. (1989) *Multiple worlds of child writers: Friends learning to write*. New York: Teachers College Press.

Dyson, Anne Haas. (2003) "Welcome to the jam": Popular culture, school literacy, and the making of childhoods. *Harvard Educational Review* 79: 328–361.

Dyson, Anne Hass. (2013) *Rewriting the basics: Literacy learning in children's cultures*. New York: Teachers College Press.

Elkins, James, ed. (2008) *Visual literacy*. Milton Park, Abingdon, and New York: Routledge.

Esrock, Ellen J. (1994) *The reader's eye: Visual imaging as reader response*. Baltimore: Johns Hopkins University Press.

Ferguson, Eugene S. (1977) The mind's eye: Nonverbal thought in technology. *Science* 197: 827–836.

Ferguson, Eugene S. (1992) *Engineering and the mind's eye*. Cambridge, Mass: MIT Press.

Finnegan, Ruth. (1988). *Literacy and Orality: Studies in the technology of communication*. Oxford: Blackwell.

Gee, James Paul. (2003). *What video games have to teach us about learning and literacy*. Palgrave Macmillan.

Goldfarb, Brian. (2002) *Visual pedagogy: Media cultures in and beyond the classroom.* Durham: Duke University Press.

Golley, Frank. (1998) *A primer for environmental literacy.* New Haven: Yale University Press.

Graff, Harvey J. (2011) *Literacy myths, legacies, and lessons: New studies on literacy.* New Brunswick, N.J.: Transaction.

Graff, Harvey J., and John Duffy. (2007) The literacy myth. *Encyclopedia of language and education*, vol. 2, *Literacy*, ed. Brian Street, 41–52; Nancy Hornberger, general editor. Berlin and New York: Springer.

Hallett, Deborah Hughes. (2002) The role of mathematics courses in the development of quantitative literacy. In *Quantitative Literacy: Why Numeracy Matters for Schools and Colleges*, ed. Bernard L. Madison, 91–98. National Council on Education and the Disciplines, Woodrow Wilson Fellowship Foundation.

Hartley, John. (2009) *The uses of digital literacy.* New Brunswick, NJ: Transaction.

Hindman, Matthew. (2009) *The myth of digital democracy.* Princeton: Princeton University Press.

Ito, Mizuko, Heather Horst, Matteo Bittanti, Danah Boyd, Becky Herr-Stephenson, Patricia G. Lange, C. J. Pasco, and Laura Robinson. (2009) *Living and learning with new media: Summary of findings from the Digital Youth Project.* John D. and Catherine T. MacArthur Foundation Reports on Digital Media and Learning. Cambridge, Mass.: MIT Press.

Ito, Mizuko, Sonja Baumer, Matteo Bittanti, Danah Boyd, Rachel Cody, Becky Herr-Stephenson, Heather A. Horst, Patrician G. Lange, Dilan Mahendran, Katynka K. Martínez, C. J. Pascoe, Dan Perkel, Laura Robinson, Christo Sims, and Lisa Tripp, with Judd Antin, Megan Finn, Arthur Law, Annie Manion, Sarai Mitnick, David Schlossberg, and Sarita Yardi. (2010) *Hanging out, messing around, and geeking out.* John D. and Catherine T. MacArthur Foundation Reports on Digital Media and Learning. Cambridge, Mass.: MIT Press.

Jenkins, Henry, with Ravi Purushotma, Margaret Weigel, Katie Clinton, and Alice J. Robison. (2009) *Confronting the challenges of participatory culture: Media education for the 21st century.* John D. and Catherine T. MacArthur Foundation Reports on Digital Media and Learning. Cambridge, Mass: MIT Press.

Keller, Daniel. (2014) *Chasing literacy and reading and writing in an age of acceleration.* Logan: Utah State University Press.

Kertész, André. 1971. *On reading.* London: Penguin.

Klapisch-Zuber, Christiane. (2007) The tree. In Anthony Molho and Diogo Ramda Curto, eds., *Finding Europe: Discourses and margins, communities, images, ca. 16th–ca. 18th centuries*, 293–313. New York and Oxford: Berghahn.

Kress, Gunther. (2010) *Multimodalilty: A social semiotic approach to contemporary communication*. London: Routledge.

Landay, Eileen, and Kurt Wootton. (2012) *A reason to read: Linking literacy and the arts*. Cambridge, Mass.: Harvard Education Press.

Lankshear, Colin, and Peter L. McLaren, eds. (1993) *Critical literacy: Politics, praxis, and the postmodern*. Albany: State University of New York Press.

Larkin, Jill H., and Herbert A Simon. (1987) Why a diagram is (sometimes) worth ten thousand words. *Cognitive Science* 11: 65–99.

Laugksch, Rüdiger C. (2000) Scientific literacy: A conceptual overview. *Science Education* 84: 71–94.

Lima, Manuel. (2014) *The book of trees: Visualizing branches of knowledge*. New York: Princeton Architectural Press.

Linder, Cedric, Leif Östman, Douglas A. Roberts, Per-Olof Wickman, Gaalen Ericksen, and Allan MacKinnon, eds. (2011) *Exploring the landscape of scientific literacy*. London: Routledge.

Major, A. Hyatt. (1971) *Prints and people: A social history of printed pictures*. Princeton: Princeton University Press.

McChesney, Robert W. (2004) *The problem of the media: U.S. communication politics in the 21st century*. New York: Monthly Review Press.

McCloud, Scott. (1993) *Understanding comics: The invisible art*. New York: Harper.

McCloud, Scott. (2000) *Reinventing comics: How imagination and technology are revolutionizing an art form*. New York: Harper.

McCloud, Scott. (2006) *Making comics: Storytelling secrets of comics, manga and graphic novels*. New York: Harper.

Messaris, Paul. (1994) *Visual literacy: Image, mind, and reality*. Boulder, Colo.: Westview.

Miller, Arthur L. (2000) *Insights of genius: Imagery and creativity in science and art*. Cambridge, Mass: MIT Press.

Moje, Elizabeth Birr, Melanie Overby, Nicole Tysvaer, and Karen Morris. (2008) The complex world of adolescent literacy: Myths, motivations, and mysteries. *Harvard Educational Review* 78: 107–154.

Mooney, Chris, and Sheril Kirshenbaum. (2009) *Unscientific America: How scientific illiteracy threatens our future*. New York: Basic Books.

Moses, Robert P., and Charles E. Cobb Jr. 2001. *Radical equations: Civil rights from Mississippi to the Algebra Project*. Boston: Beacon Press.

Nelson, George D. (1999) Science literacy for all in the 21ˢᵗ century. *Educational Leadership* 57: 14–17.

New London Group. (1996) A pedagogy of multiliteracies: Designing social futures. *Harvard Educational Review* 66: 60–92.

Norris, Stephen P., and Linda M. Phillips. (2003) How literacy in its fundamental sense is central to scientific literacy. *Science Education* 87: 224–240.

Norris, Stephen P., and Linda M. Phillips. (2009) Scientific literacy. In David R. Olson and Nancy Torrance, eds., *The Cambridge handbook of literacy*, 271–285. Cambridge: Cambridge University Press.

Nunberg, Geoffrey, ed. (1996) *The future of the book*. Berkeley: University of California Press.

Ong, Walter J. (1958) *Ramus, method, and the decay of dialogue*. Cambridge, Mass: Harvard University Press.

Palfrey, John, and Urs Gasser. (2010) *Born digital: Understanding the first generation of digital natives*. New York: Basic Books.

Pauwels, Luc, ed. (2006) *Visual cultures of science: Rethinking representational practices in knowledge building and science communication*. Hanover, N.H.: Dartmouth College Press.

Peterson, Pamela N., Susan M. Shetterly, Christina L. Clarke, David B. Bekelman, Paul S. Chan, Larry A. Allen, Daniel D. Matlock, David J. Magid, and Frederick A. Masoudi. (2011) Health literacy and outcomes among patients with heart failure. *JAMA* 305(16): 1695–1701.

Pettersson, Rune. (2014) Information design theories. *Journal of Visual Literacy* 33: 1–94.

Powers, Shawn M., and Michael Jablonski. (2015) *The real cyber war: The political economy of Internet freedom*. Champaign: University of Illinois Press.

Riggs Leyva, Rachael. (2015) Dance literacy in the studio: Partnering movement texts and residual texts. Ph.D. diss., Ohio State University.

Roth, Wolff-Michael, and Angela Calabrese Barton. (2004) *Rethinking scientific literacy*. London: Routledge.

Samson, Ghislain. (2014) From writing to doing: The challenges of implementing integration (and interdisciplinarity) in the teaching of mathematics, sciences, and technology. *Canadian Journal of Science, Mathematics, and Technology Education* 14: 346–358.

Schiller, Dan. (1999) *Digital capitalism: Networking the global market system*. Cambridge, Mass: MIT Press.

Schiller, Dan. (2014) *Digital depression: Information technology and economic crisis*. Urbana: University of Illinois Press.

Selber, Stuart A. (2004) *Multiliteracies for a new world*. Carbondale: Southern Illinois University Press.

Shor, Ira. (1992) *Empowering education: Critical teaching for social change*. Chicago: University of Chicago Press.

Shor, Ira. (1999) What is critical literacy? *Journal for Pedagogy, Pluralism and Practice*, http://www.lesley.edu/journals/jppp/4/shor.html

Sousanis, Nick. (2015) *Unflattening*. Cambridge, Mass: Harvard University Press.

Steen, Lynn Arthur. (1999) Numeracy: The new literacy for a data-drenched society. *Educational Leadership* 57: 8–13.

Steen, Lynn Arthur. (2004) *Achieving quantitative literacy: An urgent challenge for higher education*. Washington, D.C.: Mathematical Association of America.

Stewart, Garrett. (2006) *The look of reading: Book, painting, text*. Chicago: University of Chicago Press.

Stone, Michael K., and Zenobia Barlow, eds. (2005) *Ecological literacy: Educating our children for a sustainable world*. San Francisco: Sierra Club.

Thomas, Frederick J., and Allan S. Kondo. (1978) *Towards scientific literacy. Literacy in development*. International Institute for Adult Literacy Methods. Tehran, Iran: Hulton Educational Publishing.

Trefil, James. (2008) *Why science?* New York: Teachers College Press and National Science Teachers Association Press.

Tufte, Edward T. (1983) *The visual display of quantitative information*. Cheshire, Conn.: Graphics Press.

Tufte, Edward T. (1990) *Envisioning information*. Cheshire, Conn: Graphics Press.

Tufte, Edward T. (1997) *Visual explanations: Images and quantities, evidence and narrative*. Cheshire, Conn: Graphics Press.

Tufte, Edward T. (2006) *Beautiful evidence*. Cheshire, Conn: Graphics Press.

Tyner, Kathleen. (1998) *Literacy in the digital world: Teaching and learning in the age of information*. Mahwah, NJ: Lawrence Erlbaum.

Tyner, Kathleen, ed. (2010) *Media literacy: New agendas in communication*. London: Routledge.

Van Dyke, Frances, Elizabeth J. Malloy, and Virginia Stallings. 2014. An activity to encourage writing in mathematics. *Canadian Journal of Science, Mathematics, and Technology Education* 14: 371–387.

Wajcman, Judy. (2015) *Pressed for time: The acceleration of life in digital capitalism*. Chicago: University of Chicago Press.

Welch, Kathleen E. (1999) *Electric rhetoric: Classical rhetoric, oralism, and a new literacy*. Cambridge, Mass.: MIT Press.

Whitin, David J., and Phyllis E. Whitin. (2011) *Learning to read the numbers: Integrating critical literacy and critical numeracy in K–9 classrooms*. New York: Routledge and National Council of Teachers of English.

Wolf, Maryanne. (2007) *Proust and the squid: The story and science of the reading brain*. New York: Harper.

Yates, Frances. (1966) *The arts of memory*. London: Routledge.

Zarcadoolas, Christina, Andrew Pleasant, and David S. Greer. (2006) *Advancing health literacy*. San Francisco: Jossey-Bass.

7

Historicizing Literacy and Literacy Studies: Axioms and Lessons

The history of literacy matters. All of the issues taken up in this book have a historical foundation: materially, epistemologically, and discursively. Yet when an implicit appeal is made to history, a series of dichotomous shifts constitutes the determinative narrative of literacy. Whether proclaimed positively as a literacy episteme or more critically as the literacy myth, a sense of stages in vague chronological order undergirds prevailing views of human history, with passages from mark, sign, or symbol to alphabet; oral to literate, speech to writing; memory to written record; script to print; collective to individual practice, aloud to silent activity; classical to vernacular, elite to popular; informally learned to schooled; sacred to secular; traditional to modern; printed to electronic; old to new. Dichotomies have substituted for relationships, assumptions for evidence and arguments. Although strong theories that emphasize great divides, radical transformations, and technological determinism have been modified, the presumption of epochal shifts has hardly disappeared. Literacy is linked to perceptions and expectations of *change*, when its experience is certainly as much associated with *continuities*.

The epistemology of transformation is powerful and appealing. We want to believe in the power of literacy (Graff and Duffy 2007). It is generally reassuring and confirming. For the West and for educators, it is

© The Author(s), under exclusive license to Springer Nature Switzerland AG 2022
H. J. Graff, *Searching for Literacy*, https://doi.org/10.1007/978-3-030-96981-3_7

not simply foundational; it is self-serving and often profitable. To some degree, its sway comes from the fact that it is partly true; on that basis, it has become constitutive of an embracing, hegemonic sense of reality. But that is how myths operate.

I end this book with a chapter on history because the study and understanding of literacy have not yet sufficiently assimilated the arguments and implications of the impressive body of writings in the history of literacy that has developed since the late 1970s. For example, David Olson (1994) includes references to a few works from that decade, but little that has been done since then. More importantly, he fails to read with an eye to either historical debates and historical context or significant criticisms that historians have made of dominant theories. Deborah Brandt (2015) cites the historical literature but sees only a shift from "reading over writing" to a more recent "writing over reading." The historical scholarship is central to understanding and practicing literacy. We live that out daily, conceptually, ideologically, institutionally, and in terms of policy.[1]

Literacy, History, and Myths

Until quite recently, and to a considerable extent still, the construction that I call the literacy myth substituted for a history. At the same time, it claimed to have a historical foundation. As John Duffy and I wrote in 2007:

> The Literacy Myth refers to the belief, articulated in educational, civic, religious, and other settings, contemporary and historical, that the acquisition of literacy is a necessary precursor to and invariably results in economic development, democratic practice, cognitive enhancement, and upward social mobility. Despite many unsuccessful attempts to measure it, literacy in this formulation has been invested with immeasurable and indeed almost ineffable qualities, purportedly conferring on practitioners a predilection toward social order, an elevated moral sense, and a metaphorical "state of grace." Such presumptions have a venerable historical lineage and have been expressed, in different forms, from antiquity through the Renaissance and the Reformation, and again throughout the era of the Enlightenment, during which literacy was linked to progress

order, transformation, and control. Associated with these beliefs is the conviction that the benefits ascribed to literacy cannot be attained in other ways, nor can they be attributed to other factors, whether economic, political, cultural, or individual. Rather, literacy stands alone as the independent and critical variable. (Graff and Duffy 2007, 41)

Taken together, these attitudes constitute the literacy myth.

The conception and power of the literacy myth depend, on the one hand, on the understanding of myth, including myth as a mode of understanding and communication, and, on the other hand, on history, the shaping power of the past.

History contributes a much needed sense of perspective that allows us to reach out for new, different, and even multiple understandings of ourselves and others, often in their interrelationships. History mandates focusing and refocusing the lenses of time, place, and alternative spaces and developments. It probes and prompts us to comprehend what has been, what might have been, and what might be, foregrounding choice, agency, and possibility, in both their fullness and their limits. Its values and virtues are rooted in the powers of comparison and criticism, taken together. An underutilized font of valuable critique, history can also be a source of liberation, offering us mental freedom from the fetters of the present as well as the past. Historical analysis and interpretation often have great power in stimulating fresh views, novel questions, and new understandings.

This is the past alive in the present and shaping the future, not a dead hand hanging over us. It is a human and social science. This is the practice that I have tried to develop from *The Literacy Myth* (1979, 1991) through my subsequent research on the history of literacy. The powerful hold of the assumed past over the present in the historically derivative but ahistorical literacy myth (and the so-called literacy episteme) demands no less.

Myth is a mode of analysis, understanding, and communication that draws upon but distorts history. Myth itself becomes a mode of interpretation, explaining the present by way of a narrative, and a means of communicating that understanding. The literacy myth must be recognized and criticized as both ideology and culture. A historical analysis also mandates critical exploration of the relationships among material reality, social structures and relations, institutions, policy, expectations, and social theory.

Yet the central role of myth is often misunderstood: Such attitudes about literacy represent a myth because they exist apart from and beyond empirical evidence that might clarify the actual functions, meanings, and effects of reading and writing in practice. Like all myths, the literacy myth is not so much a falsehood but an expression of the ideology of those who sanction it and are invested in its outcomes. For this reason, the literacy myth is powerful, resistant to revision, and longstanding (Graff and Duffy 2007, 42).

In contrast to popular notions, myth is not synonymous with the fictive or the false. By definition and by means of the cultural work they perform, myths cannot be wholly untrue. For a myth to gain acceptance, it must be grounded in at least some aspects of perceived reality and cannot explicitly contradict common ways of thinking or shared expectations. Partial truths are not simple falsehoods or denials; rather, they involve obfuscations and distortions that tend to reinforce certain assumptions and viewpoints.

The problems inherent in the literacy myth start with confusions over the meanings of literacy and efforts to measure it. Literacy has been defined in various ways, many offering imprecise, yet progressively grander conceptions and expectations of what it means to read and write and what might follow from those practices, attitudinally and cognitively, individually and collectively. The vagueness of these definitions allows for conceptions of literacy that go beyond what has been examined empirically, investing literacy with the status of myth. Since mythos is grounded in narrative, and since narratives are fundamentally expressions of values, literacy has been contrasted in its mythic form with a series of opposing values that have resulted in reductive dichotomies that caricature major social changes. In such hierarchical structures, the oral, preliterate, and illiterate serve as the marked and subordinate terms, whereas literate and literacy assume the status of superior terms. These hierarchies reinforce the presumed benefits of literacy and thus contribute to the power of the myth.

Only by grounding definitions of literacy in specific, contextualized, and historical particulars can we avoid conferring on literacy the status of myth. In contrast with its presumed transformative consequences, literacy historically has been characterized by tensions, continuities, and contradictions. In sum, when examined closely, literacy's history often contradicts the literacy myth.

Nonetheless, major elements of the literacy myth continue to exert powerful influence: the myth of a literacy decline; the myth of the superiority of the Greek or western alphabet; the myth of literacy's link to economic development and social advancement; and the myth of literacy as essential for, and even producing democracy. In contemporary popular discourse, literacy is represented as an unqualified good, a marker of progress, and a metaphorical light making clear the pathway to happiness and success. Illiteracy, by contrast, is associated with ignorance, incompetence, and darkness—indeed, the absence of civilization.

In this discourse, the decline of literacy is taken as an omnipresent or imminent threat and signifies the end of individual advancement, social progress, and the health of the democracy. These associations represent a powerful variant of the literacy myth. That the myth of decline is largely unsupported by empirical evidence has done little to reduce its potency in contemporary discourse (McQuillan 1998; St. Clair and Sadlin 2004; Kaestle et al. 1991). Rather, the myth is argued by anecdote and presumptions of dichotomous transformations, often rooted in nostalgia for the recent past, and selective readings of evidence. The myth of decline neglects the changing modes of communication, in particular the increasing importance of media that do not depend completely on print. Literacy myths are also rooted in culture and ideology, institutions and policies.

The bias toward the alphabet resulted in what its proponents and their critics have called a great divide, with rational, scientific, individualistic literate peoples on one side, and non-logical, credulous, communal, oral peoples on the other. (See Chaps. 2–3 above, as well as Goody and Watt 1968; compare with Duffy 2007; Finnegan 1973; Gough 1968.) The assumed link between literacy and economic success is one of the cornerstones of western modernization theories. Literacy or at least a minimal amount of education is presumed to be necessary and sufficient for overcoming poverty and surmounting limitations rooted in racial, ethnic, gender, and religious differences. Implicit in this formulation is the belief that individual achievement may reduce the effects of ascribed social status and structural inequalities. Despite these expectations, there is little evidence that increasing or high levels of literacy result directly in major economic advances; in fact, they may well follow from and depend upon those advances. The same expectations influence thinking about women's literacy provision and fertility limitation. Here, too, the evidence is mixed and the connection complex, with little support for an independent role for literacy. Although literacy and education can and have been used to stimulate democratic discourse and practices, literacy has also been used to foster political repression and maintain inequitable social conditions.

Literacy myths live on among the public, policy makers, and a number of academics. The consequences are enormous and often deleterious. The need for critical historical analysis remains compelling. The literacy myth is powerful, resilient, flexible, complex, and historically rooted. Characterized by its contradictoriness, it is marked by the long duration of its hegemony. It is also marked by its potential to work constructively and progressively but at the same time with limiting or negative force, for both individuals and groups.

For some groups, most impressively in the United States for African Americans who were denied literacy by slave codes, their history and faith joined with the literacy myth's promise of the benefits of reading and writing to push and pull many people to literacy. Those who had been excluded came to share the common belief in the value of schooling with special fervor. For others, the contradictions were too great, the opportunities to gain and practice reading and writing too limited, the payoffs neither frequent nor clear. For many blacks today and recently, the power of the literacy myth has waned, in part owing to its contradictory outcomes; in impoverished communities, even school success does not guarantee stable employment or overcome discrimination. For those with initial social and cultural advantages, by contrast, the promise seemed to be fulfilled. Their success was not always incumbent on their literacy, but their experience stood in support of ideologies rooted in access to and achievement in school. Those who did not secure the presumed benefits of literacy were often blamed for their own failure. The literacy myth serves to organize, simultaneously focus but obscure, and offer an explanation for an impressive array of social, economic, and political assumptions, expectations, observations, and theories, on the one hand, and institutions, policies, and their workings, on the other hand. Powerful contradictions lie at its core and in its consequences.

In the case of the United States, but elsewhere too, the partial truths of the literacy myth functioned within the context of the political and moral economies, political and social ideology, and dominant culture, as they developed historically. Elemental struggles took place between ideologies of social progress or individual success and those of societal decline or personal failure in the specific contexts of transformations to commercial and then industrial capitalism in an avowedly democratic republic. In the conflicts between the promise of progress and the threat of decline lay many of the ideological and practical contradictions of literacy: from literacy as liberating to literacy as restricted and socially and culturally controlling. In other words, the vexed question of success versus failure, and their social and cultural correlates, lay at the core of the development of mass compulsory schooling and its contradictions.

A larger understanding follows from the historical development of school systems in relationship with changing social hierarchies. This effort pivoted on schools' ability to create a common denominator of a relatively low level of mass literacy. This level of literacy often contributed more to social order, cultural cohesion, and political stability than other possible ends. A peculiarly American synthesis relating to what I have called the moral bases of literacy (1991) took hold despite some telling conflicts, especially the denial of literacy to slaves at a time when reading was linked with individual religious and political salvation. A single standard of language, heritage, history, values, and personal characteristics became dominant, although this diverse society was divided by class, race, ethnicity, national origins, and gender. In their own historical timing, these connections were associated with a massive shift toward the consensus that illiteracy was becoming a greater danger than literacy, especially if literacy was not acquired independently but through supervised instruction. Mass literacy required social and individual controls, standardized texts, proper tutelage, and a special environment, all embodied in the common school. Here were the engines and the hallmarks of the literacy myth.

Within the synthesis that gave rise to, promoted, and long maintained the hegemony of the literacy myth were dreams and experiences of upward social mobility—making it in America; an evangelical Protestantism rooted in salvation for the individual and safe progress for the nation; a class structure inseparable from capitalism, its needs, and its costs; meritocratic and stratified notions of egalitarianism; radical individualism rooted in social inequalities and conflict, including race, class, gender, ethnic and national origins, age, and region among other distinctions; and limits to collective action. In this constellation of factors, literacy represented an achievement, but for many people it had limited usefulness and rewards. Literacy did not guarantee social mobility, and above that threshold other factors mattered more. Failure, however, had at least as powerful an impact as success. The consequences were deemed to be the responsibility of individuals and families, not of society or schools.

In its American setting, the literacy myth also held out the promise that achievement would replace social ascription—the identities attributed to persons on the basis of their race, ethnicity, national origin, class, and gender, for example—as the main determinant of social position. In these and related ways, schools were central to the diffusion of democratic culture and ideals, but they also mediated the contradictions between those ideals and continuing social inequality. The concomitants and limitations of school achievement cut deeply into this cultural process. Literacy as symbol and as fact did not always work well together, whether for guaranteeing social order, enabling individuals to secure jobs, or entitling them to full citizenship.

Myths can be expressions of collective desires and of the differential agency and power of the many and the few. Perhaps the literacy myth expresses a hope that literacy alone is enough to end poverty, elevate human dignity, and promote a just and democratic world. A less benign reading is that the literacy myth is a means through which the rich and powerful have obscured the actual causes of social and economic inequities in Western society. In this view, literacy is a symptom and a symbol. Both beliefs have been at play at different times and for different groups. Uncritical acceptance of the literacy myth leads to serious misunderstandings of the nature of literacy, its development, uses, and potentials to foster or inhibit social and economic development.

To argue that literacy has been accorded the status of myth is not to discount the importance or reading and writing in the past or present. However, we do well to contrast the literacy myth, which seamlessly connects literacy to individual and collective advancement, with the more complex and often contradictory patterns that emerge from studies of literacy's historical and recent development and practice.

From Myths to Histories of Literacy

Research on the history of literacy has developed significantly since the 1960s and 1970s. The maturation of this field has been enormously beneficial, inside the academy and on occasion beyond its walls. This significant body of scholarship demands attention more broadly, both in terms of what it may contribute to other researchers, planners, and thinkers, and in terms of its own growing needs for inter- and intra-disciplinary cooperation and constructive criticism. For example, historical literary studies have long been marked by their attention to the use of quantitative data and to issues of its accuracy and representativeness. As important as that has been to intellectual advances, that emphasis has also become a limitation on new conceptualizations and interpretations. Distinctions between quantities and qualities and between individuals and collectivities complicate questions of interpretation and meaning, as well as source criticism and research design.

After the 1970s, the main trends in historical studies included the construction of larger, more detailed databases, usually but not always from signatory or census sources; greater concern for a better grounded and more contextual interpretation of changing patterns, especially of distributions and differentiations in levels of literacy; systematic efforts to relate trends in literacy to social and economic developments, institutional interventions, and state activities, especially such factors as the availability of formal schooling and public school systems; greater attention to the effects of political transformations and events such as the French Revolution and to the ideological aspects of the subject; concern with class formation; analysis of the uses of literacy in terms of patterns of reading and writing and of individual and group-level attitudinal and psychological changes; and an increased awareness of the contradictory nature of the subject and of the difficulties involved in building historical interpretations upon a quantitative analysis of secular trend lines and patterns of distribution and differentiation. The value of comparative frameworks was also recognized, though comparative studies remained rare.

We now know much more about literacy's social patterns over time and the fairly systematic and patterned variations in its distributions over time and place. We are perhaps also more hesitant and cautious in explanation and attribution of meaning.

At the same time as research advanced, the subject of literacy was discovered by an increasing number of other historically minded social scientists. Literacy increasing featured in studies of economic change, demographic behavior, cultural development and conflict, class formation and stratification, collective actions of all kinds, and family formation and structures. Revealingly, in these studies literacy tended to be conceptualized as an independent variable, which was presumably useful in explaining shifts in another, dependent variable that was itself the object of more direct and sustained study (Graff 2010, 2011).

In the growing numbers of studies which took literacy itself as the central object of study and discussion, literacy could be and was conceptualized as either or both dependent or independent variable. At once a source of analytic and conceptual flexibility, this ambiguity could also be a problem and a source of interpretive confusion and weakness. Unfortunately, the character of literacy as a variable is rarely examined systematically.

Historians whose primary interests lay in cultural, printing and publishing, or literary questions increasingly considered literacy within their purview. Although in early research they rarely studied levels and patterns of literacy directly, they presumed it a central factor or parameter for their own work. Such studies include histories of the press and newspapers, *l'histoire du livre* (the history of the book), studies of popular culture, which were characterized by an interest in oral culture and its interactions with the written and printed, and histories of print and publishing.

The work of Robert Darnton (1972, 1982, 1983, 1984), Elizabeth Eisenstein (1979), and Roger Chartier (1987, 1989) exemplifies these intellectual trends. We have learned much from this body of work, but it remains relatively unconnected to work focused directly on literacy itself.[2]

Virtually all this scholarly work has labored under the specter and shadows of modernization theories, with make strong assumptions about literacy's role, powers, and provenance. Some researchers have challenged the assumptions of modernization's links to and impacts upon literacy (or vice versa). Others have assimilated their work within modernization theories, suffering conceptual and interpretive difficulties as a result. In some cases, assumptions substitute for empirical research and critical examination. Modernization theory, too, carried and reinforces traditional dichotomies, none of which is interpretively rich or complex enough to advance our understanding.

Themes in the History of Literacy

Despite their limitations, more than thirty years' historiography of literacy, harvested carefully, yields a rich crop of approaches, themes, and lessons. Although my discussion of this scholarship is highly selective rather than comprehensive, it demonstrates the fruits of rigorous research and careful interpretation. At the same time, the history of literacy remains contested terrain, for it involves large questions about the relationships tying literacy to learning, schooling, and education, on the one hand, and, on the other hand, to their developmental consequences for groups and individuals. Still common assumptions of simplicity, directness, and linearity fall quickly to the quagmire that obstructs the progress of the harvester. In the themes and lessons considered, we also find important parallels between historical foundations and developments and contemporary configurations and their crises (Graff 1995b).

Historicity and Complexity

The *historicity* of literacy constitutes a first and foundational theme, from which many other key imperatives and implications follow. Several decades of serious, often revisionary, scholarship and criticism join in the conclusion that reading and writing, whatever their requirements or consequences, take on their meaning and acquire their value only in concrete historical circumstances that mediate in specific terms whatever general or supposedly universal attributes or concomitants may be claimed for literacy. Ranging from ancient literacy to proclaimed postmodern literacies, this holds true for literacy's uses both practical and symbolic, as studies of the past three millennia show. Awareness of this historicity, which gains support from contemporary research in anthropology, psychology, and literary criticism, is perhaps the single most significant contribution of recent historic al scholarship, even if the point requires wider broadcast. Indeed, the conceptualization, assumptions, and expectations we bring to considerations of reading and writing are revised radically when literacy is revisioned historically. In many ways, some indicated here, history may also serve as a special laboratory to enrich our understanding of literacy in theory and practice. Historical developments provide opportunities to test theories and evaluate policies and institutional arrangements. The challenges of precise comparison across space as well as time loom large. But it is clear that the search for and expectation of interrelationships among literacies and in theory and practice of literacy must replace the dominance of dichotomies and presumptions of transformation.

Conversely, although seldom appreciated, present-day conceptions, arrangements, and practices of literacy as well as schooling and learning are historically founded and grounded. They are also strong and powerfully resistant to change. Ignorance of the circumstances in which crucial concepts, arrangements, and expectations were fashioned, the means by which they have been maintained, and their consequences severely limit and sometimes directly contradict contemporary analysis, diagnosis, prescription. The frequent use of this medical metaphor is itself part of this history.[3]

Closely related is the idea that literacy, learning, and schooling, along with the uses of reading and writing, are simple, unproblematic notions. Studies reveal that this is a historical myth. Past and recent experiences underscore their fundamental complexity, both practically and theoretically; indeed, these concepts are enormously complicated and highly problematic.

Long-persisting problems gain new import in this revision. Among them are the many great debates surrounding human language acquisition and usage; literate as opposed to oral modes of communication and their presumed consequences; the relations of literacy to hierarchies of power and wealth as opposed to egalitarian democracy; literacy's contributions to economic, political, and social development; and the status of texts. Even elementary literacy as learned and practiced is quite complex physiologically, neurologically, and cognitively. Its social and cultural dimensions generate numerous layers of complex meanings, including continuities and contradictions (Graff 1981, 1987). How little we know about learning and about teaching, especially respecting levels of literacy.

Especially prominent among the central complications of our traditions or legacies of literacy are the extraordinary frailty of conceptions and conceptualizations of literacy, and the contradictory consequences expected from its acquisition. The presumption of literacy's unproblematic simplicity "naturally" or "essentially" accompanies assumptions that emphasize its strong, uniform, universal, unitary, unwavering nature and impact. At the same time, strong notions or theories of literacy directly and linearly associate rising levels of literacy (in some versions, once a specified threshold is achieved) with large-scale effects, especially the advancement of both individuals and societies. Termed in various formulations the consequences, correlates, or implications of literacy, the number and variety of imputed effects on individuals or societies are dizzying. Literacy, it has been claimed, correlates with economic growth and industrialization, wealth and productivity, political stability and participatory democracy, urbanization, consumption, and contraception.

These wholesale claims rarely stand up to either empirical or conceptual probing historically or contemporarily. Despite its hold on popular opinion and public policy, the strong theory of literacy has been weakened by even cursory scrutiny, as literacy's impacts are seldom shown to be so direct, unmediated, abstract, or universalistic. Taken either singly or together, literacy demands new formulations—approaches, interpretations, policies and actions—of its complexity and its social, cultural, political, and economic relationships, in theory and in practice. We know more than our normative arrangements and repeated truisms indicate. The costs of ongoing neglect are too high.[4] What is at issue is seldom admitted: it is the purpose of literacy, and other learning. Those issues are inseparable from their historical course.

Typical conceptions of literacy share not only assumptions about their unproblematical status but also the presumption that they are value neutral (which is itself often represented as beneficial, a "good"). In other words, we seldom appreciate that our extremely high valuation of literacy by itself is a judgment not an empirical conclusion. To the contrary, historical studies repeatedly demonstrate that no mode or means of learning is neutral. All knowledge and skills, however elementary, incorporate the assumptions and expectations, the biases or emphases of its production, association, prior use, maintenance and preservation.[5] With them come biases with respect to their transmission, the circumstances of learning and practice. They quite likely carry fundamental biases in their very nature, for example, the newly appreciated textual biases of formal schooling and most reading and writing shaped by such formative encounters, tutelage, and restricted or regulated practice.

Reading across Media, Multiple Literacies, and Multiple Languages over Time

New studies in the history of the book and the history of reading are especially telling. Reading was, and has long continued to be, active and collective, combining the widest variety of motivations, choices, practices, and impacts. No singular shifts or simple formulas encompass this wonderfully rich history. Historians of reading, writing, and publishing need to cooperate and collaborate more with historians of literacy and vice versa. The history of reading and the history of writing also are inseparably linked, despite the specializations of scholarship and the presumptions of students of literacy today. Literacy levels are often the missing link in studies of the circulation of print media and the foundations of readership. At the very least, literacy rates help to set parameters for closer attention to reading of different kinds. These fields have much to teach each other.[6]

Janice Radway's *Reading the Romance: Women, Patriarchy, and Popular Literature* (1984; see also Radway 1986) proposes, and with a group of contemporary romance readers illustrates, that reading can be studied usefully, critically and, as her work in particularly evidences, sympathetically in its social, cultural, and political economic contexts. Her innovative practice is informed by anthropological, feminist, and literary critical perspectives. Radway also hints at the possibilities for historical efforts at this direction. Creative research by David Vincent (1979, 1989) and Sally Mitchell (1981) shows the potential of analyzing autobiographical and literary sources, for working-class and middle-class women, respectively. The pioneering and idiosyncratic, though not always persuasive, writings of Carlo Ginzburg (1980) and Robert Darnton (1984), and more recently Roger Chartier and his associates (1987, 1989), suggest the depths and insights that close study of reading practices set into sociocultturally informed communicative contexts may yield. In these examples, I add, the limits of the work are as rich as are the real achievements.[7]

Studies of the media of literacy, from script to print and screen, only begin to suggest the intricately interacting relationships; contemporary confusions about print compared to the visuality and aurality of electronic media have an impressively lengthy set of precedents.[8] This history, which had thus far been only partially studied and understood, challenges all presumptions of unmediated, linear relations and impacts.

The past, especially the European Middle Ages and the early modern era have an enormous amount to teach us about multiple literacies, including the visual, and multilinguality. Neither awaited the modern or postmodern worlds. For contemporary scholars of literacy, multiple literacies across media and modes of expression compete for attention and a place on both research agendas and, increasingly, school and university curricula. From digital and visual to scientific and spatial, and beyond, the domains of the many proclaimed new literacies are opposed to traditional alphabetic or textual literacy.

Medieval and early modern scholars reveal the powerful presence of multiple modes of expression and communication, especially the visual, centuries earlier. Major examples include Michael Clanchy's *From Memory to Written Record: England, 1066–1307* (1993) and Stuart Clark's *Vanities of the Eye: Vision in Early Modern European Culture* (2007). They are joined by historians of science, technology, and the arts high and everyday who demonstrate, sometimes brilliantly, the centrality of visual and experimental modes of reading, writing, and thinking in creativity, discovery, invention, and other forms of innovation.[9] They point toward the need to criticize and possibly rethink the roles we assign to literacy in historical development in significant part because of the centrality of what we must recognize as persistent visual literacies in art, science, religion, architecture, and technology.

Clanchy describes in telling detail critical elements of how many in the population of England came to the written record while their realms of life, religion, society, polity, culture, and economics remained fundamentally oral. In the medieval world, the oral and the written shaped each other. Reading symbols, including material objects and marks that confirmed the veracity of writing both legally and culturally, mediated centuries-long transitions. Ordinary people learned, confirmed, renewed, and transmitted their beliefs in church and state by reading images in stained glass, the built environment, and illuminated manuscripts. It is no accident that early mechanically printed works emulated the work of manuscript scribes.

Moreover, it was and long remained a multilingual world. Clanchy traces the separate and the intertwined strands of medieval Latin, French, emerging Saxon and English vernaculars, and theological and scholarly specialists in Greek and Hebrew in England, as elsewhere in the early centuries of the second millennium of the common era. These times and places are a rich laboratory for studying multilingualism across media, modes of communication, and dimensions of life. This was also a world in which the official descriptor of *litteratus* and *illiteratus*—the ability to use proper Latin—represented, in Clanchy's terms "an ideal type," not a description of popular or individual literacy abilities. Formally, only the clergy could be literate.

In *The Cheese and the Worms* (1980), Carlo Ginzburg immortalized Menocchio—Domenico

Scandella, a peculiarly literate, independent thinking, and gregarious miller who lived in the Fiuli region of Italy in the sixteenth century. Although Ginzburg finds in Menocchio an example of a timeless anarchist oral political culture of the region, the story has other, broader readings. The miller, whose occupation, location, interests, and inclinations placed him on multiple crossroads, gained direct access to a surprising variety of printed secular and religious texts in several languages, some of them translations from other languages. These texts could be borrowed as well as purchased. Menocchio was an attentive but also an inventive reader who formed independent, sometimes creative opinions that stimulated his own understanding of the creation of the world, which conflicted with that of the Catholic Church. He honed his views in conversations with a variety of friends and neighbors. In time, his anticlerical opinions came to the attention of the Inquisition, whose inquiries revealed his writing abilities. Eventually, his strong personal beliefs and his pressing need to talk about them cost him his life. Early modern literacy exceeds the bounds we have set for it.[10]

Numeracy, to take another key example, is among the multiple modes of literacy. In *The Literacy Myth*, I offered anecdotal evidence that workers who were unable to read alphabetic texts were able to count and that colors were sometimes substituted for alphabetic markers (1979, Chap. 5). In exciting new research, Brian A'Hearn, Jorg Baten, and Dorothee Crayen (2009) argue that numeracy may have been more broadly based than literacy in Western Europe than in the east, even by 1600. They conceptualize it as a form of human capital. Its contribution to economic growth and development may have exceeded that of popular literacy, especially in advance of both mass schooling and industrialization.

Contexts, Expectations, and Consequences for Learning and Practice

Recent studies in cognitive psychology and anthropology demonstrate the consequences for literacy of the specific contexts or circumstances of its acquisition, practice, and uses and of its cultural relationships. Raising more questions than it answers and challenging the received wisdom, this research joins other cognitive, linguistic, and historical studies in pointing toward more refined conceptions of skills, abilities, competencies, and knowledge in relatively precise but flexible learning, social, cultural, and communicative contexts (Scribner and Cole 1981; see discussion of their work Chap. 3 above).

Research in cultural psychology and anthropology underscores that alphabetic literacy is only one, albeit an exceptionally valuable, set of abilities and competencies, and it interacts with many others. This recognition slowly influences thinking about schooling and learning. Here, for example, long-standing and theoretically touted claims of the all but boundless potentials of literacy contrast sharply with more common levels of ability and everyday practices. Here, too, we find contradictions in literacy's history, in part from traditions of overvaluing alphabetic literacy by itself and slighting or ignoring other literacies. We neglect the extent to which school literacy is a very special use of literacy and language. Words are not only taken out of "the context for action," but they are also removed from other, non-school uses, including much of oral language usage and writing (Olson 1977). Historically, we locate the persistent and powerful structures of authority erected on these bases, as certain forms of literacy and language abilities support social differentiation, social stigmatization, reinforcement of inequality, and school failure.

Enormous implications for teaching and learning and for developing more effective literacies follow from placing traditional alphabetic literacy within appropriate communicative contexts alongside numeracy and scientific literacy, oral and aural abilities, spatial literacy (or graphicacy, as some geographers put it), visual and aesthetic literacies. Historians of science suggest that invention and discovery may owe more to visual than to alphabetic literacy. It may be difficult to formulate satisfactory notions of functional literacies without expanding our understanding of communicative contexts and channels. For such study, history provides a rich laboratory that has been only partly used.

Historical studies amply document the damages and human costs that follow from the long domination of practical and theoretical presumptions that elevate the literate over the nonliterate to a position of dominance. In part the arrogance of the imperial West, but more broadly reflecting the triumph of what Goody calls the "technology of the intellect" over the intellect and the human spirit, traditions of narrowly construed intellectualism and rationalism rationalized their reification of light over darkness, civilization over barbarity, developed over primitive, formally schooled over natural, written over spoken, literate over oral.

Hand in hand with simplicity and superiority have gone the presumed ease of learning and expectation of individual and societal progress. Despite our tardiness in recognizing its implications, historical studies repeatedly reiterate the difficulties that are normally experienced in gaining, practicing, and mastering the elements of alphabetic literacy.

Acquiring even basic elements of abilities that may--or may not--prove necessary and useful in acquiring further skills, information, knowledge, or mentalities is seldom easy, for reasons both obvious and devious.

Learning literacy, and whatever lies beyond it, has always been hard work.

The expectation and common practice of learning literacy as part of elementary education, all the formal schooling that most people experienced until the late nineteenth and early twentieth centuries, are themselves historical developments. Advocates assumed that, given the availability of written texts and elementary instruction, a foundation in reading and writing is sufficient for the development of individuals' literacy and subsequent education, as well as their occupational and cultural advancement. No serious obstacle to achieving a desired degree of literacy or additional learning need trouble those hungry for more. No matter that the cognitive and psychological place of reading and writing as foundations is not well understood, that reading has so long been poorly taught, or that debates over reading methodologies persist over centuries with much heat and little light. Among the corollaries is the presumption that failure reflected overwhelmingly on the individuals or on their race, ethnicity, class, and gender, rather than on schools, society, or the polity. This conclusion amounts to blaming the victim.

Only in part a matter of instructional media, technology, pedagogy, institutional setting, age, or social circumstances, motivation, our studies agree, is a great stimulus toward the effort to learn one's letters. Historically, those motives have varied widely, as perceptions of need have sometimes been defensive or fearful and sometimes carried anticipations of pleasure and satisfaction. Sometimes motivations are individual; sometimes they are collective. This demand or need is often associated, directly or indirectly, explicitly or implicitly, with social class, gender, race, ethnicity, age, and location, among other social structures and relationships. Unfortunately, scholars like ourselves, who live by and depend upon our manipulation of the tools of traditional learning, are not well placed to appreciate common experiences past or present.

Recent research has revealed the complicated historical and richly human images that are missing from our common operational and legitimizing myths: of multiple paths of learning literacy; the employment of an extraordinary range of instructors, institutions and other environments; the variety of beginning texts; and the diversity of sometimes conflicting or contradictory motivations pushing and pulling people toward literacy. We rediscover the informality and possibility of elementary learning without the lock-step, forced march of agegrading and wholesale psychologies of human cognition and learning based on simplistic presumptions of maturation. In this respect, both the early modern "discovery" of children and a special stage of childhood and the last two centuries' efforts to institutionalize them constitute more complicated relationships than are usually recognized.

In contrast to the variety of paths people follows in the past, the great reforming dream was formal, compulsory, mass public schools as sites for virtually universal transmission of a minimal level of literacy disseminated along with the tenets of secular morality. This type of literacy was presumed to be useful and to promote social stability, as opposed to literacy gained outside of carefully crafted learning environments with routine methods and carefully chosen materials. The first dreamers long predated the massive nineteenth-century efforts to construct school systems, which did not arrive in many areas until the twentieth and even the twenty-first centuries. Distrust, even fear, of the unwashed masses predominated, although for centuries before the fear of schooled masses had predominated over fear of the ignorant or those who learned outside the bounds of formal educational institutions. Before that reversal and the subsequent achievement of mass schooling, and long accompanying its development in many places, looser arrangements continued whose poor press was written by reformers who sought to destroy them. Those arrangements have much to tell us.[11]

While these histories underscore the relative recency and historical constructedness of the means of mass literacy provision and most of other education and thus correct prevailing notions of their inevitability, caution and hindsight also demand that we resist the temptation to romanticize the premodern past. Mass public school systems, despite their failings, have undoubtedly increased opportunities and elevated educational achievement. The price we have paid includes restrictions on literacy that arise from cultural differences and economic inequalities, as circumstances led many pupils to disdain or undervalue literacy and other forms of learning. It also included persistent inequalities of opportunity and outcomes, with greater rewards for the well-off than for the poor. Dependence on literacy, which is itself restricted and often poorly disseminated, sets rigid constraints on the contribution from schools to the polity and culture as well as the economy. More fortunately, nearly universal elementary schooling never halted popular cultural practices that include the "improper" use of literacy to read scorned or censured writing across diverse media.

Nevertheless, a great many persons learned to read and sometimes to write in a widest variety of informal, as well as formal circumstances, and at a wide range of chronological ages. These forms includes self-teaching, interpersonal learning, and episodic instruction in households, workplaces ranging from the fields to artisan shops, public marketplaces, dame schools, political gatherings, cultural settings, carceral institutions, and chance occurrences. Literacy was often acquired at much older ages than the limited span of childhood and early adolescence that came to be constructed as appropriate for school attendance. The construction of mass school systems rested in part on the closure or denial of previously common courses or paths toward proficiency. Simultaneously, approved practices respecting institution and age hardened into expectations, policies, and theories, all with their authoritative guardians. In the wake of these reform legacies, adult education attracted relatively little attention or investment. Recently, however, communitybased, alternative, and adult literacy programs are being developed to meet urgent needs.

Ironically, the long traditions of adult education are seldom called into play (Levine 1985).

Paths to Literacy and Paths of Development

Just as individuals followed different paths to literacy and learning, societies historically and more recently took different paths toward achieving rising levels of popular literacy. Despite the prevalent idea that there is only one sure road to progress, historical research emphasizes that no single route culminated in universal literacy and its modern concomitants. Similarly, with respect to the contributions of literacy and education, there has been no one route to economic development, industrialization, or political democracy. In some cases, at some times, literacy worked as causal agent, either indirectly or directly; in others, it did not. In some circumstances, literacy was influenced by economic development, making it an effect rather than a contributing cause. In still other cases, such as the first phases of industrialization in Europe, economic growth had a negative impact on literacy and education. Comparative research has revealed that sequencing and timing mattered, both chronologically and causally, in shaping the nature and degree of social unrest during industrialization, or the adaptation of large numbers of immigrants. Still, those relationships vary widely. Literacy often has served noncognitively, attitudinally, behaviorally, and symbolically in furthering social and economic development.

That is no small contribution, but it is not typically touted.

Consider patterns of economic growth in the past. They are debated and carry major implications for theory and practice. In *The Literacy Myth* (1979), I joined Roger Schofield and others in questioning a direct connection between popular literacy levels and rates of literacy's spread and the main lines of growth and development. That connection lay at the heart of the literacy myth. We argued for a weaker and more indirect connection between literacy and industrialization, compared with literacy's more direct relationships with commercial capitalism. I urged greater attention to the importance of workplace experience and learning on the job, on the one hand, and schooling's impact on attitudinal, behavioral, and other noncognitive attributes, on the other.

No one denied the importance of literacy and education. But they were reconfigured as less direct and independent relationships. For formulations with human capital at their core and for proponents of the literacy myth, such skepticism verged on sacrilege.

For the past and the present, debate continues about literacy and other levels of education as forms of or as direct contributions to human capital. In various formulations, the literacy myth may be located and assessed differently, yet it remains influential. In a careful review of education and economic growth, David Mitch points to the variety of relationships examined by scholars. "Correlation is not causation.... Thus, the contribution of rising schooling [or literacy] to economic growth should be examined more directly." With respect to the British industrial revolution, Mitch concludes, "other factors contributed to economic growth other than schooling or human capital more generally" (2005 page).

The British industrial revolution remains a prominent instance in which human capital conventionally defined as schooling stagnated in the presence of a notable upsurge in economic growth, despite expectations to the contrary. Such historical instances "call into question the common assumption that education is a necessary prerequisite for economic growth" (Mitch 2005, page; see also Mitch 1999; Vincent 2000).[12]

What of the fate of the literacy myth in more recent decades and the present? Has the postindustrial economy's dependence on advanced technology and the knowledge industry's dependence on advanced education proved it correct or made it obsolete? Mitch offers a mixed verdict, finding that increases in mass schooling seem to explain growth over relatively short periods of time, "with a more modest impact over longer time…. . Schooling should not be seen as either a necessary or sufficient condition for generating economic growth" (Mitch 2005, page). There are many other possible influences.

Others disagree (Becker and Woessmann 2015).[13] In *The Race between Education and Technology* (2008), economists Claudia Goldin and Lawrence Katz offer the fullest brief for the United States' economic and political dependence on human capital whose foundation is rooted in education. In their view, technologies stimulate advances in productivity when they are used by workers prepared to operate new machines. Rising levels of education constitute that preparation and account for what they proclaim "the human capital century." Goldin and Katz believe that today's economy requires an even higher level of education and fear that may not be developing.

The argument is powerful but not completely persuasive. It shares much with the beliefs regarding education and technology that underlay the literacy myth, although adjusted for inflation over time. In a trenchant review, political scientist Andrew Hacker responded: "I'll grant that their correlations show that education and economic growth have risen in tandem. But it just might be that the causation runs the other way. As the production of goods and services becomes more efficient, not only does national wealth increase, but there is less need for teenage labor.

So society finds itself able to underwrite more schools and colleges, and keep more young people in them longer."[14] Schofield (1968), Mitch (1999, 2005), and others have noted the same relationships for earlier periods of economic development.

Hacker, along with other political economists, points to complications in the connections among education, high technology, and jobs. While the income gap between college graduates and others has widened, the "outsized sums accruing to the very top tiers" account for a great deal of the difference, not the earnings of graduates as a whole. The intellectual emphasis in much of the college curriculum and the job skills mandated for the workforce do not match well. Even more important is the fact that the chasm between the rising numbers of graduates in technological fields and the more limited number of jobs expected to be available for them continues to grow. For example, the estimated number of engineers graduating by 2016 is four times greater than the expected number of new jobs.[15] Evidence of these trends is growing.

Cutting across these relationships is another pattern that raises even more questions for the literacy myth. Hacker notes that the *Occupational Outlook Handbook* "lists hundreds of jobs involved with high-tech instruments, including installing, repairing, and debugging them. These workers outnumber college-trained scientists, and even engineers."[16] These technicians are most often high school graduates who meet the demands of their jobs primarily with the knowledge gained at work. High-tech employers do not always seek workers with degrees. In addition, there is an imperfect match between demands for formal credentials and both job skill requirements and rewards. Yet these technicians are central to the needs of a postindustrial knowledge economy as we know it, despite their uncomfortable connection with the expectations derived from the literacy myth.

Moreover, there is good reason to envision today's economy in different terms. Connecting the present with the past in *One Nation Divisible*, Michael Katz and Mark Stern write: "Much like early twentieth-century America, ... abrupt economic change—the introduction of new technologies and modes of organizing work—led in two quite different directions, toward a high and a low road to increased productivity." The resulting bifurcation of work creates a great divide between a high path to raising productivity through high-performance workplaces, worker training and participation, wage incentives, and job security. The low road reduces labor costs by outsourcing labor, employing fixed-term and part-time contracts, and lobbying government to reduce real minimum wages and the power of unions (2006, 180–181).[17] It owes little to literacy and education by themselves.

Many of the fastest growing jobs cluster on the low road. According to one analysis, jobs in the lowest quartile of earnings will account for about 40 percent of growth in the top thirty occupations, which include many food and service workers, clerks, security guards, nurses, and computer software engineers. Katz and Stern summarize: "Less than 25 percent of the top thirty jobs will require a bachelor's degree or higher; 54 percent will require short on-the-job training. Outside the top thirty, 25 percent of new jobs will require a bachelor's degree or more—but almost 50 percent will require no more than short-to-medium-term on-the-job training" (2006, 181). Three quarters will require less than an associate's degree. Poorly paid, dead-end jobs that lack benefits appear within the most technologically sophisticated industries. Contrary to many predictions, models, and expectations, the literacy myth remains very much with us in the early twenty-first century, often contradictorily as the postindustrial economy takes this bifurcated form.

The last century and a half witnessed what we may call the globalization of the literacy myth. Literacy—usually in one or another form of the literacy myth—takes pride of place, at least symbolically, in many designs for rapid economic and social development. In some cases, the inspiration lies in an image, rather than a clear and accurate vision, of an earlier developing West. In others, it may be an elaborate blueprint. In some cases, the imperative or stimulus has been internal to the target state, as in Tokugawa Japan, Russia and the Soviet Union, or China. In others, especially after World War II, a detailed plan, complete with "aid," was exported by the victorious Allied powers and carried by their occupying armies, and by development specialists in universities, NGOs, government agencies, and the United Nations. Both impulses could be embedded in national literacy campaigns (Arnove and Graff 2008). Both derived to some extent from myths about the place of literacy in modernization. Ironically, a number of efforts included alphabetic or linguistic reform and simplification based on erroneous assumptions about indigenous alphabets or characters that followed from the literacy myth's canonization of the classical Greek alphabet.

The adoption of the literacy myth could derive from a limited understanding, or a better comprehension of efforts at making societies, economies, or polities more literate, and their limits—in effect, acts of imitation or mimesis. At stake was the effort to compete, catch-up with, or surpass other nations, sometimes from a foundation in a different or opposing political ideology or organization. We know too little about the actual operation and effects of these programs aimed at mass literacy. There is reason to believe that they may be more effective at raising literacy rates and beginning accelerated development in the short term than in the long run. In the longer term, both literacy and other stimuli for growth may stall or decline. Further growth depends on internal developments aimed at supporting it, greater resources, institutional articulation, and social and cultural changes, at home and abroad, that sometimes precede but at other times follow economic development.

With its decidedly mixed record of assisting literacy and development, UNESCO remains one of the last bastions of unqualified literacy myths. Its most recent World Literacy Decade, 2003– 2012, was proclaimed under the banner of *Literacy as Freedom*: *Education for All, Literacy for Life*. At the launch in February 2003, deputy secretary general Louise Frechette stressed that "literacy remains part of the unfinished business of the 20th century. One of the success stories of the 21st century must be the extension of literacy to include all humankind" (UNESCO 2005). Emphasizing that two thirds of all illiterate adults are women, Frechette declared literacy a prerequisite for a "healthy, just and prosperous world." "When women are educated and empowered, the benefits can be seen immediately: families are healthier; they are better fed; their income, savings and reinvestments go up. And what is true of families is true of communities—ultimately, indeed, of whole countries." "Literacy and Gender" constituted the focus of the first two years. With its emphasis on literacy as freedom, the initiative was designed to "free people from ignorance, incapacity and exclusion" and "empower them for action, choices and participation" (UNESCO 2003).[18] Ironically, UNESCO lacked the funds to tell the world about its latest campaign.

The great danger today is one that twentieth- and twenty-first century education on all levels shares with literacy models: the simple presumption that economic growth and development depend simply and directly on investment in and high rates of productivity from systems of formal education. Quantity and quality are confused; educational purpose is distorted. The consequent fears of crisis and decline rigidly narrow the frame of education, including literacy, and all but guarantee disappointment and repetition of the cycle.

A Future for the History of Literacy and for Literacy Studies

The history of literacy is firmly established as a field of study. I hope that I have made a compelling case that literacy studies needs to learn from its research and conclusions. At the same time, historical studies of literacy themselves demand renewed interest and critical attention. The achievements of historical literacy studies are many and clear. They impinge on what directions historical studies related to literacy will take, how history can constructively collaborate with other disciplines, and how historical analysis may contributes to public policy.

Persisting patterns of limitations also mark the historical field. We recognize limits of quantitative analysis alone, as well as those of aggregative and ecological methods and research designs. In some ways, I aver, we are only now coming to the most important questions and issues. There has been a shattering of received wisdom, expectations, assumptions, and that is no small accomplishment.

The obverse, however, is the question of what will replace them, which is in part a theoretical issue. The great debates about literacy's relationships to other social forces and patterns all reflect questions surrounding commercial and industrial and social development, political mobilization, religion, social mobility, class formation, work and leisure life, and social change more generally. Issues of method, such as those of dependent versus independent variables, levels of aggregation, and problems of correlational analysis, follow. The demand for critical reflection now falls upon conceptualization, method, and interpretation.

By now it should be clear that the path forward lies in moving beyond literacy as a dichotomous variable, perceived as useful or not, as either conservative and controlling or liberating. We could well aim at a historical cultural politics and a historical political economy of literacy.

Most generally, historical literacy studies must build upon their own past while also moving beyond it. The work of foundational groups such as François Furet and Jacques Ozouf (1977, 1983), David Cressy (1980), and Lee Soltow and Edward Stevens (1981) delineates parameters, baselines, and key interrelationships. Those relationships in turn offer opportunities to investigate the linkages more precisely and to seek refinements in specifying factors and their interactions. The questions that can be most fruitfully analyzed range from literacy's relations with class, gender, age, and culture to overarching themes of economic development, social order, mobility and stratification, education and schooling, actual uses of literacy, and language and culture.

One demand falls upon much sharper contextual grounding, often in clearly delineated localities. Others encompass the completion of time series, among other quantitative analyses. Major opportunities for close, critical contextualization and connective interpretation exist in contemporary research in Carl Kaestle and his colleagues' "history of readers and reading" (1991), l'histoire du livre, and Chartier's history of "texts, printing, readings" (1987, 1989; see also Gilmore 1989; Allen 1991). Groundbreaking studies by Clanchy (1979) and Ginzburg (1980) point the way. Despite sometimes brilliant openings, the potential of these scholarly practices is unfulfilled; their integration into social, cultural, economic, or political histories remains a major challenge.

Comparative studies, despite their complications, must advance. The promise of historical and contextual understanding cannot be fulfilled without them. This requires a greater appreciation and emphasis on source criticism and recognition of the different meanings of different measures of literacy (as well as literacy's uses) among different populations as evidenced from varying sources. Contextualization, for example, of the acquisition and the uses of reading and writing, is also critical for comparisons, as the work of Egil Johansson (1977, 1981, 1985; Graff, et al., 2009) and R. A. Houston (1985) in particular illustrates. No less important is the search for indicators of the levels and the quality of literacy, permitting us to advance beyond the constraining dichotomy of literate versus illiterate (compare, for example, Graff 1979, with Kaestle et al. 1991). Novel approaches to combining records and to record linkage stand out on this agenda.

Moving in this direction requires identifying new conceptualizations of context in the historical study of literacy. Recognizing that literacy only acquires meaning and significance within specified historical contexts does not in itself reduce the risks of abstracted analysis. Novel work in anthropology and psychology, such as that of Shirley Brice Heath (1983) and Sylvia Scribner and Michael Cole (1981), provides important suggestions and valuable guidelines for historians. The tasks lie not only in defining and specifying contexts for study and interpretation but also in delineating the varying levels of context—vertically or horizontally, for example—and in experimenting with ways to operationalize them. Edward Stevens's (1985, 1988) focus on illiterate persons in judicial settings and Johansson's (1977, 1981, 1985) perspective on church and community indicate two opportunities to probe more intensively. Microhistories and studies of autobiographical materials offer special opportunities, as noted earlier. William Gilmore's (1989) localized regional case study reiterates the richness of records. For the recent past, oral histories, library use records, and participant observation, or ethnographies of communications, offer other possibilities.

Contexts for analysis are many and diverse. They range from those of acquisition, use, and action, to those of individual, family, group, or community, gender, or social class, individual and collective. The scope for defined study is itself variable, but should include material conditions, motivations, opportunities, needs and demands, traditions, and transformations. In this way, linguistic forms, dialects, communication channels and networks, pushes and pulls from religion, culture, politics, the economy, and so forth, may be incorporated. Literacy's relationship to personal and/or collective efficacy and activism or agency, which is subject to intense debate, may also be explored further, in part in analysis of specific events and processes and in part in terms of patterns of communications and mobilization within defined contexts.

Class formation and vital behavior are just two of the many key topics calling for examination.

Are historical ethnographies of literacy possible, if they are conceptualized fully in terms of literacy among the many modes and relations of communications? Recent work contains fascinating hints in that direction which merit fuller examination. A number of studies in popular culture in the past may serve as stimulating models, including those of Peter Burke (1978, 1987), LeRoy Ladurie (1978), R. W. Scribner (1981, 1984), and Keith Wrightson and David Levine (1979). Clearly, the subject and its significance require a fair test. Current interests in an anthropology of communications and in ethnographies of reading and writing at varying levels of context and generality are guides to follow.

On one hand, literacy may be viewed as one among other media and its roles and impacts evaluated. On the other hand, ethnographic and communicative approaches have the potential to expand perspectives while simultaneously grounding them more precisely for meaningful interpretation. Novel contextualization can also be a boost to the renewal and refinement of quantitative studies, past and present. Attention to context, in sum, offers both new and better cases for study, opportunities for explanation, and approaches to literacy's changing and variable historical meanings and contributions.

Also spanning historical studies and research in other disciplines is the difficult but necessary demand for critical examination of the conceptualization of literacy itself. Recent research teaches us about the contradictions central to literacy's history. It has revealed the problems in treating literacy as an independent variable and the confusions that inhere in treating literacy as either or both dependent and independent. Questions of contextualization may well limit analysis of literacy as an autonomous or independent factor; they will also, I think, stimulate new formulations of the nature of literacy as a dependent variable. This task is inseparable from developing new relational and dialectical conceptions. In the process, new considerations about levels and quality of literacy must transcend the conceptualization of literacy as a dichotomous variable. Psychological and anthropological studies promise to contribute here too. To transcend these lacunae requires excavation of other relevant aspects of cultural communications among which literacy, in shifting degrees and mediations, takes its place.

A relatively small step takes us to the question of literacy and what might well be termed the creation of meaning. Historical studies of literacy have been little influenced by recent debates in intellectual and cultural history, literary criticism and philosophy, cognitive psychology, cultural anthropology and ethnography, or critical theories of communication. To some extent, these emphases stem from dissatisfaction with traditional approaches to texts, their reading, understanding, and communication. More recently, the entire enterprise of grasping the creation, maintenance, and communication of meaning has changed in major ways related to issues central to literacy. The parallels with literacy studies have not mandated a parallel course.[19]

Cultural and intellectual histories are themselves, along with many areas of the humanities and the social sciences in a significant time of ferment and exploration; so too are literary criticism, cognitive and cultural psychology, and some areas of philosophy (Graff 2014). Concerns about interactions between readers and texts, reader responses to writing and print, the shaping of individual and collective processes of cognition, and the ways in which meaning is created, influenced, transmitted, and changed are common, if not always clarified. Chartier (1989), for example, raises questions and advances hypotheses about modes and practices of early modern French reading, reading as active and creative, reception aesthetics and horizons, appropriation, interpretive communities, textuality and orality, printing and circulation. Kaestle and his collaborators (1991) confront readers, readership, and readability in twentieth-century American society.

At least partly to its detriment, the history of literacy, and literacy studies in general, largely stand in isolation from interdisciplinary rapprochement. Questions about literacy's contribution to individual, class, and collective awareness, patterns of cognitive and noncognitive attitudinal formation, and cultural behavior more generally all underscore this need. The nagging issue of the uses of literacy and their consequences demands further new exploration.

The need for a sharper theoretical awareness of the relevance of the history of literacy for many important aspects of social, economic, and psychological theory across those disciplines, constitutes a further point. This is implied in the foregoing, and too frequently implied rather than argued directly in the literature. Historical studies of literacy provide significant opportunities for testing theories. Insofar as their results continue to raise criticisms of normative theoretical expectations and assumptions, there may also be prospects for essaying new formulations. Both historical practice and historians' contributions to other interested parties can only benefit from this.

A question of methodology, indeed of epistemology, links all of the above. Has the tradition of taking literacy as primary object of analysis—the history of literacy, or literacy studies, per se—approached an end point? Should a new generation refocus itself in terms of literacy as a significant—indeed, a necessary—component of other relevant investigations? The question, simply put, is that of shifting from historical studies of literacy to histories that encompass literacy within their context and conceptualization, from the history of literacy to literacy in history. To move in this direction is no simple task, yet the implications for historians and for studies of contemporary literacy are momentous. This book provides many leads in that direction.

Finally, I call attention to the relevance of the history of literacy for a number of policy issues in societies developed and underdeveloped today, and to the contributions that reconceptualization might bring to them. Historical analysis can contribute to understanding and fashioning responses to deal with those problems that are sometimes deemed literacy crises. In grasping that there are many paths to literacy, that literacy's relations to social and economic development are complex, that the quantity and the quality of literacy are not linearly related, that the consequences of literacy are neither direct nor simple, and that literacy is never neutral, historians have much to share with their fellow students and to offer those who formulate social policies. That is no small contribution.

The past provides a set of experiences that tends to call into question rather than sustain common expectations. Although neither all the research nor the balance sheet of historical interpretation is in, we may argue that historical experiences provide a better guide to such crucial questions as how and to what extent basic literacy contributes to the economic and individual wellbeing of persons in different socioeconomic and cultural contexts, and under what circumstances universal literacy can be achieved. The costs and benefits of alternative paths can be discerned, and estimated, too. Thus, the connections and disconnections between literacy and commercial development, a generally positive relationship, and literacy and industrial development, often an unfavorable linkage at least in the short run of decades and half-centuries, offer important case studies and analogs for analysis. The data of the past strongly suggest that a simple, linear, modernization model of literacy as prerequisite for development and development as stimulant to increased levels of schooling will not suffice. Too many periods of lags, backward linkages, setbacks, and contradictions exist to permit such cavalier theorizing to continue without serious challenge and criticism.

Literacy's relationships with paths to economic development present cases in point. So, too, do the connections of literacy with social development. There too, we discover a history of continuities and contradictions, and of variable paths to societal change and development. From the classical era forward, leaders of polities and churches, reformers as well as conservers, have recognized the uses of literacy and schooling. Often they have perceived unbridled, untempered literacy as potentially dangerous, a threat to social order, political integration, economic productivity, and patterns of authority. Increasingly, however, they came to conclude that literacy, if provided in carefully controlled, structured, formal institutions created expressly for the purposes of education and transmission of literacy and supervised closely, could be a powerful and useful force in achieving a variety of important ends. Precedents long predated the first systematic mass efforts to put this conception of literacy into practice, in Rome, for example, and in the visionary proposals of the fifteenth- and sixteenth-century Christian humanists. For our purposes, the Reformations of the sixteenth century represented the first great literacy campaigns. They were hardly homogeneous efforts, as Sweden reminds us, in either design or degree of success. Nonetheless, they were precedent-setting and epochal in their significance for the future of social and educational development throughout the world.

With the Enlightenment and its heritage came the final ideological underpinnings for the modern and liberal reforms of popular schooling and institutional building that established the network of educational,

social, political, cultural, and economic relationships central to the dominant ideologies and their theoretical and practical expressions for the past
two centuries. Prussia took the lead, and provided a laboratory that
United States, Canadian, English, French, and Scandinavian school promoters and reformers regularly came to study. North Americans and
Swedes followed in Prussia's wake, and, in time and in their own ways, so
did the English, French, Italians, and more recently vast areas of the
underdeveloping world.

Of course, other important uses of literacy—for personal advancement, entertainment, study, collective action, and the like—cannot be
slighted. The significance and potential of literacy to individuals and to
groups throughout history, even if sometimes taken out of context and
exaggerated, are undoubted. The role of social class and group-specific
demands for literacy's skills, the impact of motivation, and the growing
perceptions of its value and benefits are among the major factors that
explain the historical contours of changing rates of popular literacy. In
other words, demand must be appreciated, as well as supply, stimuli from
below as well as force and compulsion from above: in intricately reciprocal and dialectical relationships. Historical studies call attention to literacy's limits and its roles in promoting and maintaining hegemony.

Recognizing the history of literacy and its relevance to nonhistorians is
at once a first step and a paradigmatic one.

Notes

1. This chapter draws particularly on Graff, "Whither the history of literacy?" (1988); Graff, "Assessing the history of literacy in the 1990s"
   (1995c); *Labyrinths of literacy* (1995a); *Literacy and historical development* (2007); "*Literacy Myth* at thirty" (2010); *Literacy myths, legacies,
   and lessons* (2011); and "Epilogue: Literacy studies and interdisciplinary
   studies with notes on the place of Deborah Brandt" (2014). For fuller
   bibliographies, see my Syllabus for History of Literacy graduate seminar,
   available at https://u.osu.edu/gratt.40/files/2041/12/ENG-7884-HIS-
   775-Grad-Hist-of-Lit-Spr-2014-Updated-BiblioRevd-26uqqo8.pdf

2. For interesting examples in this field, see Allen, *In the public eye* (1991); Burke, *Popular culture* (1978); Carpenter, *Books and society in history* (1983); Davidson, *Revolution in the word* (1986); Davidson, *Reading in America* (1989); Feather, *Provincial book trade* (1985); Febvre and Martin, *L'apparition du livre* (1958); Gilmore, *Reading becomes a necessity* (1989); Ginzburg, *Cheese and the worms* (1980); Hall, "Uses of literacy" (1983); Hall, *Worlds of wonder* (1992); Hall, *Cultures of print* (1996); Hall and Hench, *Needs and opportunities* (1987); Joyce et al., *Printing and society* (1983); Kaestle et al., *Literacy in the United States* (1991); Spufford, *Small books and pleasant histories* (1981); Stock, *Implications of literacy* (1983); Stock, *Listening for the text* (1990). See also the journals *Revue française d'histoire du livre* (Société des Bibliophiles de Guyenne), *Publishing History*, and more recently *Book History*.

3. On literacy metaphors, see Barton, *Literacy* (2006); Hamilton, *Literacy and the politics of representation* (2012).

4. For some of the human costs of such dominant notions, see for example Aronowitz and Giroux, "Schooling, culture, and literacy," 1988; Botstein, "Damaged Literacy" (1990); Graubard, *Literacy in America* (1990); Katz, "New educational panic" (1988); Kozol, *Illiterate America* (1985); Levine, *Social context of literacy* (1985). For historical and international comparisons, see Arnove and Graff, *National literacy campaigns* (2008).

5. The almost cyclical debate over skills versus content, which spans the entire educational realm from literacy learning to graduate training, is another version of this confusion. There is a large literature on vocational schooling, among the functional and/or utilitarian literacies. See Levine, *Social context of literacy* (1985); Katz, "New educational panic" (1988).

6. For some of the possibilities, see Casper et al., *Industrial book, 1840–1880* (2007); Graff, *Literacy myth*, 1979, Chap. 7.

7. See also Allen, *In the public eye* (1991); Davidson, *Revolution in the* word (1986); Davidson, *Reading in America* (1989); Gilmore, *Reading becomes a necessity* (1989); Gross, *Books and libraries* (1988a); Gross, *Much instruction from little reading* (1988b); Isaac, "Dramatizing the ideology of revolution" (1976a); Isaac, "Preachers and patriots" (1976b); Isaac, *Transformation of Virginia* (1982); Kaestle et al., *Literacy in the United States* (1991); Sicherman, "Sense and sensibility" (1989); Sicherman, "Reading and ambition" (1993); Sicherman, "Connecting lives" (2006); Sicherman, "Ideologies and practices" (2007); Steedman (1982);

Steedman, "Woman writing a letter" (1999); Steedman, "Poetical maids and cooks who wrote" (2005); Stout, "Religion, communications, and the ideological origins of the American Revolution" (1977); Thomas, "Meaning of literacy" (1986).

8. See in particular Clanchy, *From memory to Written Record* (1991); see also the literature on visuality, science, and related areas cited in Chap. 6.

9. For science and technology, see especially Ferguson, "Mind's eye," 1977; Esrock, *Reader's eye* (1994); Miller, *Insights of genius* (2000); Pauwels, *Visual cultures of science* (2006).

10. Among the reviews of *The Cheese and the Worms*, see Dominick LaCapra, "*The Cheese and the Worms*: The Cosmos of a Twentieth-Century Historian," in his *History and Criticism* (Ithaca: Cornell, 1985), 45–69; David Levine and Zubedeh Vahed, "Ginzburg's Menocchio: Refutations and Conjectures," *Histoire sociale* 34 (2001): 437–464; Keith Luria, "The Paradoxical Carlo Ginzburg," *Radical History Review* 35 (1986): 80–87; John Martin, "Journeys to the World of the Dead: The Work of Carlo Ginzburg," *Journal of Social History* 25 (1992): 613–626; Anne Jacobson Schutte, "Carlo Ginzburg: Review Article," *Journal of Modern History* 48 (1976): 296–315; Paola Zambelli, "From Menocchio to Piero Della Francesa: The Work of Carlo Ginzburg," *Historical Journal* 28 (1985): 983–999.

11. Suggestive studies include Galenson, "Literacy and age" (1981); Laqueur, "Working-class demand," 1976, Spufford, *Small books and pleasant histories* (1981). On early modern Sweden, where exceptionally high levels of reading but not writing literacy and of female literacy were achieved largely without mass institutional schooling, see Johansson, *History of literacy in Sweden* (1977); Johansson, "History of literacy" (1981); Johansson, "Popular literacy in Scandinavia" (1985).

12. Note that literacy and schooling are not perfectly synonymous or interchangeable. Nor are specific job skills and more general cognitive advances.

13. For a very different economic analysis, see Pritchett, "Does learning to add up add up?" 2006. For an interesting argument for an increasing value of literacy, specifically of writing, as a development of the so-called knowledge economy or society, see Brandt, "Changing literacy," 2003; Brandt, "Drafting U.S. literacy" (2004); Brandt, "Writing for a living" (2005). In this view, writing itself is productive and a force of productivity; see Chap. 5.

14. Andrew Hacker, "Can we make America smarter?" *NYRB*, April 30, 2009.
15. Ibid.
16. Ibid.
17. See also Henwood, *After the new economy*, 2003; Jeff Madrick, "Goodbye, Horatio Alger," *The Nation* Feb. 5, 2007.
18. See also UNESCO 2005, 2005–2006, 2007; Farrell, "Literacy and international development" (2009); Arnove and Graff, *National literacy campaigns* (2008).
19. Chartier, *Cultural uses of print* (1987), Chartier, *Culture of print* (1989), and Hall, "Uses of literacy" (1983), are exceptions.

References

A'Hearn, Brian, Jorg Baten, and Dorothee Crayen. (2009) Quantifying quantitative literacy: Age heaping and the history of human capital. *Journal of Economic History* 69: 783–808.

Allen, James Smith. (1991) *In the public eye: A history of reading in modern France, 1800–1940.* Princeton: Princeton University Press.

Arnove, Robert F., and Harvey J. Graff, eds. (2008) *National literacy campaigns and movements: Historical and comparative perspectives.* New Brunswick, N.J.: Transaction Publishers.

Aronowitz, Stanley, and Giroux, Henry. (1988) Schooling, culture, and literacy in the age of broken dreams: A Review of Bloom and Hirsch. *Harvard Educational Review* 58: 172–194.

Barton, David. (2006) *Literacy: An introduction to the ecology of written language.* Oxford: Blackwell.

Becker, Sascha O., and Ludger Woessmann. (2015) Was Weber wrong? A human capital theory of Protestant economic history. *Quarterly Journal of Economics* 124: 531–596.

Botstein, Leon. (1990) Damaged literacy: Illiteracies and American democracy. *Daedalus* 119: 55–84.

Brandt, Deborah. (2003) Changing literacy. *Teachers College Record* 105: 245–260.

Brandt, Deborah. (2004) Drafting U.S. literacy. *College English* 66: 485–502.

Brandt, Deborah. (2005) Writing for a living: Literacy and the knowledge economy. *Written Communication* 22: 166–197.

Brandt, Deborah. (2015) *The rise of writing: Redefining mass literacy.* Cambridge: Cambridge University Press.

Burke, Peter. (1978) *Popular culture in early modern Europe.* New York: Harper and Row.

Burke, Peter. (1987) *The historical anthropology of early modern Italy.* Cambridge: Cambridge University Press.

Carpenter, Kenneth E., ed. (1983) *Books and society in history.* New York: Bowker.

Casper, Scott E., Jeffery D. Groves, Stephen W. Nissenbaum, and Michael Winship, eds. (2007) *The Industrial Book, 1840–1880,* vol. 3 of *A history of the book in America.* Chapel Hill: University of North Carolina Press.

Chartier, Roger. (1987) *The cultural uses of print in early modern France,* trans. Lydia G. Cochrane. Princeton: Princeton University Press.

Chartier, Roger, ed. (1989) *The culture of print: Power and the uses of print in early modern Europe,* trans. Lydia G. Cochrane. Princeton: Princeton University Press.

Clanchy, Michael T. (1993) *From memory to written record: England, 1066–1307.* Rev. ed., Oxford: Blackwell.

Clark, Stuart. (2007) *Vanities of the eye: Vision in early modern European culture.* Oxford: Oxford University Press.

Cressy, David. (1980) *Literacy and the social order: Reading and writing in Tudor and Stuart England.* Cambridge: Cambridge University Press.

Darnton, Robert. (1972) Reading, writing, and publishing in eighteenth-century France. In Felix Gilbert and Stephen R. Graubard, eds, *Historical studies today,* 238–250. New York: Norton.

Darnton, Robert. (1982) *The literary underground of the Old Regime.* Cambridge, Mass: Harvard University Press.

Darnton, Robert. (1983) What is the history of books? In Kenneth E. Carpenter, ed., *Books and society in history,* 3–28. New York: Bowker.

Darnton, Robert. (1984) *The great cat massacre and other episodes in cultural history.* New York: Basic Books.

Davidson, Cathy N. (1986) *Revolution in the word: The rise of the novel in America.* New York: Oxford University Press.

Davidson, Cathy N., ed. (1989) *Reading in America: Literature and social history.* Baltimore: Johns Hopkins University Press.

Duffy, John M. (2007) *Writing from these roots: Literacy in a Hmong-American community.* Honolulu: University of Hawai'i Press.

Eisenstein, Elizabeth L. (1979) *The printing press as an agent of change: Communications and cultural transformations in early modern Europe.* 2 vols. Cambridge: Cambridge University Press.

Esrock, Ellen J. (1994) *The reader's eye: Visual imaging as reader response.* Baltimore: Johns Hopkins University Press.

Farrell, Joseph P. (2009) Literacy and international development: Education and literacy as basic human rights. In David R. Olson and Nancy Torrance, eds, *The Cambridge handbook of literacy*, 518–534. Cambridge: Cambridge: University Press.

Feather, John. (1985) *The provincial book trade in eighteenth-century England.* Cambridge: Cambridge University Press.

Febvre, Lucien, and Henri-Jean Martin. (1958) *L'apparition du livre.* Paris: Editions Albin Michel.

Ferguson, Eugene S. (1977) The mind's eye: Nonverbal thought in technology. *Science* 197: 827–836.

Finnegan, Ruth. (1973) Literacy versus non-literacy: The great divide. In Robin Horton and Ruth Finnegan, *Modes of thought*, 112–144. London: Faber and Faber.

Furet, François, and Jacques Ozouf. (1977) *Lire et écrire: L'alphabétisation des Français de Calvin à Jules Ferry.* 2 vols. Paris: Editions de Minuit.

Furet, François, and Jacques Ozouf. (1983) *Reading and writing: Literacy in France from Calvin to Ferry.* Cambridge: Cambridge University Press.

Galenson, David. (1981) Literacy and age in pre-industrial England. *Economic Development and Cultural Change* 29: 815–829.

Gilmore, William J. (1989) *Reading becomes a necessity of life: Material and cultural life in rural New England, 1780–1835.* Knoxville: University of Tennessee Press.

Ginzburg, Carlo. (1980) *The cheese and the worms: The cosmos of a sixteenth century miller.* Baltimore: Johns Hopkins University Press.

Goldin, Claudia, and Lawrence F. Katz. (2008) *The race between education and technology.* Cambridge, Mass: Harvard University Press.

Goody, Jack, and Ian Watt. 1968. The consequences of literacy. In Jack Goody, ed., *Literacy in traditional societies*, 27–68. Cambridge: Cambridge University Press.

Gough, Kathleen. (1968) Implications of literacy in traditional China and India. In Jack Goody, ed., *Literacy in traditional societies*, 69–84. Cambridge: Cambridge University Press.

Graff, Harvey J. (1979) *The literacy myth: Literacy and social structure in the nineteenthcentury city.* New York and London: Academic Press.

Graff, Harvey J. (1981) Reflections on the history of literacy: Overview, critique, and proposals. *Humanities in Society* 4: 303–333.

Graff, Harvey J. (1987) *The legacies of literacy: Continuities and contradictions in Western society and culture.* Bloomington: Indiana University Press.

Graff, Harvey J. (1988) Whither the history of literacy? The future of the past. *Communication* 11: 5–22.

Graff, Harvey J. (1991) *The literacy myth,* with new introduction. New Brunswick, N.J.: Transaction.

Graff, Harvey J. (1995a) *The labyrinths of literacy: Reflections on literacy past and present.* Rev. and exp. ed. Pittsburgh: University of Pittsburgh Press.

Graff, Harvey J. (1995b) Literacy, myths, and legacies: Lessons from the history of literacy. In Harvey J. Graff, *The labyrinths of literacy,* 318–349. Pittsburgh: University of Pittsburgh Press.

Graff, Harvey J. (1995c) Assessing the history of literacy in the 1990s: Themes and questions. In Armando Petrucci and M. Gimeno Blay, eds., *Escribir y leer en Occidente,* 5–46. Valencia, Spain: Universitat de Valencia.

Graff, Harvey J., ed. (2007) *Literacy and historical development.* Carbondale: Southern Illinois University Press.

Graff, Harvey J. (2010) *The Literacy Myth* at thirty. *Journal of Social History* 43: 635–661.

Graff, Harvey J. (2011) *Literacy myths, legacies, and lessons: New studies on literacy.* New Brunswick, N.J.: Transaction.

Graff, Harvey J. (2014) Epilogue: Literacy studies and interdisciplinary studies with notes on the place of Deborah Brandt. In Julie Nelson Christoph, John Duffy, Eli Goldblatt, Nelson Graff, Rebecca Nowacek, and Bryan Trabold, eds, *Literacy, economy, and power: Writing and research after Literacy in American lives,* 202–226. Carbondale: Southern Illinois University Press.

Graff, Harvey J., and John Duffy. (2007) The literacy myth. *Encyclopedia of language and education,* vol. 2, *Literacy,* ed. Brian Street, 41–52; Nancy Hornberger, general editor. Berlin and New York: Springer.

Graff, Harvey J., Alison McKinnon, Bengt Sandin, and Ian Winchester, eds. (2009) *Understanding literacy in its historical contexts: Socio-cultural history and the legacy of Egil Johansson.* Lund: Nordic Academic Press

Graubard, Stephen, ed. 1990. *Literacy in America.* Special issue, *Daedalus* 119 (Spring).

Gross, Robert A. (1988a) *Books and libraries in Thoreau's Concord: Two essays.* Worcester, Mass: American Antiquarian Society.

Gross, Robert A. (1988b) *Much instruction from little reading: Books and libraries in Thoreau's Concord.* Charlottesville: University of Virginia Press.

Hall, David D. (1983) The uses of literacy in New England, 1600–1850. In William L. Joyce, David D. Hall, Richard D. Brown, and John B. Hench, eds, *Printing and society in early America*, 1–47. Worcester, Mass: American Antiquarian Society.

Hall, David D. (1992) *Worlds of wonder, days of judgment: Popular religious belief in early New England.* Cambridge, Mass: Harvard University Press.

Hall, David D. (1996) *Cultures of print: Essays in the history of the book.* Amherst: University of Massachusetts Press.

Hall, David D., and John Hench, eds. (1987) *Needs and opportunities in the history of the book: America, 1639–1876.* Worcester, Mass: American Antiquarian Society.

Hamilton, Mary. (2012) *Literacy and the politics of representation.* London: Routledge.

Heath, Shirley Brice. 1983. *Ways with words: Language, life, and work in communities and classrooms.* Cambridge: Cambridge University Press, 1983; with new epilogue, 1996.

Henwood, Doug. (2003) *After the new economy: The binge … and the hangover that won't go away.* New York: New Press.

Houston, R. A. (1985) *Scottish literacy and the Scottish identity: Illiteracy and society in Scotland and northern England, 1600–1800.* Cambridge: Cambridge University Press.

Isaac, Rhys. (1976a) Dramatizing the ideology of revolution: Popular mobilization in Virginia, 1774 to 1776. *William and Mary Quarterly* 33: 357–385.

Isaac, Rhys. (1976b) Preachers and patriots: Popular culture and the revolution in Virginia. In Alfred F. Young, ed., *The American Revolution*, 125–156. DeKalb: Northern Illinois University Press.

Isaac, Rhys. (1982) *The transformation of Virginia.* Chapel Hill: University of North Carolina Press.

Johansson, Egil. (1977) *The history of literacy in Sweden, in comparison with some other countries.* Educational Reports No. 12. Umea, Sweden: Umea University and School of Education.

Johansson, Egil. (1981) The history of literacy in Sweden. In Harvey J. Graff, ed., *Literacy and social development in the West*, 151–182. Cambridge: Cambridge University Press.

Johansson, Egil. (1985) Popular literacy in Scandinavia about 1600–1900. *Historical Social Research* 34: 60–64.

Joyce, William L., David D. Hall, Richard D. Brown, and John B. Hench, eds. (1983) *Printing and society in early America.* Worcester, Mass.: American Antiquarian Society.

Kaestle, Carl, Helen Damon-Moore, Lawrence C. Stedman, Katherine Tinsley, and William Vance Trollinger Jr. (1991) *Literacy in the United States: Readers and reading since 1880.* New Haven: Yale University Press.

Katz, Michael B. (1988) The new educational panic. In Leslie Berlowitz, Denis Donohue, and Louis Menand, eds, *America in theory*, 178–194. New York: Oxford University Press.

Katz, Michael B., and Mark J. Stern. 2006. *One nation divisible: What America was and what it is becoming.* New York: Russell Sage.

Kozol, Jonathan. (1985) *Illiterate America.* Garden City, NJ: Doubleday.

Laqueur, Thomas W. (1976) Working-class demand and the growth of English elementary education, 1750–1850. In Lawrence Stone, ed., *Schooling and Society*, 192–205. Baltimore: Johns Hopkins University Press.

LeRoy Ladurie, Emmanuel. (1978) *Montaillou: The promised land of error*, trans. Barbara Bray. New York: Braziller.

Levine, Kenneth. (1985) *The social context of literacy.* London: Routledge and Kegan Paul.

McQuillan, Jeff. (1998) Seven myths about literacy in the United States. *Practical Assessment, Research & Evaluation* 6. Excerpted from Jeff McQuillan (1998) *The Literacy Crisis: False Claims, Real Solutions* (Portsmouth, N.H.: Heinemann), retrieved 12-31-2015 from https://www.heinemann.com/shared/onlineresources/e00063/7myths.html and also available at http://PAREonline.net/getvn.asp?v=6&n=1

Miller, Arthur I. (2000) *Insights of genius: Imagery and creativity in science and art.* Cambridge, Mass.: MIT Press.

Mitch, David. (1999) The role of education and skill in the British Industrial Revolution. In Joel Mokyr, ed., *The British Industrial Revolution: An economic perspective*, 241–279. Boulder, Colo.: Westview Press.

Mitch, David. (2005) Education and economic growth in historical perspective. *EH.Net encyclopedia*, ed. Robert Whaples, July 26, 2005, http://eh.net/encyclopedia/article/mitch.education

Mitchell, Sally. (1981) *The fallen angel: Chastity, class and women's reading, 1835–1880.* Bowling Green, Ohio: Popular Press.

Olson, David R. (1977) From utterance to text: The bias of language in speech and writing. *Harvard Educational Review* 47: 257–281.

Olson, David R. (1994) *The world on paper: The conceptual and cognitive implications of writing and reading.* Cambridge: Cambridge University Press.

Pauwels, Luc, ed. (2006) *Visual cultures of science: Rethinking representational practices in knowledge building and science communication.* Hanover, N.H.: Dartmouth College Press.

Pritchett, Lant. (2006) Does learning to add up add up? The returns to schooling in aggregate data. In Eric A. Hanushek and Finis Welch, eds, *Handbook of the economics of education*, vol. 1, 635–695. Amsterdam: North Holland.

Radway, Janice A. (1984) *Reading the romance: Women, patriarchy, and popular literature*. Chapel Hill: University of North Carolina Press.

Radway, Janice A. (1986) Reading is not eating: Mass-produced literature and the theoretical, methodological, and political consequences of a metaphor. *Book Research Quarterly* 2: 7–29.

Schofield, Roger S. (1968) The measurement of literacy in pre-industrial England. In Jack Goody, ed., *Literacy in traditional societies*, 311–325. Cambridge: Cambridge University Press.

Scribner, R. W. (1981) *For the sake of simple folk: Popular propaganda for the German Reformation*. Cambridge: Cambridge University Press.

Scribner, R. W. (1984) Oral culture and the diffusion of Reformation Ideas. *History of European Ideas* 5: 237–256.

Scribner, Sylvia, and Michael Cole. (1981) *The psychology of literacy*. Cambridge, Mass.: Harvard University Press.

Sicherman, Barbara. (1989) Sense and sensibility: A case study of women's reading in late Victorian America. In Cathy Davidson, ed., *Reading in America*, 201–225. Baltimore: Johns Hopkins University Press.

Sicherman, Barbara. (1993) Reading and ambition: M. Carey Thomas and female heroism. *American Quarterly* 45: 73–103.

Sicherman, Barbara. (2006) Connecting lives: Women and reading, then and now. In James P. Danky and Wayne A. Wiegand, eds., *Women in print: Essays on the print culture of American women in the nineteenth and twentieth centuries*, 3–24. Madison: University of Wisconsin Press.

Sicherman, Barbara. (2007) Ideologies and practices of reading. In Scott E. Casper, Jeffrey D. Groves, Stephen W. Nissenbaum, and Michael Winship, eds, *The Industrial Book, 1840–1880* (vol. 3 of *A History of the Book in America*), 279–302. Chapel Hill: University of North Carolina Press.

Soltow, Lee, and Edward Stevens. (1981) *The rise of literacy and the common school in the United States*. Chicago: University of Chicago Press.

Spufford, Margaret. (1981) *Small books and pleasant histories: Popular fiction and its readership in seventeenth-century England*. London: Methuen.

St. Clair, Ralf, and Jennifer Sadlin. (2004) Incompetence and intrusion: On the metaphorical use of illiteracy in U.S. political discourse. *Adult Basic Education* 14: 45–59.

Steedman, Carolyn. (1982) *The tidy house*. London: Virago.

Steedman, Carolyn. (1999) A woman writing a letter. In Rebecca Earle, ed., *Epistolary selves: Letters and letter writers, 1600–1945*, 111–133. Farnham, Surrey: Ashgate.

Steedman, Carolyn. (2005) Poetical maids and cooks who write. *Eighteenth-Century Studies* 39: 1–27.

Stevens, Edward. (1985) Literacy and the worth of liberty. *Historical Social Research* 34: 65–81.

Stevens, Edward. (1988) *Literacy, law, and social order.* DeKalb: Northern Illinois University Press

Stock, Brian. (1983) *The implications of literacy: Written language and models of interpretation in the eleventh and twelfth centuries.* Princeton: Princeton University Press.

Stock, Brian. (1990) *Listening for the text.* Baltimore: Johns Hopkins University Press.

Stout, Harry S. (1977) Religion, communications, and the ideological origins of the American Revolution. *William and Mary Quarterly* 34: 519–541.

Thomas, Keith. (1986) The meaning of literacy in early modern England. In Gerd Baumann, ed., *The written word: Literacy in transition*, 97–131. Oxford: Oxford University Press.

UNESCO. 2005. *Literacy for life. Education for all global monitoring report, 2006.* Paris: UNESCO.

UNESCO. 2005–2006. *United Nations literacy decade: Education for all*, Second Progress Report to the General Assembly for the period 2005–2006. Paris: UNESCO.

UNESCO. 2007. *Education for all by 2015: Will we make it? EFA global monitoring report 2008.* Paris: UNESCO.

Vincent, David. (1979) *Bread, knowledge, and freedom. A study of nineteenth century working class autobiography.* London: Europa.

Vincent, David. (1989) *Literacy and popular culture: England 1750–1914.* Cambridge: Cambridge University Press.

Vincent, David. (2000) *The rise of mass literacy: Reading and writing in modern Europe.* Cambridge: Polity Press.

Wrightson, Keith, and David Levine. (1979) *Poverty and piety: Terling, 1525–1700.* New York and London: Academic Press.

8

Epilogue: Many Pasts, Many Futures

To advance constructively, theoretically, empirically, and humanely, literacy studies needs to be framed as historical, comparative, and critical. Literacy studies scholars should stop congratulating themselves and end their sometimes reckless pursuit and celebration of the "new." In many ways, literacy studies should learn from, though not return to, its roots.

I propose five paths to revised, renewed literacy studies.

Literacy and Literacies Are Relational and Dialectical

The conceptualization and investigation of interrelationships must replace the presumption of dichotomies and divides. The explosion of many, multi-, and multiple literacies without an explicit search for their relationships, connections, and associations, including their dialectical shaping and reshaping of one another, jeopardizes both the original breakthroughs and risks the loss of recognizable forms of literacy in theory and practice. We must trace relationships among literacies and languages across media and modes of comprehension and expression, from the alphabetic to other symbolic, visual, spatial, embodied, and performative.

Historical Awareness Is Fundamental

Conceptions and practices of literacies are historically constructed, established, institutionalized, revised, and transmitted. This awareness of the direct and indirect, explicit and implicit, persistence of theories and expectations should inform scholars' analysis of what is new and what is, instead, the familiar presented in a new guise. Similarly, it moderates the usual overemphasis on change and underestimation of the power of continuities.

Context Gives Meaning to Literacy and Creates the Ground for Its Study and Practice

The most effective path to avoid the conundrums and contradictions that result from formulaic notions of progress and decline in the historical study of literacy lies in the specification of context. Fundamentally, literacy has no meaning outside of distinct temporal and spatial locations, which are neither local nor global but are defined by their connections to and differences from other settings.

Translation Is Inseparably Intertwined with Matters of Literacy

Literacy involves making and communicating meaning across media and modes of understanding and expression from one person or set of persons to others via the symbol and sign systems that constitute languages. Acts of reading and writing that cross time and space and link disparate groups are usefully viewed in terms of the theory and practice of translation. This recognition facilitates placing literacy in its proper comparative communicative contexts. No less importantly, it reduces the need to invent redundant neologisms such as transliterate, translingual, and transnational, which proliferate the varieties of literacies and segregate rather than interrelate them. This path also promotes learning from the wide range of theories and practices of translation and the critical distinctions they offer.

Negotiation Provides an Especially Human Approach to the Study and Practice of Literacy and Literacies

In recent years, literacy studies scholars have sought new concepts and metaphors for reading, writing, and beyond. In a critical discussion of hybrid literacies, Elizabeth Moje mentions the transcendence of either/or binaries via third-space or "thirdness" as one articulation with respect to identities and locations. After reviewing alternative terms, Moje favors navigation as a "term of distinction." "The concept of navigating thus acknowledges the roles of space, time, and context in how people engage in literate practice or enact identities in a new way that hybridity or hybrid literacies cannot" (Moje et al. 2008, 366). Moje's primary focus falls on teaching and learning in a relatively formal and normative sense.[1]

My focus is broader; it aims to include but go beyond schooling. For that reason, I find the concept, theory, practice, metaphor, and notion of negotiation more fitting, flexible, relational, and deeply human than notions of navigation or hybridity. It parallels translation. Negotiation is not deterministic, essentialist, limited, or oriented toward a finite goal; it is more adaptive and can be individual or group-centered. If a person can navigate as part the process of negotiation, the term recognizes the agency as well as the constraints and contradictions, of leaders and learners, their choices and options, experiential learning by doing amidst the give and take of the widest variety of contexts or environments. It embraces both individual and collective, formal and informal activities. I believe it is more amenable to exploring and practicing a dialectical interrelational approach to multiple literacies across different media and modes of understanding and communication.

Anne Haas Dyson (1989, 2003) offers the fullest demonstration of negotiation in the development of literacy in her study of elementary school learners in Oakland, California. Dyson's pioneering use of the concept of negotiation is richly suggestive. Although I developed and adopted the term developed independently, this concurrence shows its potential. We learn from Dyson's example and her description of how young people recontextualize across media and modes of understanding and expression.

Following her interest in how youngsters "tinker with drawn and written worlds" (1989, 76), Dyson shows how they negotiate social compromises among themselves and the styles and genres they use to move between their media sources. She portrays an elementary school student "negotiating among his imaginary, social, and experiential worlds" (182) and "negotiating between symbolic media: visual and verbal magic" (186) as they developed and changed. In the process, these first and second graders "renegotiated the relationship between drawing and writing." Manuel, a first grader, learned "to coordinate his pictures and his texts more closely, not by making art notes but by finding words for visual images without abandoning narrative action." He "worked to bring his drawn and written art closer together, capturing the physical beauty of his pictures in his texts" (186). "In his search, Manuel also kept in mind the language of the story he was developing. He was creating visual art, but he was working within the tension between language, on the one hand, and line, color, and shape, on the other" (197). "Discovering a way to bring his own visual sense and his reflective style into his dramatic texts would contribute to Manuel's emergence as an acknowledged artist—a social star—in the second grade" (183).

Negotiation claims a central place in new studies of literacy, I suggest.

Following these and other paths, literacy studies, old and new, may change for the better.

Why does it matter?

That is a question I ask each of us to ponder and to answer for ourselves and together. I quote the Norwegian scholar Johan Galtung:

What would happen if the whole world became literate? Answer: not so very much, for the world is by and large structured in such a way that it is capable of absorbing the impact. But if the whole world consisted of literate, autonomous, critical, constructive people, capable of translating ideas into action, individually or collectively—the world would change. (1976, 93)

Note

1. The words "negotiation" and "navigation" appear fairly often in writings about children's and adolescents' reading, but a thorough bibliographic search turned up no work that developed or reflected on these concepts.

References

Dyson, Anne Haas. (1989) *Multiple worlds of child writers: Friends learning to write*. New York: Teachers College Press.

Dyson, Anne Haas. (2003) "Welcome to the jam": Popular culture, school literacy, and the making of childhoods. *Harvard Educational Review* 79: 328–361.

Galtung, Johan. 1976. Literacy, education and schooling for what?" In Léon Bataille, ed., *A turning point for literacy: Adult education for development the spirit and declaration of Persepolis*, 93–105. Oxford: Pergamon Press.

Moje, Elizabeth Birr, Melanie Overby, Nicole Tysvaer, and Karen Morris. 2008. The complex world of adolescent literacy: Myths, motivations, and mysteries. *Harvard Educational Review* 78: 107–154.

Part II

2021: Looking Forward and Backward

Abstract In Part 2, 2021, I take stock with a set of specific foci. In One, I assess the rise and partial success of the New Literacy Studies from the 1970s on, and the fact of a resurgent set of literacy myths and a continuing proliferation of "many" and "new" literacies. In Two, I confront today's unprecedented rise of a New Illiteracy and campaigns to ban books without reading them and knowing the supposedly offending or dangerous contents. In Three, I examine in greater detail the persistent promotional claims of "financial literacy" in a new iteration FL4ALL as a combined marketing ploy and misrepresentation to the public.

9

The New Literacy Studies and the Resurgent Literacy Myth

The roots of the once "new literacy studies" lay in the 1960s and spread in the 1970s and 1980s. By the early 2000s they were ascendant, with new journals like *Literacy in Composition Studies* and significant presence in journals, book publications, conference sessions, and course catalogues. The transformation of our understanding of literacy remains far from complete, and fundamental lessons remain to be learned.

Accelerating in the 21st century, the same period witnessed the contradictory trend toward an uninformed battle between new literacies and old ones, and the endless proliferation of "multiple literacies." The different bodies of writing and publicity seldom acknowledge each other. To a considerable degree, both the "new" and the "multi-literacies" are marketing campaigns serving corporate profit-making with the promotion of degrees, certificates, courses, consultants, how-to books, and now apps. The conflicts and contradictions are insufficiently appreciated.

I date the foundations of the new literacy studies in the groundbreaking revelations, critiques, and reform proposals in the classic books by Paul Goodman, *Growing Up Absurd* (1960) and *Compulsory Miseducation* (1964); Paulo Freire (1970), *Pedagogy of the Oppressed;* and Jonathan Kozol (1967), *Death at an Early Age*), among others of that exciting time.

H. J. Graff, *Searching for Literacy*, https://doi.org/10.1007/978-3-030-96981-3_9

Socially and culturally, there was a relatively small step to a next generation influenced by this literature but more academic. I helped to pioneer it with *The Literacy Myth* (1979, and subsequent historical works), a study of nineteenth century Canada in comparative perspective. Other authors followed in a series of interrelated books that together created a new field of study and interpretations of literacy in theory and practice.

These constitute a collection of now-classic works across disciplines: psychologists Sylvia Scribner and Michael Cole (1981), *The Psychology of Literacy*); anthropologist Shirley Brice Heath (1983), *Ways with Words: Language, Life, and Work in Communities and Classrooms*); anthropologist Brian Street (1984), *Literacy in Theory and Practice*); and compositionist Deborah Brandt (2001), *Literacy in American Lives.* Each derived from original research in historical or personal sources or ethnography. Together they form an intellectual foundation with international influence. (See among others, Galvao et al (2017),"An Interview with Harvey J. Graff and Brian Street" (also "Literacy Studies and Composition through the work of Harvey J. Graff," 2017.)

From a wide range of approaches and disciplinary orientations, the new literacy studies revised what I designated as "the literacy myth" with concrete research, clear logic of inquiry and interpretation, evidence, comparisons, grounded criticism, new hypotheses, and novel theories. The "literacy myth" dated from antiquity but was articulated and promoted by the "invention" of alphabets especially the Greek alphabet; the diffusion of the printing press and movable typography; progressive elements of the Renaissance and Enlightenment; nineteenth-century institutional school reforms; and twentieth-century presumptions of the essentialist demands of modern civilization. The "literacy myth" presumed *the unique and innate power of "literacy by itself."*

With no need for documentation, qualification, or definition, literacy held *limitless power regardless of individual, collective, or historical context.* Literacy was synonymous with progress, illiteracy with *stagnation and decay.* Remediation for individuals or groups was never presumed likely. When defined at all, literacy meant "reading and writing" with the level of ability unexamined. A later generation would deem literacy in this mythical conception to be essentialist and universalist, a false value, and the confusion of untested inherited ideas with any documented reality. To many, this was an excessively overdetermined form of "modernization theory."

The "mere possession" of literacy was presumed to lead to *superiority and advancement*. Lack of literacy represented an all but *irreparable limitation*. Individuals, age groups, gender groups, racial and ethnic groups, tribes, territories, regions, nations, and even continents were *labeled essentially as superior or inferior*. Literacy and illiteracy, reciprocally, stood as both cause and effect.

As I summarized in 2010, "The Literacy Myth refers to the belief, articulated in educational, civic, religious, and other settings, contemporary and historical, that the acquisition of literacy is a necessary precursor to and inevitably results in economic development, democratic practice, cognitive enhancement, and upward social mobility…" ("The Literacy Myth at 30," 635)

By reference to myth, I did not argue that these foundational assumptions were completely false. If that were the case, the "myth" would never have achieved its hegemony. To the contrary, the new literacy studies reformulated our understanding by demonstrating across time and space that literacy always reflected the conditions of its transmission and practice: its specific contexts. Literacy is never a "neutral skill"; it is always historically determined and value-laden. It always requires definition and contextualization. (Graff and John Duffy (2014), "Literacy Myths;" Graff (2010), "The Literacy Myth at 30;" Graff (2011), *Literacy Myths, Legacies, and Lessons*. See also, for example, Stephen Black and Keiko Yasukawa (2014), "The literacy myth continues;" Zoe Druick (2016), "The Myth of Media Literacy.")

Heath, Street, Scribner and Cole, and Brandt all elaborated my arguments, with separate paths, independent orientations, and their own emphases. Heath introduced us to Trackton, a black community and its neighboring, more prosperous, white community. Over the course of a multiyear ethnography, she demonstrated that the presumption of inherited and transmissible deprivation was prejudicial and false. She also revealed the divergent literacy orientations of the two communities.

For Street, literacy is never "autonomous." More often it is "ideological." He showed this in his ethnographic research in Iran and in his critiques of prevailing ideas including those of anthropologist Jack Goody and medievalist Walter Ong.

Cross-cultural experimental psychologists Scribner and Cole compared the dynamics of learning literacy and using the abilities in a region in Africa. Although they hesitated to unsubscribe from all tenets of literacy's independent attributes, they emphasized the power of context.

In her examinations of different kinds of writing, Brandt documented the importance of values, writing formats and traditions, and practices. Each of us revealed the customs and practices of our own disciplines as well as our shared concerns.

Review of the scholarly and higher-educational domains demonstrates the striking influence of the new literacy studies by the 1980s and 1990s. There was a visible effect on many disciplines and fields within them. These included social history and history of education; educational studies including foundations, teaching, and learning; composition studies; and various specializations within each of the social sciences. Publications and curricula support my view.

Yet the replacement of the literacy myth by the new literacy studies was never complete. There is reason to believe that its influence has been diminishing. This question demands more complete study.

My review of the past decade or so suggests an undeclared and insufficiently noticed conflict between the new literacy studies and the resurrected myth in the form of proliferating "new literacies" and "multiple literacies." The latter represent Street's autonomous literacies as they evoke the independent power of reading and writing in numerous forms of "literacies" and "skills" in the face of "illiteracies" old and new.

Almost never are these literacies related to foundations in reading, writing, or sometimes arithmetic. Typically, their interconnections and shared contexts of both learning and practice are ignored. Tellingly, their literature almost never cites the new literacy studies' founding and subsequent works.

Instead, the literature of the "new," "many," and "multiple literacies" acknowledges few empirical or theoretical studies. Overwhelmingly, the references are to declarative, applied, and promotional writings. For example, the *Journal of Education and Practice* published in 2017 the less-than-four-page "Expanded Territories of 'Literacy': New Literacies and Multiliteracies," by Yuan Sang, with a slim and outdated reference list.

The literature reflects the state of this field. It is promotional, confused, and contradictory with little interest in elaborating arguments or documenting definitions or applications. It is dominated by lists of "literacies," literally 3, 5, 6, 7, 10, 13, and 20 in a rapid online search. Online promotional pieces include "Redefining literacy in the 21st century" (2018), which refers to new technologies but offers no redefinition. Or "Literacies for lifelong learning: A quality enhancement plan proposal" (2020). This "proposal… focuses on students achieving multiple literacies to further strengthen their ability to engage in lifelong learning after graduating from the University of Houston-Clear Lake." Neither demonstrates awareness with the basic texts of old, new, or "multiple" literacy studies.

The variable listings of "literacies" are extraordinary. Repetitive and redundant, even within the same list, some—like agricultural or racial literacy— are bizarre. These "literacies" have boundless claims; essential or transformative are among the milder ones. The different "literacies" are seldom compared, interrelated, or evaluated. Of course, all "encompass a wide range of skills… all of which are necessary to succeed."

Many derive from formal organizations founded to promote and sell them, figuratively and literally. Many claim to replace the ever "dying" domain of print. Some repeat the most traditional practices of basic reading and writing (and sometimes arithmetic). Some repeat the outmoded notion of "functional literacy." Most of them resemble illogical, unfounded metaphors rather than reputable literacies. There is no self-awareness, self-criticism, or admission of multiple contradictions. Despite a half-century of the new literacy studies, these "literacies" proliferate in violation of all its tenets.

Astonishingly, they include reading and writing literacy; functional literacy; writing literacy; prose literacy; document literacy; content literacy; disciplinary literacy; visual literacy; scientific literacy; ecological literacy; numerical literacy; quantitative literacy; data literacy; digital literacy; coding and computational literacy; multimodal literacy; technological literacy; critical literacy; balanced literacy; media literacy; news literacy;

informational literacy; trans-literacy (transfer not trans-sexual); game literacy; civic literacy; civic and ethical literacy; multicultural literacy; financial literacy; health and financial literacy; early literacy; developmental literacy; health literacy; mental health literacy; emotional literacy; emotional/physical literacy; racial literacy; agricultural literacy; and recreational literacy.

The sense of chaos, incoherency, and redundancy derives directly from these lists of "many literacies." Among the complications is the blurring of the lines between scholarship and education, on the one hand, and promotion and sales, on the other.

Of the lengthy listing of "literacies," I draw special attention to a "new literacy" recently promoted in a full-page advertisement in the *New York Times* (Aug. 3, 2021). This is a form of financial literacy touted as "FL4ALL." In an original formulation that blends elements of cheerleading with the work of a flailing ad agency, this awkward promotion dubs financial literacy as FL, a first in the murky annals of "multiple literacies" rhetoric.

FL4ALL derives from a group of banking and financial institutions and one online "education academy," with other corporate "partners." Neither the ad nor the uninformative website shows any familiarity with new literacy studies or multiple literacies. No thought is given to how FL relates to reading and writing or other forms of literacy. FL is never defined. The poorly composed text misappropriates language from the civil rights movement. It makes many boasts about the need and value for FL4ALL. It quickly descends into contradictions. Its promises and prose are a caricature of several hundred years of the literacy myth. Matters of learning and practice do not occur to these marketers peddling a fabricated product.

Writing and composition continue to straddle the line between literacy as an integrative form of reading and writing in specific contexts of learning and practice, and composition as writing alone. The latter by itself does not qualify as an old or new literacy or one of "many" literacies.

This often purposeful confusion is part of a license to exaggerate, promote, and sell writing or composition.

A contemporary example is Global Society of Online Literacy Educators (GSOLE), according to its website "an inclusive organization of teachers, tutors, and administrators across ranks, all working to improve access to quality literacy education at all levels." They advance this goal through virtual conferences, webinars, and an "online certification" program. This virtual world is solely concerned with writing and composition but choses "literacy" for its name and its sales pitches.

Despite the development and institutionalization of the new literacy studies, the gross exaggeration of the power of literacy by itself continues, outside of any meaningful context including foundational reading, writing, and in some cases arithmetic. Often tied to commercialization, the effort to gain credibility by proclaiming anything and everything a "literacy" carries on. The temptations and the appeal are too great. More than four decades after its formal identification, the literacy myth continues to compete with established, trusted research and understanding.

Originally published in *Literacy in Composition Studies*, Fall 2021

10

Literacy, Politics, Culture, and Society: The New Illiteracy and the Banning of Books, Past and Present

As a student of the history of literacy for the past 50 years, I coined the phrase "the literacy myth" to identify, explain, and criticize the former consensus that reading and writing (and sometimes arithmetic) are sufficient in themselves, regardless of degree of proficiency or social context, to transform the lives of individuals and their societies. (See Graff (1979), *The Literacy Myth*, new edition with new introduction, 1991; *Literacy Myths, Legacies & Lessons: New Studies on Literacy*, Transaction, 2011,; and most recently "The new literacy studies and the resurgent literacy myth," *Literacy in Composition Studies*, Fall 2021.) Anthropologist Brian Street (1984) called this "the autonomous" theory of literacy (Street, *Literacy in Theory and Practice*).

In late 2021, I confront what I can only understand and explain as an unprecedented "new illiteracy," yet another version of the ever-shifting "literacy myth." This time the historical continuities are shattered by, first, the call to ban books in innumerable circumstances; second, the banning of written literature without taking the expected step of reading it; and, third, calls for not only banning but also burning books. Together, this constitutes a movement for illiteracy not a recognizable campaign for approved or selective uses of reading and writing. (See also "PEN America Report, 2021; Hank Reichman (2021), "From 'Critical Race Theory,'" 2021.)

Banning books from curricula, erasing them from supplementary reading lists, and ridding them from library shelves has mid-20th century precedents; the *burn* books movement does not. Nor does the banning of books without censors reading them in order to identify and publicize their offending content. In Virginia, "'conservative school board members ... proposed not just banning certain books deemed to be sexually explicit, but burning them .... 'I think we should throw those books in a fire' [one stated; he continued] that allowing one particular book to remain on the shelves even briefly meant the school 'would rather have our kids reading gay pornography than about Christ.'" (See Aaron Blake (2021), "'I think we should throw those books in a fire;'" see also Hannah Knowles and Hannah Natanson (2021), "Backlash to school books centering on race, sex, and LGBTQ people turns into conservative rallying cry;" Michelle Goldberg (2021), "A frenzy of book banning;" Bump, Phillip (2021), "The symbolism of burning books is stark. But in 2021, symbolism is all it is.")

Banning—and in its most militant form burning—books is an effort, unknowingly and unacknowledged, to resurrect the late-medieval and early modern Roman Catholic Counter-Reformation in its contest with both radical Catholics and early post-Martin Lutheran Protestants. That was an attempt to halt unauthorized reading, including the ability of individuals to read for themselves. Individual writing was not yet an issue.

Then seen as a "protest," individual access to written or printed texts was perceived as threatening in ways that the controlled oral reading to the "masses" by a priest or other leader was not. It was a politics of enforcing orthodoxy and countering both collective and individual autonomy.

The similarities as well as the differences between today and more than a half millennium ago are powerful. (For an ahistorical snapshot of supposed book burnings, see Gillian Brocknell (2021), "Burning books: 6 outrageous, tragic and weird examples in history.) Both movements are inseparable from the politics of ignorance, rooted in fear, and expressed in both legal and extra-levels struggles for control and power. Both are inextricably linked to other efforts to restrict free speech, choice and control over one's body, political and civil rights, public protests, and much more.

Where they were once led by the Established Church, today right-wing politicians, their parties, radical evangelical Protestants, and supporting activists supercharge censorship crusades to ban written materials of all sorts. In the eyes of some commentators, these politicians are being "opportunistic."

Despites comments in the media and condemnation by professors, teachers, librarians, and First Amendment attorneys, these issues are not well understood. Parents of school-aged children are confused. The young, supposedly to be protected, face the greatest threat to their intellectual and psychological development. That danger is most severe for the racially and gender diverse, who see themselves being erased or banned.

To a historian of literacy, this movement harkens back well beyond the "Ban Books" and "Read Banned Books" movements of the 1950s and 1960s, with their now seemingly innocuous obsession with J.D. Salinger's *Catcher in the Rye*, Harper Lee's *To Kill a Mocking Bird*, or Maya Angelou's *I Know Why the Caged Bird Sings*. My dated "Read Banned Books" T-shirt that I wore for certain sessions in my courses on the history of literacy seems tame and quaint.

Even Anthony Comstock, secretary of the New York Society for the Suppression of Vice, who tried to use the U.S. Postal Service to limit the circulation of obscene literature and destroyed books, did not aim to empty libraries. Nor did the now-laughable "Ban in Boston" follies of the 20th century.

Compare this history to efforts in Virginia to ban without much explanation Nobel and Pulitzer Prize-winning author Toni Morrison's classic novels *The Bluest Eye* and *Beloved*. Or Texas school districts' banning young adult novelist Ashley Hope Perez's (2015) award-winning *Out of Darkness*. The latter effort is based on a single paragraph taken out of context, in a 400-page book. Perez, my colleague, receives vile and abusive hate mail on social media and in postal mail. In all these cases, the new illiterates either do not, or cannot, read the supposedly offending texts.

Perhaps the most revealing example so far is Texas Republican state representative and candidate for Texas Attorney General Matt Krause's campaign stunt of releasing a list of 850 books that he wants to be "investigated" for possible violation of something or other. He demands that school superintendents provide him with lists of texts on bookshelves that deal with certain subjects relating to race and sex. He and his office refuse to respond to questions about either list or demand. Texas school officials state flatly that they lack the time and resources to respond to a probably illegal fishing expedition. (See Cassandra Pollock and Brian Lopez (2021), "Texas lawmaker keeping mum on inquiry into what books students can access," *Texas Tribune*, Oct. 29.)

Krause struggles to position himself to the political right of scandal-plagued A.G. Ken Paxton.

He alleges that these titles may violate Texas H.B. 3979, known as the "critical race theory law."

Almost none of the 850 books have anything to do directly or indirectly with critical race theory. (See Mariana Alfaro (2021), "Texas GOP lawmaker launches investigation of books on race and sexuality;" Karen Attiah (2021), "Why books have become a battlefield in Texas." This article has a link to Krause's list.)

What is immediately apparent from a look at Krause's list is that it is compiled from an Internet search of keywords. It is also organized by publication date, which has no relationship to the content of the texts. There is a numerical bias favoring most recent years. Once more we find the new illiteracy: no familiarity with actual contents of the listed volumes and no concern to examine them directly. Sixteenth-century orthodox Catholics and Anthony Comstock would turn over in their graves.

Previous banning movements did not so overtly concentrate on race, aim to empty libraries, and associate so closely with one political party and bids for election. They prided themselves on their direct familiarity with the explicit contents of that which they wished to ban (or even burn).

They used their *literacy* in their brazen efforts to control the uses of others' literacy.

Today's banners and burners, by contrast, are the new *illiterates*, achieving a rare historical distinction.

11

The Economic Debasement of Literacy: The Misrepresentation and Marketing of "Financial Literacy"

A marketing campaign calling itself **FL4ALL** announced itself in a full-page ad in the *New York Times* on August 3, 2021. It represents a dangerous fiction and threat to students and unsuspecting "hard working citizens," to repeats its promotional language. The campaign's actions follow what I declared in my 1979 book, *The Literacy Myth*, the exaggerated importance of literacy by itself, taken out of context. To borrow the academic terms of literacy studies, "reading" the advertisement as "written" is revealing.

Let's begin with the ad's text. It misrepresents both literacy and economics, and is a danger to the population this corporate coalition claims to serve. It provides signposts at every point.

First, no knowledgeable person says or writes "FL" for "financial literacy." Perhaps for a football or a soccer league.

Second, no one except marketers and business corporations seeking to derive financial profits would promote a flawed slogan like "FL4ALL. The ad proclaims, "financial literacy is a civil rights issue of this generation." In parroting the language of civil rights movements, such sloganeering is an unacceptable misappropriation. "Civil rights" is a complicated term. This strategy of false-promotion is offensive to genuine civil rights activists and the public. Could FL4ALL not afford a responsible advertising agency?

© The Author(s), under exclusive license to Springer Nature Switzerland AG 2022
H. J. Graff, *Searching for Literacy*, https://doi.org/10.1007/978-3-030-96981-3_11

Third, the poorly constructed and misleading wording continues with "you can grow the economy by expanding the ladder of opportunity." Do they really mean making the "ladder of opportunity" longer? That contradicts the promotion.

Fourth, the "mission statement" ends with "We believe in embedding financial literacy into the business plan of America." Here we have the most forthright statement in the ad. The fundamental goal of the 10-year project is "the business of plan of America," not the security or the advancement of individuals young or older. Yet no business plan appears on their website.

The founding organizations comprise eight corporations, the NBA, and the NFL, with an online "education academy" the only representative of any kind of education. That's a revealing admission: as a *faux* literacy, FL has nothing to do with education despite the immediate association of the word literacy with schooling.

The public relations campaign commits "ourselves and our corporations to addressing one of America's greatest challenges: the lack of knowledge and understanding of how money—and everything that revolves around it—works." Is this what they mean by "financial literacy": Money and "everything that revolves around it"? That's not literacy or even a debatable conception of "financial literacy," but a calculated distraction.

The writing is uncertain. "American's greatest challenges" are distorted in an awkward sales pitch. Next FL4ALL either ignorantly or purposely confuses "financial stress;" the "cost" of "financial literacy"--which is not defined; and "most Americans'" lack of funds for emergencies.

This is not useful to those wishing to solidify their economic security. The "call to action" and "time to act" become more muddled with each paragraph.

Among the many problems is that FL4ALL never defines literacy or "financial literacy." At best it is a metaphor and at worst a fiction or myth. In this campaign, it is an undisguised pitch designed to sell FL4ALL as a product and lead to profits. The promotion applies most directly to co-sponsor Khan Academy but also to Bank of America, Walmart, Delta Airlines, Disney, PayPal, and other "founding organizations" and their "partners" BlackRock, IHeart Radio, MasterCard, USbank, Nextdoor, and others.

We must define literacy clearly. Literacy is a form of reading, writing, and in some cases arithmetic, based on a common set of recognized symbols, including major alphabets and numeral systems. The ceaseless proliferation of "many literacies" since the 1970s allows anything and everything to declare itself a "literacy." This multiplication ranges from "sports literacies" and "racial literacy" to "automobile literacy" and "dog or cat literacy," with "financial literacy" in between. The flood of literacies, many for profit, seizes on this moment and promotes confusion in its self-promotion. Together, these literacies threaten to destroy any agreed-upon definition of literacy, especially critical with respect to teaching, learning, and practice. FL4ALL says nothing about these vital elements.

Like many of these "new literacies," FL4ALL is devoted to corporate profit-making and the promotion of degrees, certificates, courses, consultants, how-to books, and now apps. The conflicts and contradictions are not recognized, acknowledged, or examined. This is a powerful and dangerous example of "the literacy myth." "Literacy by itself" is uniquely powerful and holds limitless power regardless of individual, collective, or historical context. This is an unabashed sales pitch, never sold with a money-back guarantee.

As a myth as defined in *The Literacy Myth*, there is with no need for documentation, qualification, or definition. As with FL4ALL, this misleading image of literacy is almost never measured directly and very rarely defined. Its "mere possession" leads to superiority and advancement. Lack of literacy is an unrepairable limitation. The myth gains its hegemony from its broad promotion and uncritical acceptance of its supposed promise. Repeated sufficiently and loudly, and anchored in a promise that the currently fashionable and superficially relevant "literacy" will pay off with interest, the imperative seems axiomatic.

To the contrary, it is critical to start with the basics and then qualify the term "literacy" when appropriate with relevant adjectives. Any responsible approach begins with a clear definition and thorough consideration of the context in which the proposed and/or promoted subject qualifies as a "literacy," based on its relationship to some forms and levels of reading, writing, and in the case of financial literacy arithmetic—and their interconnections. It must then rigorously develop the foundations of its teaching, learning at different ages and levels of complexity, and practice or specific applications. All literacies have specific contexts and expected—not simply promoted—consequences. Only then, an odd commodity like FL4ALL might be promoted seriously and with respect to its audience.

Otherwise, conceptualization, shared knowledge, and communication are impossible. Isolation and distortion follow. "Aspirational literacies" like FL4ALL have sales or related appeal among their proponents. The extent to which they have a meaningful appeal for their publics remains unclear and untested.

The unmistakable result is general confusion. FL4ALL directly contributes to that. We must join together to work for clarification and common knowledge, and to combat distortion and misappropriation. Citizens of all ages deserve it.

References

Alfaro, Mariana. (2021) "Texas GOP lawmaker launches investigation of books on race and sexuality used in school districts," *Washington Post*, Oct. 27.

Attiah, Karen. (2021) "Why books have become a battlefield in Texas," *Washington Post*, Nov. 1.

Bartsch, Robert A. (2010) "Literacies for lifelong learning: A quality enhancement plan proposal." University of Houston.

Black, Stephen and Keiko Yasukawa. (2014) "The literacy myth continues: adapting Graff's thesis to contemporary policy discourses on adult 'foundational skills' in Australia." *Critical Studies in Education*, 55: 1-21.

Blake, Aaron. (2021) "'I think we should throw those books in a fire': Movement builds on right to target books," *Washington Post*, Nov. 10.

Brandt, Deborah. (2001) *Literacy in American Lives*. Cambridge: Cambridge University Press.

Brocknell, Gillian (2021) "Burning books: 6 outrageous, tragic and weird examples in history," *Washington Post*, Nov. 13.

Bump, Philip. (2021) "The symbolism of burning books is stark. But in 2021, symbolism is all it is," *Washington Post*, Nov. 11.

Druick, Zoe. (2016) "The Myth of Media Literacy" *International Journal of Communication*, 10: 1125-1144.

Duffy, John, et al. "Literacy Studies and Composition through the work of Harvey J. Graff," Tribute Session, Conference on College Composition and Communication, 2017, forthcoming.

Freire, Paulo. *Pedagogy of the Oppressed.* First published in Portuguese, 1968, Herder and Herder, Chestnut Ridge, N.J., 1970.

Galvao, Ana Maria de Oliveira, Maria Cristina Soares de Gouvêa, and Ana Maria Rabelo Gomes (2017) "An Interview with Harvey J. Graff and Brian Street" (first published in Brazil in 2015), *Literacy in Composition Studies*, 5: 49-66.

Goldberg, Michelle. (2021) "A frenzy of book banning," *New York Times*, Nov. 12.

Goodman, Paul. (1960) *Growing Up Absurd.* New York: Random House, 1960.

Goodman, Paul. (1964) *Compulsory Miseducation.* New York: Horizon Press, 1964.

Graff, Harvey J. (1979) *The Literacy Myth: Literacy and Social Structure in the Nineteenth Century City.* New York: Academic Press.

Graff, Harvey J. (1987) *The Legacies of Literacy: Continuities and Contradictions in Western Society and Culture.* Bloomington: Indiana University Press.

Graff, Harvey J. (2010) "The Literacy Myth at 30," *Journal of Social History*, 43: 635-661.

Graff, Harvey J. (2011) *Literacy Myths, Legacies, and Lessons: New Studies on Literacy.* New Brunswick, N.J: Transaction.

Graff, Harvey J. and John Duffy. (2014) "Literacy Myths," in *Literacies and Language Education: Encyclopedia of Language and Education*, ed. B.V. Street and S. May, London: Springer, 2-11.

Heath, Shirley Brice. (1983) *Ways with Words: Language, Life, and Work in Communities and Classrooms.* Cambridge: Cambridge University Press.

Knowles, Hannah and Hannah Natanson. (2021) "Backlash to school books centering on race, sex, and LGBTQ people turns into conservative rallying cry," *Washington Post*, Nov. 12.

Kozol, Jonathan. (1967) *Death at an Early Age.* New York: Random House.

Oxford, Bethany. (2018) "Redefining literacy in the 21st century." *Medium*. (2021) "PEN America Report Warns About Dangers of Educational Gag Orders," *Academe Blog,* Nov. 8, 2021.

Pollock, Cassandra and Brian Lopez. (2021) "Texas lawmaker keeping mum on inquiry into what books students can access as school districts grapple with how to respond," *Texas Tribune*, Oct. 29.

Reichman, Hank. (2021) "From 'Critical Race Theory' to 'Pornography,' the Book Banners are Back," *Academe Blog*, Nov. 11.

Sang, Yuan. (2017) "Expanded Territories of 'Literacy': New Literacies and Multiliteracies," *Journal of Education and Practice,*8: 16-19.

Scribner, Sylvia and Michael Cole. (1981) *The Psychology of Literacy.* Cambridge: Cambridge University Press.

Street, Brian. (1984) *Literacy in Theory and Practice.* Cambridge: Cambridge University Press.

Index[1]

---

[1] Note: Page numbers followed by 'n' refer to notes.

consequences of, 20, 75, 81, 123, 127–130, 244, 280
context, 124, 130, 272
continuum, 61
controlled and restricted, 14, 20, 30, 50, 60, 148, 232
core skills, 195
crisis/declining, 20, 91, 231
culture of, 11, 34, 122
defined, 8, 16, 24n9, 111, 123, 126, 293
developmental, 125, 129
dichotomy of, 10, 30, 72, 86, 112, 160, 227, 255
digital/media/tech, 17, 32, 35, 98, 146, 192–194, 199
disciplines, 16, 21, 23
domestication and, 15, 75
economics and, 11, 20, 50, 146, 171, 197, 231, 248, 259
Enlightenment, Romanticism eras, 18
episteme, 30, 32
ethnographies, 57, 74, 85, 256
European American gaps, 73
financial, 189, 284, 291
gender and, 14, 161, 252
government and, 50
health, 190
history, 42, 150, 227, 235, 237, 244
ideology, 10, 58, 77, 233, 281
illiterate/nonliterate stereotypes, 16, 19, 30, 33, 34, 71, 76, 231
indigenous, 55, 252
judicial settings, 255
levels of, 233, 240, 246, 248

literature, 18, 22, 34, 39, 44, 46, 154, 289
Maori containment, 50
measures of, 9, 228
mediated/unmediated, 133
men and, 14
"mentality," 54, 109
metaphors, 273
modes of, 38, 189, 191, 216
moral bases of, 233
multiple, 9, 22, 96, 271, 279, 283, 293
myth of, 12, 19, 109, 173, 228, 280, 287
New Literacy Studies, 22, 71–73, 85, 86, 98
new vs. old, 202–216
nonhomogeneous, 38, 259
non-school, 133
numeracy, 209–213, 243
orality and, 15, 30, 33, 38, 45, 49, 58, 145
paraliterate system, 56
performance literacy, 214
practice and theory, 73, 83, 95, 115, 123, 124, 130
practice vs. event, 87
psychology of, 107, 109, 243
school and, 58, 126, 145, 157, 245, 246
science and, 209–213
slavery and, 148
in society, 21, 36, 48, 92, 99, 149, 258
symbolic space, 32
training center, 18
translating/understanding, 30, 158, 208, 272–273